ntents

The artist for this issue is Kathleen Forsythe

CYBERNETICS & HUMAN KNOWING
A Journal of Second-Order Cybernetics, Autopoiesis & Cyber-Semiotics

Cybernetics and Human Knowing is a quarterly international multi- and transdisciplinary journal focusing on second-order cybernetics and cybersemiotic approaches.

The journal is devoted to the new understandings of the self-organizing processes of information in human knowing that have arisen through the cybernetics of cybernetics, or second order cybernetics its relation and relevance to other interdisciplinary approaches such as C.S. Peirce's semiotics. This new development within the area of knowledge-directed processes is a non-disciplinary approach. Through the concept of self-reference it explores: cognition, communication and languaging in all of its manifestations; our understanding of organization and information in human, artificial and natural systems; and our understanding of understanding within the natural and social sciences, humanities, information and library science, and in social practices like design, education, org- anization, teaching, therapy, art, management and politics.

Because of the interdisciplinary character articles are written in such a way that people from other domains can understand them. Articles from practitioners will be accepted in a special section. All articles are peer-reviewed.

Subscription Information

Price: Individual $98/£49. Institutional: $220/£110. 50% discount on full set of back volumes. Payment by check in $US or £UK, made payable to Imprint Academic to PO Box 200, Exeter EX5 5HY, UK, or Visa/Mastercard/Amex). sandra@imprint.co.uk

Editor in Chief: Søren Brier, Professor in semiotics at the Department of International Culture and Communication Studies attached to the Centre for Language, Cognition, and Mentality, Copenhagen Business School, Dalgas Have 15, DK-2000 Frederiksberg, Denmark, Tel: +45 38153246. sb.ikk@cbs.dk

Associate editor: Jeanette Bopry, Instructional Sciences, National Institute of Education, 1 Nanyang Walk, Singapore 637616. jeanette.bopry@gmail.com

Associate editor: Dr. Paul Cobley, Reader in Communications, London Metropolitan University, 31 Jewry Street, London EC3N 2EY. p.cobley@londonmet.ac.uk

Website editor: Argyris Arnellos, Department of Product and Systems Design Engineering of the University of the Aegean, Syros, Greece. arar@aegean.gr

Managing editor: Phillip Guddemi, The Union Institute and University, Sacramento CA, USA. pguddemi@well.com

Art editor and ASC-column editor: Pille Bunnell, Royal Roads University, Victoria BC, Canada. pille@interchange.ubc.ca

Journal homepage: www.chkjournal.org
Full text: www.ingenta.com/journals/browse/imp

Copyright: It is a condition of acceptance by the editor of a typescript for publication that the publisher automatically acquires the English language copyright of the typescript throughout the world, and that translations explicitly mention *Cybernetics & Human Knowing* as original source.

Book Reviews: Publishers are invited to submit books for review to the Editor.

Instructions to Authors: To facilitate editorial work and to enhance the uniformity of presentation, authors are requested to send a file of the paper to the Editor on e-mail. If the paper is accepted after refereeing then to prepare the contribution in accordance with the stylesheet information at www.chkjournal.org

Manuscripts will not be returned except for editorial reasons. The language of publication is English. The following information should be provided on the first page: the title, the author's name and full address, a title not exceeding 40 characters including spaces and a summary/ abstract in English not exceeding 200 words. Please use italics for emphasis, quotations, etc. Email to: sbr.lpf@cbs.dk

Drawings. Drawings, graphs, figures and tables must be reproducible originals. They should be presented on separate sheets. Authors will be charged if illustrations have to be re-drawn.

Style. CHK has selected the style of the APA (*Publication Manual of the American Psychological Association*, 5th edition) because this style is commonly used by social scientists, cognitive scientists, and educators. The APA website contains information about the correct citation of electronic sources. The APA Publication Manual is available from booksellers. The Editors reserve the right to correct, or to have corrected, non-native English prose, but the authors should not expect this service. The journal has adopted U.S.English usage as its norm (this does not apply to other native users of English). For full APA style informations see: apastyle.apa.org

Accepted WP systems:
MS Word and rtf.

Forsythe, K. (2007). *Breath Flower*. 25 cm x 40 cm, collage on paper.

Cybernetics And Human Knowing. Vol. 15, nos. 3-4, pp. 5-14

Foreword: Emergence and Downward Determination

Charbel Niño El-Hani (Guest editor for thematic section), Søren Brier, Pille Bunnell,
Phillip Guddemi, and Jeanette Bopry.

The concept of emergence made a comeback on the philosophical scene in the 1990s. In this decade, the terms *emergent, emergence,* and the expressions *emergent property, emergent phenomenon,* as well as others have been increasingly employed by both philosophers and scientists. This was partly a result of the great development of the sciences of complexity – interdisciplinary fields of research concerned with the complex properties of life and mind. Another reason for the strong comeback of this philosophical doctrine lies in the criticisms and even the collapse of positivistic reductionism and its proposal for unifying science. The very term *emergence* and its derivatives have become popular in the context of computer models of non-linear dynamical systems, complex systems research, Artificial Life, consciousness studies, and so forth.

As the concept of emergence and related notions are increasingly used, it becomes more and more important to keep the exact meaning of the central ideas involved clear, inasmuch as the notion of emergence is often regarded with suspicion by both philosophers and scientists. Indeed, if we can recognize, on the one hand, the intuitive appeal of this notion, on the other hand, we cannot deny that it is interwoven with several quite important philosophical problems. Several philosophers and scientists have tried to make it clear in recent years what is at stake in the notion of emergence as well as in related notions, such as *downward causation, downward determination, supervenience,* and *levels.* Nevertheless, it is clear that there are many open issues in this field lending themselves to debate, and new avenues are certainly still waiting to be explored. We intend, with this special issue of *Cybernetics & Human Knowing,* to contribute to the opening of these new avenues by gathering innovative approaches to the problem of emergence—and related problems—from different theoretical perspectives. In particular, we emphasize the contributions of sciences of complexity and cybernetics to the treatment of emergence. After all, emergence has been a concept largely used in general systems theory and cybernetics.

The special issue is organized in the form of discussions around four position papers, followed by a commentary by another researcher (or researchers) in the field, and a reply from the authors of the original paper.

The first position paper is "Emergence and Downward Causation in Contemporary Artificial Agents: Implications for Their Autonomy and Some Design Guidelines" by Argyris Arnellos, Thomas Spyrou, and John Darzentas. They discuss the possibility of the emergence of autonomy in contemporary artificial agents. For this purpose, they take the symbol-grounding problem as a point of reference and the framework of second-order cybernetics and some other theoretical developments in the investigation of complex, self-organizing systems as a basis. In their view, autonomy has been too easily ascribed to artificial agents in the fields of AI and ALife. But, if we consider the interdependence of interactivity, intentionality, autonomy, functionality, and meaning in agents such as living beings, we will be almost obliged – they claim – to argue against the ascription of autonomy to the design results of AI and ALife. This sets the stage for the main task in their paper: to analytically ground the claim that such artificial agents cannot be called autonomous. It is in this analytical grounding that the notion of emergence appears, due to its direct relation to the functionality and autonomy of an agent. The outcome of their arguments is that the design of an artificial autonomous agent requires the design of genuinely emergent representational autonomy, something that cannot be done in silicon-based systems, but, for the moment, only in a carbon-based biology. Furthermore, interactivity, intentionality, autonomy, functionality, and meaning should genuinely emerge within the system, instead of being just a result of an imposed functionality in the course of an artificial ontogeny. The authors analytically describe the features of a framework that could, in principle, support the abovementioned emergence. Nevertheless, intrinsic meaning demands intrinsic intentionality, and, as artificial systems have no inherent, but just derivative intentionality, they can only function in accordance with their designers' anticipations, not their own. Thus, they are design limited and can never be truly autonomous, according to Arnellos and his colleagues.

Maria Eunice Quilici Gonzalez and Osvaldo Pessoa offer comments about Arnellos, Spyrou & Darzentas' paper. They consider their negative answer to the possibility of making a genuinely autonomous artificial system to be sound, but not really more than a simple consequence of the definitions the authors themselves adopt. In particular, the notions of functional emergence and meaning, as used by Arnellos et al., demand further explanation, according to their commentators. Regarding emergence and downward causation, Gonzalez and Pessoa stress the existence of weaker and stronger concepts of emergence and the ongoing controversies about which kind applies to living beings. As partly a consequence of these issues, it seems to them that Arnellos and colleagues' suppositions about the emergence of meaning in living systems need further explanation. How should we understand, say, the emergence of teleological and intentional behavior in phylogenesis, from previously non-teleological and non-intentional systems? These comments point to avenues of research that are still to be traveled, and Arnellos and colleagues' paper provide, in their view, a far-reaching and inspiring source of reflection. As a contribution to our journey, Gonzalez and Pessoa, from the perspective of the dynamics of secondary self-organization, address the role of communication and learning in the emergence of complex forms of organization. The basic idea is that, in such self-organization, mechanisms of adjustment and learning in the process of communicating with other systems give rise to criteria of relevance that underlie the emergence of meaning in secondary self-organizing systems. Then, the central issues become whether artificial systems could autonomously acquire learning mechanisms with such criteria of relevance and further, given the central role of communication, whether they can meaningfully communicate with each other. In their view, these are questions that cannot be solved only theoretically, since they involve empirical aspects.

Arnellos and colleagues provide, then, further explanations in order to better clarify what they consider to be Gonzalez and Pessoa's misunderstandings of their arguments. They take as a starting point the claim that agency is a systemic capacity. They emphasize that the novelty in their approach consists in their attempt to provide a framework in which the notions of autonomy, functionality, intentionality, and meaning can be integrated in a naturalistic position. They also explain how they view the emergence of teleological or intentional behavior in previously non-teleological and non-intentional systems within their framework. In their view, they are not committed to internalist representational conjectures, as suggested by their commentators. From Bickhard's interactivist model, they develop an argument that representations necessarily emerge in the interaction between system and environment. Representations, in turn, consist in a system's anticipations regarding its interactive capabilities towards the respective environment. They agree with Gonzalez and Pessoa in that it is necessary to bring learning into the picture to address complex forms of organization, agency, and autonomy. Finally, they discuss the problem of whether artificial systems could autonomously acquire, through evolution, learning mechanisms with indicators of relevant information in their selective interaction with the external world. For this to be possible, they argue, newer purposes should evolve on the basis of a purpose denoting self-interest. In this respect, they see some promise in robotics projects, such as the "Big-Dog," which is an artificial agent serving its own self-interest. But, generally speaking, AI is not, in their view, moving in the direction of architectures that try to support the features considered in their framework. They see their work as a contribution that shows the power of an interactivist framework for building autonomous artificial agents, shedding new light on a difficult problem faced in this endeavor. Maybe, AI can redirect their approach towards what Arnellos and colleagues take to be the grounds for strong agency and autonomy.

In the second position paper, "Emergence: Process Organization, Not Particle Configuration," Mark Bickhard begins with a short examination of the history of the metaphysical frameworks that make emergence look like a mysterious notion. That is, he goes back to the Pre-Socratics, and, particularly, to Parmenides, to address how substance metaphysics came to dominate Western thinking. He focuses, thus, on the requirement of replacing substance by process metaphysics. He points out, for instance, a basic flaw in Jaegwon Kim's well-known arguments against emergence, namely that it assumes a particle framework, according to which physical causality is constituted as particle causality, denying the legitimacy of organization as a potential locus of causality. Nevertheless, the particle framework assumed by Kim is false, since a metaphysics consisting of only particles would yield a world in which nothing ever happens; after all, particles have zero probability of hitting each other. Another reason for its falsehood lies in the fact that the world is thought today to be constituted not only by particles, but also by fields in terms of which the particles interact. Thus, these fields must have causal powers, and they can only show such powers as a consequence, in part, of their organization. This restores the legitimacy of organization as a locus of causality. Finally, the same conclusion is reached by considering that our best physics does not support a world constituted of particles, but, rather, of quantum fields, which are processes, possessing, as any fields (and processes in general), causality in virtue of their organization. From this process philosophical perspective, change becomes the default, and it is stability that needs to be explained. Emergent causal powers are not precluded, they take place in higher-level organizations of processes (not in configurations of particles). Further, normativity, intentionality, and other mental phenomena can be treated as emergent from non-normative, non-intentional phenomena. It is not that this stance tells us how such emergent phenomena should be modeled, but they at least make them feasible and understandable.

João Queiroz and Floyd Merrell focus on Peirce's theory of signs and process metaphysics when commenting upon Bickhard's paper. They highlight how Peirce's theory, alongside with Wheeler's notion of a *co-participatory* universe and Prigogine's conception of a *self-organizing* universe, gives support to Bickhard's process metaphysical approach to emergence. Meaning is a fundamental notion in Peirce's philosophy. Thus, they give great attention to his general theory of meaning, discussing several aspects in which it radically differs from the standard view in philosophy of language, theoretical linguistics, and cognitive science. Why does meaning matter when discussing process philosophy? They argue that process metaphysics is a necessary presupposition for an adequate concept of meaning to be built. Meaning cannot be dissociated from the concept of becoming, of a flux through which signs act, semiosis is instantiated. They also discuss abduction, as a complement to induction and deduction. They argue that meaning entails a process of imagination (abduction), which merges with a process of considering possible consequences (deduction), and interacting with features of the physical world (induction). This argument leads them to endorse Bickhard's theses that change becomes the default, emergence is self-organizing, and mental phenomena can emerge from non-normative, non-intentional phenomena. But, they add, Bickhard's account of process philosophy should also include sign processes and the emergence of meaning.

In his answer to Queiroz and Merrell, Mark Bickhard expresses his agreement with the claim that there are strong convergences between Peirce's model of meaning and process metaphysics, on the one hand, and his own process-based emergence account and interactivist model of representation, on the other. He takes the opportunity given by his commentators to discuss some additional process metaphysical frameworks. He also elaborates on further consequences of a shift towards process metaphysics, and raise some questions about Peirce's philosophy. Here, we would like to call attention to Bickhard's claim that several ontological notions, such as individuation, supervenience, and boundaries, will necessarily come into question when we shift to a process metaphysical framework. The notion of boundaries, for instance, becomes more problematic in a process framework. This can be readily seen when we ask what would be the boundaries of a flame, or, to consider a central issue in ecology and its philosophy, when we ask how we establish the boundaries of an ecosystem. In our view, it is both correct and stimulating to consider how we still only deal with a small part of the vast range of issues that are raised by a shift from particle to process metaphysics. As Bickhard says, we have a long way to go, but what a way it will be! Finally, we should mention here that, despite his general agreement on a number of convergences between Peirce's model of meaning and his own view, Bickhard also raises quite relevant and difficult questions concerning the differences between these frameworks. In doing so, he poses interesting challenges to Peircean thinkers, which can be the basis for fruitful investigations.

The third position paper, by John Collier, is entitled "A Dynamical Account of Emergence," and addresses the dynamical conditions necessary and sufficient for emergence. He first considers logical conditions for emergence, disregarding a number of mysterious and not well supported notions sometimes invoked in emergentist works, such as separate substances or causal independence. Then, he focuses his attention on irreducibility, unpredictability, and novelty, which any adequate account of emergence should explain. However, these qualitative characteristics should be made more precise. In order to obtain more precise accounts of them, Collier addresses computational conditions for emergence, considering that in a system that is unpredictable and/or irreducible, one of three assumptions should be violated: 1) either the system is not closed, or 2) it is non-Hamiltonian, or, 3) computational resources are not sufficient to compute the macrostate of the system from the trajectories of the microcomponents. When at least one of these assumptions is not satisfied, computability fails and there is room for emergence. After considering these logical conditions for emergence, he takes the metaphysics he developed with C. A. Hooker, namely dynamical realism, as a basis for hooking up the computational characterizations to a dynamical world. Dissipative and nonholonomic processes are regarded by Collier as the dynamical basis for emergent properties and objects. These processes are found in systems showing what he calls radically non-Hamiltonian behavior, which underlies, in his view, all emergence. Collier describes, then, five necessary and sufficient—but not independent—conditions for emergence: 1) non-integrability (implying irreducibility), 2) energetic and/or informational openness (entailing dynamic boundary conditions), 3) existence of multiple attractors in the system's dynamics, 4) radically non-Hamiltonian behavior, and 5) essentiality of at least one (emergent) property of the system. Finally, he shows that systems satisfying these conditions are irreducible and unpredictable, and can also be treated as novel.

Eugenio Andrade offers comments about John Collier's paper, stating from the very beginning that he agrees with the physicalist account of emergence put forward by this author. This is partly because such an account is consistent with the principle of continuity (Peirce's synechism), which is the best way, in Andrade's view, to overcome the polarization between reduction and emergence. He intends, however, to examine the applicability of Collier's account to the emergence of living systems. Andrade stresses that, to account for these systems, one needs to propose an intermediary model of information processing agency, building a bridge between dynamics and semiosis (i.e., the action of signs). In order to do so, one needs to consider how information processing can be treated as a form of causation. This demands that one is clear, first of all, about what is meant by *information processing*. To clarify the meaning of this expression, Andrade appeals to the distinction between analog and digital information, as introduced by Hoffmeyer and Emmeche. As a source of intermediary models of physical systems, situated in the way from dynamics to semiosis, Andrade contrasts Collier's physical information systems with Zurek's information gathering and using systems. He regards the latter as better suited to account for the emergence of semiosis, since they fulfill the properties of Peircean signs as dynamical systems that serve as media for the communication of forms.

John Collier answers Andrade by trying to clarify some arguments in his paper. He stresses, for example, one advantage of a dynamical account of emergence, namely that dynamical conditions can be measured. Normally it is difficult to tell whether or not logical conditions like computability are really obtained in a system, or just seem to hold, because of specific system models that may or may not be correct. Another advantage of a dynamical account is that it can help to distinguish accidental and necessary conditions associated with emergence. Indeed, Collier thinks that Andrade mentions a number of accidental conditions as if they were necessary for emergence. One example would be the assumption that closed systems cannot be emergent. The universe, Collier argues, is both closed and isolated, and, yet, exhibits emergent properties. Moreover, neither far-from-equilibrium conditions nor complexity are regarded by Collier as necessary to emergence, even though they can be associated with it. In the end of his piece, he expresses his agreement with Andrade's arguments about information and semiosis, appraising them as a putative basis for a dynamical account of semiosis, as he himself tried to produce in other papers. We cannot but agree that, even though important steps have already been taken, there is still much to be done before a more precise account of the connections between information, semiosis, and dynamics is available.

In several papers included in this special number, the controversial nature of the concept of downward causation is considered. Vieira and El-Hani's paper focuses precisely on this concept. The problem of downward causation is the problem of how a higher-level phenomenon can cause or determine or structure a lower-level phenomenon. It is both a central concept in emergentist thinking and a highly debated issue in the literature on emergence. Vieira and El-Hani begin by considering previous attempts to advance in neo-Aristotelian approaches to this problem. These approaches claim that additional causal modes—besides efficient causation—should come into play if one wants to understand downward causation, in particular, formal and functional causal modes. Vieira and El-Hani's argument is, rather, that one should move towards conceptualizing other kinds of determination, besides causal determination, as we can see, for instance, in discussions about supervenience and physical realization. They offer, then, an account of downward determination with the intent of establishing what is determining and determined, and, moreover, what the meaning of *determining* is in such a phenomenon. The idea is to contribute to the development of a coherent account about how principles of organization constrain and, thus, partially determine the behavior of a system's lower-level constituents. They formulate the determining influence of a higher-level general organizational principle on particular lower-level processes as follows: if lower-level entities $a,b,c,...,n$ are under the influence of a general organizational principle, W, then they will show a tendency, a disposition, to instantiate process p or a set of processes $\{P\}$, rather than some other, also possible processes. Further, the changes in disposition in downward determination can be treated in terms of Popper's propensities, in such a manner that their probability is not just in our minds, but is, instead, instantiated in the world.

Alvaro Moreno stresses, in his comment to Vieira and El-Hani's paper, his agreement with the central assumption that downward causation plays an important role in our current understanding of biological phenomena. Still, he disagrees with the idea of moving from a concept of causation to a concept of downward determination. Moreno also seems puzzled by Vieira and El-Hani's apparent agreement with arguments against downward causation, while not stating so clearly their rejection of such criticisms. He rightly calls attention to the many problems that would result from putting the notion of downward causation aside, in our attempts to understand complex systems. Moreno also expresses his agreement with the understanding of constraints as embodied boundary conditions harnessing lower-level dynamics. But, he adds, to validly justify downward causation based on the concept of constraint, one should assess the ontological status of constraints, and further, it is necessary to adopt a naturalized perspective about that concept. He goes on, then, to explain why an ontological concept of constraint enters the scene when we consider thermodynamically dissipative systems. He argues that in dissipative systems the maintenance of the global structure depends not only on a specific set of boundary conditions, but also on the effect they produce on the microscopic dynamics, so that they become self-maintaining structures. This type of constraint is possible due to the creation of a causal loop, crucially involving downward causation. Hence, Moreno reaches a naturalized concept of constraints, in which they are treated as material structures embedded in a closed organization that they contribute to maintain. His next step, then, is to show how in the case of enzymes a new type of constraint is reached from these former types of constraints found in dissipative structures. Enzymes constitute a flexible and specific, relatively stable form of constraint, which harnesses both the rate and specificity of the low level processes. Enzymes also make it possible that highly specific and unlikely recursive networks of chemical reactions are produced. These networks, in turn, renew the very enzymes, turning them into more persistent structures than they were at first. We are, then, at the realm of living systems as we know them. To the end of his commentary, Moreno shows his disagreement with Vieira and El-Hani's proposal of replacing causation by non-causal determination in the treatment of whole-to-part relationships. He does so by arguing that determination, as opposed to causation, means purely formal entailment, and constraints appear as rate-dependent, material processes.

When addressing downward determination, Vieira and El-Hani consider a flexible, specific, and relatively stable type of constraint, harnessing the rate and specificity of lower-level processes, as one finds in enzymes and other biological entities and processes. In their reply, they call attention to the fact that, while they are discussing logical conditions for emergence, Moreno's emphasis lies on dynamics. It is indeed the case that a proper discussion about emergence and downward determination should include a consideration of both aspects, but Vieira and El-Hani focus on the former in the paper included in this issue. They do not think that one can just overcome the problems surrounding the idea of downward causation by appealing to a concept such as meta-efficient causation. Despite the recourse to this concept, the philosophical problems are still there. When addressing these problems, they stress that they do not intend to argue for downward determination in a disembodied way. This is why they appealed to Popper's propensities theory of probability, since it puts probability in the world. In this case, one is not dealing with purely formal entailments, but, rather, with material processes. Vieira and El-Hani intend to propose that there are advantages in talking about downward determination, rather than causation, when addressing the many philosophical problems related to the synchronic influence of wholes over parts. This was precisely the move in the understanding of another mereological relation, the physical realization or constitution of wholes by their parts. Physical realization has been conceived as a synchronic, non-causal determinative relationship even by strong critics of downward causation and emergence, such as Jaegwon Kim. They see many advantages in moving towards determination, and not only strategic ones, but also in the sense of conceptual clarification. It seems to them that the formulation of downward determination in terms of Popperian propensities may make it clearer what is at stake when a higher-level subsystem constrains or harnesses the dynamics of lower-level subsystems. The need to clarify some central issues related to downward causation explains why Vieira and El-Hani gave so much attention to the philosophical strategy of carefully running through arguments against this notion, so as to provide answers to them. They argue that it is true that rejecting the notion of downward causation would create many more problems than accepting it, but this does not relieve us of providing conceptual clarifications about the meaning of that notion. They finish their reply by stating that, in order to move on to a discussion about the contributions of downward determination to the understanding of complex biological systems, it will be important to build a case for naturalized constraints, as Moreno stresses, and, also, to shift from logical to dynamical conditions for emergence, as Collier prompts us to do.

Ranulph Glanville's column: A Cybernetic Musing is this time called "Five Friends;" one may add "of second-order cybernetics." Roughly these friends are as follows: (1) The principle that a description of a thing is not the thing described. This is the basic premise of representation. (2) Circularity of form leading by iterative recursion. (3) The Turing Test, a conceptual tool defining intelligence based on recognizing the quality of intelligence attributed by an observer to an object, based on their interaction. (4) The black box, which allows us to remain profoundly ignorant, yet to build descriptions allowing us to act as if we knew. Glanville considers the black box the best available description of how we confront the world and the root device of radical constructivism. Finally, (5) The principle of mutual reciprocity, which states that, if we draw a distinction based on a quality, we must also permit the possibility of the same quality being given to the other side of that distinction. Glanville writes: "In distinguishing ourselves, we must also distinguish another: there is no distinction in a world of one!" This is also what the Turing test and circularity do. Thus the attribution of intelligence to an object cannot with certainty be deemed an essence of that object, but is in the description of interaction; and we have circulated back again!

In this issue we have also included two contributions from Klaus Krippendorff: a paper titled "Social Organizations as Reconstitutable Networks of Conversation" and this month's ASC Column, titled "Cybernetics's Reflexive Turns." These two interlinked papers were not planned as part of the volume theme, but emergence as a phenomenon is not totally absent from the notions inherent in the ideas. The dynamics of conversation can be regarded as always emergent, always arising in the present. The meaning of actions is created and accepted or dismissed according to the dynamics of each conversation. As Krippendorff discusses, the meaning of texts also arises in the process of reading, and the coordination of one's reading in conversations with others. Thus meanings are dialogical accomplishments.

Though the underlying passion of this paper is a plea against trivializing human agency, the body of the paper is centered around the claim that the ability of individual actors to reconstitute a social organization supersedes all other conditions of a social organization's viability. Several metaphors of social organization (e.g., family, machine, biological, person, and network) are shown to be variously lacking or misleading. Given that organizations exist according to how their members constitute and reconstitute them at any moment, regardless of how the organization may be described, one could also consider organizations as emergent phenomena. But as stated before, this paper was not solicited in the context of the theme of this issue; it is presented here as it is so closely linked to the current ASC column.

In the ASC column Krippendorff discusses the implications to cybernetics of some of the ideas in his paper on reconstitutable organizations. Krippendorff is concerned that second-order cybernetics's is constrained by three implications of its commitment to cognitive autonomy: cognitivism, observation, and representation. The paper offers an epistemology of constructive participation in social systems by adding three reflexive turns to the epistemological consequences of cognitive autonomy. Two of these have historical roots in cybernetics, but have not been fully examined. Krippendorff invites us to consider further the implications of 1) participation in (responding to, designing, and constituting) systems; 2) involvement in the epistemologies of various discourses; and 3) the social contextualization of the discourse of cybernetics. Regarding the latter, he reads Margaret Mead's call for a "cybernetics of cybernetics" as an invitation to cyberneticians to recognize and embrace responsibility for the complexification that cybernetics is bringing to society – a reflexive participation in an unprecedented, and perhaps emerging path of social changes. Krippendorff summarizes the column with an emerging definition of cybernetics: namely "an inter-disciplinary discourse that brings forth radically reflexive realities."

Phillip Guddemi, in this issue, reviews a book on the relevance of Gregory Bateson to biosemiotics. The editor of this book is Jesper Hoffmeyer, the originator of the concept and field of biosemiotics. In 2005, as one of the last commemorations of the 100th anniversary of Bateson's birth, Hoffmeyer and others organized the Copenhagen Bateson Symposium. The book is composed of articles based on papers given at that conference. In his review, Phillip Guddemi, who was also a participant, constructs a perspective on how the papers comprising this book relate to Bateson's ideas and to each other's. He hopes thereby to encourage a continued conversation, begun with the symposium and with this book, about Bateson's legacy and its potential for inspiring creative work today.

The artist for this issue, Kathleen Forsythe, has incorporated her understanding of circularity and reflexivity in most of her work; including her art. She paints for pleasure, for the sense of renewal and aliveness that creativity offers. For her the act of painting is always a surprise; as she says "just like life!" For Kathleen the experience of painting, and of observing not only the evolving painting but the process of participating in that, helps her "to unfold the infinite interior and to see the act of creation in the process of it happening."

Forsythe, K. (2006). *Saragasso Sea*. 45 cm x 75 cm, acrylic on paper.

Cybernetics And Human Knowing. Vol. 15, nos. 3-4, pp. 15-41

Emergence and Downward Causation in Contemporary Artificial Agents:
Implications for their Autonomy and Some Design Guidelines

Argyris Arnellos, Thomas Spyrou, John Darzentas[1]

Contemporary research in artificial environments has marked the need for autonomy in artificial agents. Autonomy has many interpretations in terms of the field within which it is being used and analyzed, but the majority of the researchers in artificial environments are arguing in favor of a strong and life-like notion of autonomy. Departing from this point the main aim of this paper is to examine the possibility of the emergence of autonomy in contemporary artificial agents. The theoretical findings of research in the areas of living and cognitive systems, suggests that the study of autonomous agents should adopt a systemic and emergent perspective for the analysis of the evolutionary development of the notions/properties of autonomy, functionality, intentionality and meaning, as the fundamental and characteristic properties of a natural agent. An analytic indication of the functional emergence of these concepts and properties is provided, based on the characteristics of the more general systemic framework of second-order cybernetic and of the interactivist framework. The notion of emergence is a key concept in such an analysis which in turn provides the ground for the theoretical evaluation of the autonomy of contemporary artificial agents with respect to the functional emergence of their capacities. The fundamental problems for the emergence of genuine autonomy in artificial agents are critically discussed and some design guidelines are provided.

Keywords: Autonomy, Emergence, Functionality, Meaning, Self-organization, Normativity, Agency, Intentionality, Downward Causation

1 Autonomy and Agency

Autonomy is a property that is quite easily ascribed to almost every contemporary artificial agent independently of its constructive, developmental, and functional characteristics (see e.g., Hexmoor, Castelfranchi, & Falcone, 2003). However, and not surprisingly though, the same happens with the notion of agency for almost all artificial systems that are able for at least the most basic interaction with their environment, independently of the ways this interaction is realized. As a result, any artificial system that can be observed to exhibit some kind of pro-activeness in terms of taking the initiative, to have a self-ruling and independent ability to perceive its environment, to reason in order to interpret its perceptions, to draw inferences in order to act in its environment, to solve problems, to communicate with other artificial or natural systems and in general, to socialize, is called as *autonomous agent*. Is this

1. Department of Product and Systems Design Engineering - University of the Aegean, 84100, Syros, Greece.
   Email: arar@aegean.gr, tsp@aegean.gr, idarz@aegean.gr

justified for every artificial system which is the design result of the research being held in the areas of AI, robotics, ALife, multi-agent systems, and so forth.?

The term *autonomous* derives from a Greek composite word (auto = self) and (nomos = law) and although it has many interpretations, it literally means that a system is free of external control and constraint in its action and judgment, that is self-governing, self-steering. In its most basic version it means that a system exists and acts as an independent entity, that is, it self-generates the rules that govern its functioning, or in other terms, it self-generates its self-regulation. In more specific terms, as (Collier, 2002) argues, an autonomous system exhibits a special form of functional organization that contributes to its own governance and uses this governance for its own maintenance in a variable environment. Consequently, the organization of an autonomous system is both the subject and the object of its functionality.

Autonomous systems primarily act in the world for their self-maintenance. The ability to act upon an environment in order to effect a goal-oriented attribution of a certain purpose belongs to an agent and hence, autonomous systems are ultimately agents. Of course, there are several natural systems that can be considered as autonomous agents, but these systems demonstrate different degrees of agency. Concepts such as autonomy and pro-activity, even though "simple" properties such as perception and inference are not a black and white issue, at all. This should be quite expectable for agency, as well, as it does not also come in an all or nothing package, but it has a gradual nature and there are various many different levels of agency in the biological realm. Actually, autonomy drives interaction and profits from it, and as a result enhances the capacity for agency (Arnellos, Spyrou and Darzentas, in press). Agents are not static things, but complex systems interacting with dynamic and complex environments and therefore exhibiting a dynamic nature. Adopting a dynamic and evolutionary view and attempting to project an agent in a future time horizon, one may suggest that there are some dynamic and gradual conceptual and material ingredients that are complexly integrated together to form an agent in various degrees and in various points of evolution.

Considering the above mentioned, and keeping artificial agents in mind, one may conclude that a complete definition of the term *agent* is out of any question and any prospective definition towards this direction should express agency as a capacity with a gradual and evolutionary nature. In order to pursue such definition we try to modify Kampis's (1999) evolutionary definition of agency, which comes as a list of somewhat ad hoc properties of an agent, in a way that the suggested definition is more susceptible to an analysis of its functional characteristics. We suggest that such a strong notion of agency calls for: interactivity – the ability of an agent/cognitive system to perceive and act upon its environment by taking the initiative; intentionality – the ability of an agent to effect a goal-oriented interaction by attributing purposes, beliefs and desires to its actions; and autonomy – which can be characterized as the ability of an agent to function/operate intentionally and interactively based on its own resources.

This definition mentions three fundamental capacities that an agent should exhibit in a somewhat nested way regarding their existence and evolutionary development. Therefore, according to this definition, agency requires interactivity, which in turn implies action upon the environment. This action is not an accidental but an intentional one, as it is a purposeful action directed towards a goal and it is driven by content such as beliefs and desires. Additionally, such an agent exhibits the property of autonomy, as it interacts with the environment in an intentional manner based on its own resources, hence, also based on its internal content. These three properties seem to be quite interdependent, especially when one attempts to understand if it is possible for each one of them to increase qualitatively while the others remain at the same level.

On the other hand, notions such as autonomy, intentionality, beliefs, goal-orientation, cognition, and so forth are philosophically-loaded and quite heavy terms, which bring about controversies in relevant discussions even in the highly theoretical and interdisciplinary scientific domains. Considering that a theoretical and naturalized analysis of an autonomous agent should also be used as an inspiration and a guide for the design of artificial agency, one should be very careful regarding the conceptual burden that may be raised by the theoretical load of the respective terminology. It is not unlikely, at all, that this is one of the reasons that contemporary artificial systems are so easily called autonomous agents. In the desired direction, Collier (1999), from a critical perspective on the domain of complex systems research, suggests that there is a very interesting interdependence between the three above-mentioned properties. Specifically, Collier suggests that there is no function without autonomy, no intentionality without function, and no meaning without intentionality. The interdependence is completed by considering meaning as a prerequisite for the maintenance of a system's autonomy during its purposeful interaction with the environment.

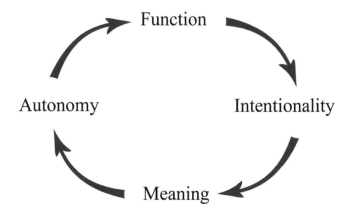

Fig. 1 - Interdependence between autonomy, functionality, intentionality and meaning in an autonomous agent.

At this point some may say that this is just a conceptual interdependence. However, as analyzed below, it is also a theoretical interdependence with a functional grounding, and as such, it sets some interesting constraints in the capacities that contribute to agency and it brings about some requirements in terms of the properties that an agent should exhibit independently of its agential level or in other words, of its level of autonomy and as such, of its cognitive capacity (see Arnellos, Spyrou, Darzentas, 2007b, in press). These properties and their interdependence are characteristics of the strong notion of agency (i.e. the one exhibited by living systems), which is considered as emergent in the functional organization of the living/ cognitive system, that is, the autonomous agent. The term *functional* is used here to denote the processes of the network of components that contribute to the autonomy of the agent and particularly, to the maintenance of the autonomous system as a whole (see e.g., Ruiz-Mirazo & Moreno, 2004).

On the other hand, meaning, if it is not to be considered as an ascription of an observer, should be linked with the functional structures of the agent. Hence, meaning should guide the constructive and interactive processes of the functional components of the autonomous system in such a way that these processes maintain and enhance its autonomy. In this perspective, the enhancement of autonomy places certain goals by the autonomous system itself and hence, the intentionality of the system is functionally guiding its behavior through meaning.

At this point, one may ask again the same question, namely if the design results of the broad areas of AI and ALife can be called as autonomous agents. It seems that if one decides to rely upon the analysis so far, he is almost obliged to answer in the negative, although he is not in a very comfortable position with his answer as he still has no means to analytically ground his decision. In the rest of this paper an attempt is made to provide an analysis for such an answer, based on a more analytic indication of the functional formation of the above mentioned concepts and properties that constitute an autonomous agent during its development and evolution. The notion of emergence will prove to be a key concept and the ground for such an answer, as it is directly related to the functionality and the autonomy of an agent.

2   Emergent Functionality in Autonomous Agents

One should always keep in mind that in such an autonomous system, intentionality is not reducible to the processing of meanings, nor are the combinations of meanings bringing forth any "aboutness." On the contrary, meaning and its functional substratum are properties that may emerge when an autonomous agent acts intentionally. In other words, an autonomous system may act intentionally if its actions are mediated by meaning. Hence, it appears that for a system to exhibit the capacity of agency, it needs to exhibit the degree of autonomy that will provide for the functionality that is needed, in order to support its intentional and purposeful interaction with the environment, the result of which will emerge new meanings that will further enhance its autonomy. The foundations of such a functional emergence have been established in the systems-theoretic framework of second-order cybernetics.

2.1 Emergence through Organizational Closure and Self-Reference

In the second-order cybernetic epistemology a cognitive system is able to carry out the fundamental actions of distinction and observation. It observes its boundaries and it is thus differentiated from its environment. As the cognitive system is able to observe the distinctions it makes, it is able to refer the result of its actions back to itself. This makes it a self-referential system, providing it with the ability to create new distinctions (actions) based on previous ones, to judge its distinctions, and to increase its complexity by emerging new meanings in order to interact. The self-referential loop can only exist in relation to an environment, but it also disregards the classical system-environment models, which hold that the external control of a cognitive system's adaptation to its environment is replaced by a model of systemic and operational/organizational closure (von Foerster, 1960/2003, 1981).

Due to that closure, the self-reference of an observation emerges meaning inside the cognitive system, which is used as a model for further observations in order to compensate for external complexity. The system which operates on meaning activates only internal functions and structures, (eigenvalues), a set of some stable structures, which are maintained in the functions of the cognitive system's organizational dynamics (Rocha, 1996) and which serve as points of departure for further operations during its interaction with the environment. Indeed, this closure is functional in so far as the effects produced by the cognitive system are the causes for the maintenance of its systemic equilibrium through the emergence of more complex organizations.

With system closure, environmental complexity is based solely on system observations, thus, system reality is observation-based. As von Foerster (1976/2003) argued, the results of an observation do not refer directly to the objects of the real world, but instead, they are the results of recurrent cognitive functions in the structural coupling between the cognitive system and the environment. In particular, von Foerster states that "ontologically, Eigenvalues and objects, and likewise, ontogenetically, stable behavior and the manifestation of a subject's 'grasp' of an object cannot be distinguished" (von Foerster, 1976/2003, p. 266). Thus, each emergent function based on observations is a construction, it is an increase of the organization and cognitive complexity of the agent. This process of emergent increment of order through the internal construction of functional organizations and simultaneous classification of the environment is a process of self-organization (von Foerster, 1960/2003, 1981).

There are two interesting issues at this point. First, self-organizing systems appear to have an emergent functionality which provides the means for self-maintained, self-enhanced and self-regulated organizational dynamics. This functionality originates from a network of processes with a high degree of recursivity that produces and maintains internal invariances in the case of internal and external perturbations. This may be seen as an abstract conception of an autonomous agent, although, as it will be shown below, it is not (see Fig. 2), but nevertheless, it appears to be a model close enough to many realizations in different biological scales and domains. As such, in the second-order cybernetic framework of autopoiesis (Maturana & Varela, 1980), life is defined as this special kind of basic autonomy (Varela, 1979; Varela & Bourgine, 1992). Actually, Varela says that:

> Autonomous systems are mechanistic (dynamic) systems defined as a unity by their organization. We shall say that autonomous systems are organizationally closed. That is, their organization is characterized by processes such that (1) the processes are related as a network, so that they recursively depend on each other in the generation and realization of the processes themselves, and (2) they constitute the system as a unity recognizable in the space (domain) in which the processes exist. (Varela, 1979, p. 55)

The basis of Varela's conception of autonomy is its active role in the contribution of the self-maintenance of the autopoietic system and especially in the production of its active components, but also in the effective alteration of its boundary conditions in order for the system to be able to maintain its necessary variables in a homeostatic way. What is emphasized in autopoiesis and in self-organization, in general, is the systemic and emergent nature of the whole organism as an autonomous agent. The functionality of the processes of such an autonomous system, as it is described by the two characteristic features in Varela's quotation, can be mapped to an organizational code which executes three functions/operations: a selection of the structural components of the system; their interrelation/correlation in order to emerge a functional whole; and a continuous self-referential control/steering in order to make sure that the respective selection and interrelation are fulfilling the goals of the system.

This code belongs to the designer of the autonomous system, and for the moment, that which primarily distinguishes between a self-organizing and an artificial system is that in the former case the goal comes from within the system, that is the system designs itself and for itself (Arnellos, Spyrou, & Darzentas, 2007a), while in the latter case, the goal comes from an external designer. For the moment, we are not going to comment in the respective difference. What is really important is that a certain kind of functionality emerges out of the code's selection and interrelation processes and it emerges in such a way, that one is justified to say that it is the new functional organization that establishes the autonomy of the system (no. 2 in Varela's quotation), but it is also responsible for its maintenance, as it is the code which continuously selects and interrelates the emergent processes with a focus on the goal of their regeneration and realization (downward causation), that is, with a focus on its self-maintenance (no. 1 in Varela's quotation). It appears that for Varela, from an epistemological perspective, autonomy is equivalent to the notion of self-referentiality, which in turn, it is connected to the concept of organizational closure (Luisi, 2003). The basis of Varela's conception of autonomy is its active role in the contribution of the self-maintenance of the autopoietic system and especially in the production of its active components, but also in the effective alteration of its boundary conditions in order for the system to be able to maintain its necessary variables in a homeostatic way.

On the same track, cognitive behavior is the result of a higher level of autonomy, where the neural system creates invariant patterns of sensorimotor correspondences in order to determine the behavior of the living system as a unit that exists and acts in space. Specifically, von Foerster, in his really enlightening attempt to describe the self-referential nature of the nervous system, he makes a model of it as a matrix (Fig. 2) in which the squares are nervous cells and in between them are the synaptic gaps, which can be filled with transmitters and says that:

The black squares labelled N represent bundles of neurons that synapse with neurons of other bundles over the (synaptic) gaps indicated by the spaces between squares. The sensory surface (SS) of the organism is to the left, its motor surface (MS) to the right, and the neuropituitary (NP), the strongly innervated master gland that regulates the entire endocrine system, is the stippled lower boundary of the array of squares. Nerve impulses travelling horizontally (from left to right) ultimately act on the motor surface (MS) whose changes (movements) are immediately sensed by the sensory surface (SS), as suggested by the "external" pathway following the arrows. Impulses travelling vertically (from top to bottom) stimulate the neuropituitary (NP), whose activity release steroids into the synaptic gaps, as suggested by the wiggly terminations of the lines following the arrow, and thus modify the modus operandi of all synaptic junctures, hence, the modus operandi of the system as a whole. Note the double closure of the system that now recursively operates not only on what it "sees", but on its operators as well. (von Foerster, 1988/2003, p. 225)

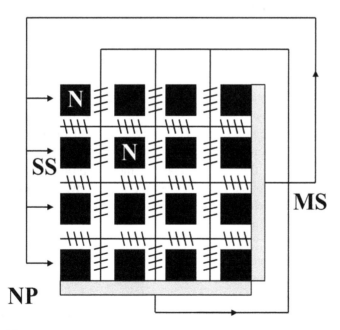

Fig. 2. Double closure of the senso-motoric and inner-secretoric-neuronal circuits

He then continues by arguing that this double closure between these two non-trivial machines are making computations which are subject to a non-trivial constraint, which is postulated as cognitive homeostasis, namely that "The nervous system is organized (or organizes itself) so that it computes a stable reality" (von Foerster, 1988/ 2003, p. 225).

Again, instances of emergence and downward causation are present in this organization, based on which, the autonomous system is able to perceive and act in its environment by internally creating meaningful information about its external environment. Specifically, a new functional meaning (modus operandi) emerges out of the self-organizing activity of the sensorimotor system with the activity of the neurohypophysis that produces steroids and releases them in the synaptic gaps. This emergent functionality forms the neural system as a whole, through which the agent interacts with the world and then immediately feeds back into it the respective environmental changes, which, through the receptors, return to the motor system, and in turn, regulate its self-organization (downward causation).

Another important issue that should be noticed is that in the second-order cybernetic framework a certain kind of autonomy is established, where the cognitive capacities are directly related with the capacity of the system to be alive. Particularly, in this perspective of agency, intentionality and especially, the endogenous production of purpose are located at the level of the origin of life and of biological functionality. Therefore, this inclination of a self-organizing cognitive system to maintain its own self-organization constitutes the core of its intentional and purposeful (goal-oriented) interaction with the environment. This is another characteristic of autonomous self-organizing and autopoietic agents, which distinguishes them from artificial agents (see section 3).

The analysis of the functional formation of the main concepts related to autonomous agents, presented so far, could also be used as a basis for judging the autonomy of artificial agents. However, the respective description is not adequately naturalized (Arnellos, Spyrou, & Darzentas, in press). Although we managed to ground autonomous agency on the functionality of the self-organizing system and to introduce some requirements for it, this is not as far as we may go in terms of naturalization and hence, this will not be the most appropriate theoretical ground based on which we will be able to judge for their autonomy, and most importantly, to advise their design. Therefore, we continue our analysis with the relevant, to our problem, notion of cohesion.

2.2 Emergence of Cohesion via Process Closure

In section 2.1 it was argued that what defines an autonomous system is a global network of relations that establishes some self-maintained dynamics, where action and constitution are identical properties of the system itself. Practically, this means that the activity of the system is constituted of the constant regeneration of all the processes and of the components that constitute the system as an emergent functional whole. It is due to self-reference that the organizationally closed nature of such an autonomous system is not considered as circular. Actually, the internal productive interrelations acquire a cohesive functional meaning in a collective way, since they contribute to the overall maintenance of the system. In the respective organization the whole and the parts are correlated to each other in a highly dynamic and reciprocal way. This systemic pattern of organizational (functional) dynamics is observed in every self-organizing system. Collier (1988) and Collier and Muller (1998) have called this pattern of organizational dynamics as cohesion, which is an inclusive capacity of an autonomous system and it indicates the existence of causal interactions among the components of the system in which certain capacities emerge and hence, the respective components are constituents for the system itself. Cohesion is not an epiphenomenal property, but on the contrary, it is exactly the emergence of this functional cohesion that avoids meaningless circularity and as such, the organization of the respective autonomous systems disregards the classical mechanistic opposition between the constituent parts and the global properties of the system itself.

Cohesion is an emergent property and as such, it can only be explained with respect to the causal roles that the constituent components and the relations among them acquire in the dynamic organization of the system.

Cohesive systems exhibit different kinds of correlations between different processes with respect to the degree (or the type) of cohesion that they exhibit. Systems with very strong and highly local bonds exhibit a powerful cohesion, which does not necessarily provide them with genuine autonomy and agency. Nevertheless, in the level of autopoiesis, or in what Ruiz-Mirazo & Moreno (2000) call the level of metabolic agency, the respective cohesion emerges in systems that are thermodynamically open and function in far-from-equilibrium conditions (Collier & Hooker, 1999). Such systems exhibit a kind of long-range correlations between different processes (certainly longer than the correlations that one can meet in a rock or in a self-organized crystal). As Collier (2007) has stressed, since there is an internal need for the coordination of the processes in order for them to achieve viability (self-maintenance), one should expect to find in such an autonomous system a holistic organization in which organizationally/operationally open aspects of lower level are closed at higher organizational levels. As it has already been argued, this is a highly constructive type of autonomy and it requires what Collier (1999) suggests as process closure (in accordance with organizational/operational closure), in order to mention the fact that in such autonomous systems there are some internal constraints controlling the internal flow of matter and energy, and by doing so, the whole system acquires the capacity to carry out the respective processes, since these processes will contribute to its self-maintenance.

Furthermore, and as it appears from Varela's quotation, the nature of the emergent process closure implies that all the interactive alternatives of the cognitive system are internally generated and their selection is an entirely internal process. Therefore, such autonomous systems must construct their reality by using internally available structures. Their functionality is entirely dependent on its structural components and their interrelationships that establish the respective dynamics. Hence, the functionality of the cognitive system is immediately related to the maintenance of its systemic cohesion and consequently of its self-organizational dynamics. At this point, one should notice the interesting relation between second-order cybernetic systems, or systems that emerge functional cohesion mainly through process closure, with von Uexküll's theories about the functionality of living systems (von Uexküll, 1982). For von Uexküll, living organisms contain a functional rule or a building plan (i.e. an organizational code), which has an inherent meaning quality and thus, living systems are acting plans (i.e. they design themselves and for themselves, see also Arnellos, Spyrou, & Darzentas, 2007a), in contrast to machines that act according to the plans of their designers. This capacity makes them autonomous systems, such as the autopoietic systems, in contrast to machines, which are allopoietic systems.

What is really important regarding this type of emergent coherence is that since, in the more general second-order cybernetic framework of autopoiesis, functional closure enables the recursively interdependent generation and realization of the involved processes themselves, what really emerges is a distinct autonomous agent with a simultaneously configured world of perception and action. This is exactly what von Uexküll calls the coming together of the organism's components to form a coherent whole, which acts as a subject. This is the reason for arguing that this emergent coherence forms a system whose cognitive capacities are directly related with the capacity of the system to be alive. The emergent coherence is a result of a functional embedding, and it provides such autonomous systems with a certain kind of embodiment, which make the study of their behavior irreducible to physics and chemistry. For von Uexküll, this kind of embodiment emerges the Umwelt (i.e. the subjective world) of the autonomous agent.

In the autonomous systems described so far, perception and action are so closely related to the self-constructive and self-maintaining dynamics of the system. As a result, any downward causation, as the constraining of the function of the system's parts from the whole, will also acquire very fast and local characteristics in order to be able to be synchronized with the next step of the functional emergence, since the fundamental purpose of such systems is to maintain themselves. This is a kind of strong downward causation that comes in a greater degree from the higher levels of the system than from the environment.

Nevertheless, rocks and crystals show great degrees of cohesion with the respective emergent and downward constraining characteristics, but they are not exhibiting any significant intentionality, let alone experiencing any Umwelt, and as such, they cannot be considered as genuine agents. Agency do comes in a lot of degrees and different levels in nature (Arnellos, Spyrou, & Darzentas, in press), but almost everybody would agree that living systems are quite different from rocks. The main difference lies in the fact that genuine autonomous systems, such as living systems, exhibit a high degree of disentanglement from the environment, not in terms of their interactive processes, but, in terms of their ability to adapt in different environmental perturbations. On the contrary, systems merely exhibiting cohesion via process closure emerge a functional organization that is too tight with their environments, but with minimal interactive characteristics, and as such, they cannot evolve beyond a certain threshold. Hence, such systems are at the threshold of autonomy exhibiting, at most, a reactive type of agency.

It will then be safe to argue that cohesion via process closure is a necessary but not a sufficient condition for genuine autonomy and agency. Again, there are enough tools to judge and criticize the autonomy of contemporary artificial agents, but there are also some other important issues that should be considered in order to better to advise their design. Particularly, genuinely autonomous agency is open-ended and emerges out of intentional and mostly ill-defined goals and purposes of the respective systems (Arnellos, Spyrou, & Darzentas, 2007b). Therefore, agency cannot be solely a matter of internal constructive processes and process closure. The need for open-endedness calls for interaction of the autonomous agent with the environment, while, the functional aspects of such an embodiment and its anticipatory content calls for advanced and efficient mechanisms of controlling and managing these interactions.

2.3 Emergence of Normative Functionality

As it was described in 2.2, and due to the organization code – the functional rule, or the building plan of the system – a qualitative and quantitative imbalance emerges that indicates an asymmetry between the system and its environment. Specifically, in the self-organizing systems described so far, this asymmetry is created and maintained by the functionality of the system through the establishment of internal constructive relations that differentiate the system from its environment organizationally, and further, specify its autonomy and its identity. Hoffmeyer (1998) strongly argues that the secret of life and the development of agency are constructed upon this fundamental asymmetry. From a biological point of view, Hoffmeyer (1998), and others (see e.g. Ruiz-Mirazo & Moreno, 2000, 2004) suggest that this asymmetry is produced via a semi-permeable membrane. This membrane plays the role of dynamic boundaries, which has a functional basis of a chemical nature as they are the result of a productive organization and of the activity of the self-regulating and self-modifying processes of their systems.

This self-regulation aims in the maintenance of the system. The autopoietic model exemplifies this active relation between the boundary and the recursive production processes of the system's constitutive components, but with an emphasis in the absoluteness of the control and constrain of the flows of energy and matter in the system from the environment (Collier, 2004b). As also suggested by Hoffmeyer, this relation is a relation of regulation, hence, it cannot be an absolute one. Although the material basis of the complex boundary that supports the asymmetry is crucial for the functional emergence of such a boundary, for the moment, let's stay with the logical implications of such an asymmetry.

Bickhard (1993, 2000) exemplifies the implications of this asymmetry by postulating a recursive self-maintenant system, which is a self-organizing system that has more than one means at its disposal in order to maintain its ability of being self-maintenant in various environmental conditions. This is a self-organizing system which functions far-from the thermodynamic equilibrium by continuously interacting with the environment, from where it finds the appropriate conditions for the success of its functional processes. Far from equilibrium processes cannot be kept in isolation, as they will run out of their dynamic functional stability. Consequently, the interactive opening of the system to the environment is considered as the most important point in its evolution towards genuine autonomy and agency, as it first of all enhances the stability of the system and its ability to maintain its maintenance. Specifically, the interactions in which an autonomous agent engages will be functional and dysfunctional (Moreno & Barandiaran, 2004). The former corresponds to the interactions which are integrated in the functional organization of the agent and in this way they contribute to its self-maintenance. The latter corresponds to the interactions that cannot be properly integrated in the functional organization and hence, they do not contribute or/and disturb the self-maintenance of the system.

Therefore, the primary goal of such a self-organizing system is to maintain its autonomy in the course of interactions. Since it is a self-organizing system, its embodiment is of a kind that its functionality is immediately related to its autonomy, through the fact that its apparent inclination to maintain its autonomy, in terms of its self-maintenance (its purpose), constitutes the intentionality of its actions and hence, of its interaction with the environment. As such, autonomous systems do not only exhibit process closure, but also interaction closure (Collier, 1999, 2000, 2007), a situation where the internal outcomes of the interactions of the autonomous system with its environment contributes to the maintenance of the functional (constructive/ interactive) processes of the system that are responsible for these specific interactions. It is cohesion via process and interaction closure that distinguishes truly autonomous systems from other kind of cohesive systems. In this case, an autonomous system is not only able to maintain itself, but it can also meaningfully alter its internal functionality in order to adapt to complex and changing conditions around the environment. This capacity for meaningful critique regarding the functional and the dysfunctional with respect to the maintenance of the system is a normative one. Self-maintenant systems that exhibit normative functionality are truly autonomous systems and they present genuine agency (for more details on normativity and agency see Moreno & Barandiaran, 2004; Bickhard, 2005; Arnellos, Spyrou, & Darzentas, in press).

In this way, the overall functional closure (process and interaction closure) of an agent is guided by its autonomy, in the sense of the former contributing for the maintenance of the latter, while its intentionality derives from this specific normative functionality, as the latter is being directed towards the primary purpose of maintaining the self-maintenance. This cohesive combination of process and interaction closure is responsible for the emergence of functional norms within the autonomous system and for the autonomous system itself. Emmeche (2000), being on the same track, says that "the notion of function in biology is the teleological notion of 'a part existing for the good of the whole,' or 'having the purpose of' doing something in relation to the whole." (Emmeche, 2000, p. 194). As such, he also adopts the normative perspective of emergent functionality, while he also suggests that functionality is only possible under a closure of operations, but as the capacity for interaction closure suggests, he also argues in favor of an only partial and relatively open functional closure. Specifically, Emmeche says that:

> Only when the causal chain from one part to the next closes or feeds back in a closed loop -- at once a feed-back on the level of parts and an emergent function defined (as mentioned) as a part-whole relation -- can we talk about a genuine function. In other words: It is because function is the function of a part that works effectively to produce (part-part efficient causation) influences on other parts within the same whole (the same form, the organism's) -- where each part is constrained by the same whole (formal causation) -- the total of parts interacting under these constraints in a coherent emergent pattern *is* the whole organism, whose maintenance (final causation) as form is the goal of each part. Here, final causation -- i.e., the dual process of *downward* constraints (formal cause) on the behavior of the parts and the *emergent* pattern of the parts forming a functioning organism (final causation), which is made of parts (material causation) -- is the causation of a physical part within a biological whole being committed to a specific role in the internal organization of that whole, thus the internal ascription (*de re*) of a role to the part is the emergence of that part's function. (Emmeche, 2000, p. 195)

What Emmeche tries to indicate is that a certain part or process of a system serves a function as far as it, first of all, contributes to the maintenance of this system and the role of this part or process is emergent in the internal organization of the respective whole, while this whole is downwardly constraining the emergent pattern/form of this part or process. Hence, normative functions emerge as a contribution for the autonomy of the agent, and with the goal of satisfying the respective functional norms.

What is still missing is meaning, on the basis of which the cognitive system decides which of the available functional processes should make use of, in order to successfully interact with a specific environment, that is, in order to fulfill its goal, that is, to satisfy its functional norms. In this case, an autonomous system uses its anticipations with the respective representational content (meaning). But, where exactly is this content to be found?

2.4 Anticipations and the Emergence of Representational Content

Bickhard argues that such an autonomous system should have a way of differentiating the environments with which it interacts, and a switching mechanism to choose among the appropriate internal functional processes that it will use in the interaction. The differentiations are implicitly and interactively defined, as the internal outcomes of the interaction, which in turn depends on the functional organization of the participating subsystems and of the environment. These differentiations create an epistemic contact with the environment, but they do not carry, in any way, any representational content. However, they are indications of the interactive potentiality of the functional processes of the autonomous system itself. As such, these differentiations functionally indicate that some type of interaction is available in the specific environment and hence, implicitly predicate that the environment exhibits the appropriate conditions for the success of the indicated interaction.

In this model (Bickhard, 1993, 2000), such differentiated indications constitute emergent representations. The conditions of the environment that are functionally and implicitly predicated by the differentiation, as well as, the internal conditions of the autonomous cognitive system (i.e. other functional processes or conditions), that are supposed to be supporting the selected type of interaction, constitute the dynamic presuppositions of the functional processes that will guide the interaction. These presuppositions constitute the representational content of the autonomous cognitive system regarding the differentiated environment. This content emerges in the interaction of the system with the environment. What remains to be shown is how this representational content is related to the anticipations of an autonomous system.

Anticipation relates the present action of an agent with its future state. An anticipatory system has the ability to organize its functional state, in such a way that its current behavior will provide the ability to successfully interact with its environment in the future. An anticipatory system needs to be able to take into consideration the possible results of its actions in advance (that is, prior to its action and as such, purely reactive systems are not capable of anticipative functionality), hence, anticipation is immediately related to the meaning of the representations of the autonomous cognitive system (Collier, 1999). In this way, anticipation is one of the most characteristic aspects of autonomous systems due to their need to shape their dynamic interaction with the environment so as to achieve future outcomes (goals of the system) that will enhance their autonomy. In the context of the autonomous systems discussed so far, these future outcomes should satisfy the demand for process and interaction closure of the system and in general, for system's normative functionality.

Normative functionality is evaluated on the basis of the functional outcomes of the autonomous system, therefore, anticipation is immediately related to functionality (Collier, 2007). Even the simplest function requires anticipation in order to be effective. As mentioned before, anticipation is goal-directed. As a matter of fact, anticipation almost always requires functionality, which is, by default, a goal-oriented process. In this perspective, anticipation guides the functionality of the system through its representational content. In the model of the emergence of representations in the special case of an autonomous agent presented above, the representational content emerges in system's anticipation of interactive capabilities (Bickhard, 2001). In other words, the interactive capabilities are constituted as anticipation and it is this anticipation that could be inappropriate and this is detectable by the system itself, since such anticipation is embedded in the functional context of a goal-directed system (the emergent normativity).

These anticipations are guiding the interpretive interactions of an autonomous agent, that is, the recursive regulatory relations between itself and its environment. In case these interactions contribute to the agent's self-maintenance, its capability for interactive anticipation progressively increases and as such its intentional capacity increases too (Christensen & Hooker, 2002; Arnellos, Spyrou, & Darzentas, 2007b, in press).

So far, an analysis of the functional emergence of the fundamental properties of an autonomous agent has been provided. In the next section, this analysis will be used as a theoretical ground for the evaluation of the autonomy of contemporary artificial agents. The point of reference for this evaluation will be the symbol-grounding problem, which as it will be shown below, it is directly related to the emergence of functionality in an autonomous system.

3   How Autonomous is an Artificial Agent?

3.1 The Symbol-Grounding Problem as an Implication of non-Emergent Functionality
Almost every attempt to build an artificial agent begins by trying to connect the internal world of an agent with its external environment. Most times this connection is being made through the use of symbols, where each one of them has a meaning related to a state of affairs in the external environment. These symbols are playing the role of representations connected with the action modules of the artificial system (i.e. software, hardware or any degree of their combination). The processing of these symbols results in new meanings which guide the action of the system towards its environment. The disembodied nature of these symbolic systems results in the formulation of representations with no connection or/and correlation with the structure and the functionality of the system. This is the essence of the symbol-grounding problem, which comes as a set of problems posed by (Harnad, 1990), who founded his attack on Searle's Chinese Room Argument (Searle, 1980).

Harnad's argument was that an artificial agent does not have access to the meaning of the symbols it manipulates, but, the observer ascribes meaning in its actions. This is like somebody is trying to learn Chinese from a Chinese to Chinese dictionary. He will be able to reply to a Chinese question with a Chinese answer (provided that this is a super-efficient dictionary), but he will never be able to grasp the meaning of Chinese words. In other words, how can syntax ever acquire a semantic content? Therefore, based on the direct analogy, Harnad argues that computers and the respective agents will never be able to grasp the meaning of the symbols they manipulate, and as such, they will never be able to semantically connect these symbols with the respective state of affairs of the environment with which they interact. Artificial agents will never be able to develop the capacity for autonomy.

The source of the symbol-grounding problem is the grounding of meaning within the autonomous system itself. If we accept the analysis of section 2, then, intrinsic meaning requires intrinsic intentionality, which will provide the appropriate functionality for the emergence of meaning, that is, for the emergence of new types of functionality, which will result in new meanings, which will contribute to the autonomy of the system. Along the same lines, Collier (1999) suggests that the prerequisite for representational autonomy (which will immediately vanishes the symbol-grounding problem) is the emergence of functional autonomy from embodied intentionality. As it was argued in 2.4, the meaning of representations is directly related to the anticipations of the system. In case anticipations are not functional emergents of the system, the latter will not be able to confront any environmental change beyond those for which it has been designed to. This is an artificial system with no inherent but with a derivative intentionality, and any such system functions in accordance to the anticipations of its designer, hence, it is design limited. Moreover, such artificial systems cannot alter or enhance their anticipations on their own in order to achieve greater flexibility for their interaction with the environment.

As it has already been shown, these problems will prevent anyone from calling the respective artificial systems as autonomous agents. However, as it was mentioned in the beginning of section 2, almost all the design results of the disciplines of the new AI and of robotics are called as autonomous agents. This is, primarily, because most of the researchers consider symbol-grounding as a problem concerning only the computational framework of cognition (see e.g., Fodor, 1990) and its cornerstone, the physical symbol systems hypothesis (Newell, 1980). Additionally, there is a huge amount of research trying to analyze or/and solve the symbol-grounding problem (see e.g., Chalmers, 1992; Ziemke, 1999; Coradeschi & Saffioti, 2003), and a lot of researchers arguing in favor of it having been solved (for a different kind of analysis regarding the efficiency of several proposed architectures for solving the symbol-grounding problem, see Taddeo & Floridi, 2005). In the next sections we will examine the main approaches in the solution of the symbol-grounding problem having as a basis the theoretical analysis of the functional emergence of a genuine autonomous agent that was presented in section 2.

3.2 Emergence in Computational/Representational Agents
3.2.1   Computationalism provides emergent correspondences
As a solution to the symbol-grounding problem, Harnad suggested a hybrid symbolic/ connectionistic system where symbolic representations are grounded in two types of non-symbolic representations: a. in the iconic representations, which are analog transformations of sensorial perceptions and b. in categorical representations, which take advantage of the sensorimotor invariants for the active transduction of sensorial perceptions to basic symbols (e.g. horse, stripes), from which more composite symbolic representations can be build (e.g. zebra = horse + stripes). In other words, categorical representations are the elements of a systematically combinatorial system. Harnad proposes the use of neural networks for the bottom-up transformation of the real world's objects to individual symbolic representations through the use of non-symbolic representations (Harnad, 1990, 1993).

Harnad argues that the respective categorical representations result from keeping only the invariant properties of an iconic representation, so the cognitive agent will be able to recognize and not only to discriminate an object. He of course admits that this is very difficult to be implemented as it involves the physiology of perception of the natural cognitive systems. Another difficulty, which is also recognized by Harnad, is that in his approach (and in almost all approaches in building an artificial agent) there are some logical operators that should be externally imposed (by the designer) in order the system that combines the categorical representations to function and to configure the respective symbolisms.

The problem is concentrated on the way that the meaning of these operators will be imposed to the system. It is obvious that this kind of meaning does not emerge within the system and the same goes for the respective functionality which is driven by this very meaning. Harnad (1995) argues that such architecture needs a robotic functionality and not a merely computational system, in order for the categorical invariants to be grounded in a realistic (and not in a virtual) sensorimotor interaction between the system and its environment.

What is missing from Harnad's solution regarding the symbol-grounding problem, and, indeed, from every solution which is provided under the cognitivistic/ connectionistic framework, is not the way that the categorical representations are formed, but the need for a clarification of the relation between the external signal and of its iconic representation as its analogue. If this is to be made via a simple transduction of the respective signal, then, the respective correspondence would count as a representation. The problem at this point is that one cannot analyze this transduction and hence, nobody knows if such a correspondence could really count as a representation. Indeed, if one considers the framework of second-order cybernetics described in section 2.1, he will conclude that there is no space for any kind of direct or indirect correspondences, and furthermore, one is not justified to say that *aboutness* comes as a function of such correspondences.

On the other hand, one should also try to explain how such correspondence pre-exists in a respective representation, which is equivalent to explain the whole physiology of perception. Harnad and all other similar approaches use the notion of information as a magical quantity which exists in the external signal and somehow is passed in the representation. This would be acceptable if we had such a theory. For the moment we do not, and considering the approaches presented in section 2, it is highly likely that information is not something that can be passed from one cognitive agent to another, but it is rather the result of the functional formation of a system, and as such, it belongs to it and it stays within it. This is highly related and of course, in accordance with Bickhard's (1993) suggestion, namely that emergent representation, that is, emergent meaning needs inherent aims and goals, otherwise, all one may have is correspondences with no grounded meaning in the artificial agent, but grounded only in the mind of its designer.

3.2.2   Computational and Weak Emergence

There are numerous approaches under the cognitivist/representationalist umbrella, which are all facing the same fundamental problem: what emerge are correspondences and not representations because of the derivative nature of the respective functionality, and as such, there is no emergent meaning, hence, there is no genuine autonomy. Such examples are the approaches of (Cangelosi, Greco, & Harnad, 2000) and (Cangelosi & Harnad, 2001), where they use a very complicated three-layered feedforward neural network as the transformer of categorical perception into grounded low-level labels and then, into higher-level symbols. Although the main problem, that is, the transformation of external data to semantic content for the machine, remains, there are some other issues that should be taken under consideration.

In a feedforward neural network activation is propagated in only one direction (from input to output) and after some time, where the network will have been trained and the weights of its connections will have been stabilized, the respective mappings will remain the same, as the network cannot alter its transfer function. In this case, as Ziemke and Sharkey (2001) argue, the network becomes a trivial machine (to use von Foerster's words), or in other words, a passive action-reaction system. Therefore, these kinds of architectures are breaking down to systems that solely emerge correspondences and not in an open-ended way, as after some time the mapping remains invariant.

However, for their authors, the merit of these architectures is not only the very powerful transduction mechanism, but also the combinatorial strength of the learning modules that are fed by the transducer and they can provide the artificial agent with a very rich vocabulary of higher-order concepts and of language. The appearance of a variety of high-level concepts in these systems is considered as a case of genuine emergent behavior, and the respective systems are considered as autonomous. The reasons for the lack of some concepts in these systems is that the selected underlying functionality or/and the learning mechanism is not the best possible, or that they system has not still interacted with the variety of the environments that a natural agent needs to interact in order to emerge a great variety of meaning.

The acceptance of this kind of emergence, either in concepts or in primitive behaviors is also evident in the domain of ALife Representative paradigms are the ones of Langton (1989) and of Baas (1994). Langton argues in favor of the emergence of genuine life in artificial systems as the result of a mapping of the low-level behaviors of the simulated natural systems (e.g., bird flocking) into informational computer processes. The emergence of a higher-level behavior is not only simulated, but it realizes the same thing with the natural phenomenon. Baas proposes complexity, hierarchies emergence and evolution as four interrelated phenomena which every biological system presents and which are also supported in ALife simulations. He also suggests that in ALife simulations one can observe both emergence and downward causation, and he also argues that these two properties can only empirically be proved that are being exhibited by a natural system.

The theoretical justification of these claims comes from the work of Bedau (1997; 2002), who proposes that in such computational simulations there is the appearance of weak emergence as there are new emergent macroscopic states that can be derived from the microscopic dynamics but only through simulations. This kind of emergence is in principle predictable, but not in every detail, as the weakly emergent properties arise from the top-down feedback processes (downward causation). In weak emergence there is no unique direction of causality from the microscopic to the macroscopic level (as for example in feedforward neural networks), but there are causal relations in both directions. It is probably of no need to say that this kind of approach to the emergence of new behavior in artificial systems is dominant in ALife.

However, the problems are numerous and this kind of emergence has been attacked from many thinkers (see e.g., Cariani, 1991; Kampis, 1991; Emmeche, 1992, 1994) with respect to its relation to genuine emergence and the consequent autonomy. The conclusion of these critiques is that this is a computational emergence in which global patterns arise from local micro-deterministic computational interaction. Any finite-state machine which is used in these computations is a determined machine with predetermined transition rules and predefined primitives. As such, it is like somebody trying to simulate via prior selected rules the interpretations of a specific process, while this very interpretation has already been realized by an external natural cognitive system (the designer of the simulation). Additionally, such kinds of simulations are by default disembodied, while as argued in section 2, autonomy requires a body and a respective embeddedness in the environment from which it emerges. As Kampis (1991), Emmeche (1992), have suggested, formal computation does not have the causality of natural causation, or as von Neumman (1966) argues, by adopting only the logical part of a process (its abstraction) we may lose the most interesting part, that is, its material basis and the respective causality.

So, computational emergence is in no way a genuine functional emergence, and on a basic level, it is not significantly different from any other kind of computationalism. The interrelations between intentionality, functionality and meaning do not hold, or to be more specific, they do not even exist, hence, these kinds of systems cannot be considered as autonomous systems.

3.3 Emergence in Physically Grounded Artificial Agents
3.3.1   Emergence in the subsumption architecture
As it was mentioned in the previous section, one of the main points in Harnad's approach to the solution of the symbol-grounding problem was that symbol-grounding is an empirical issue and then, one needs a robotic functionality for the perceptive invariants to be grounded in a realistic and not in a virtual (simulated in software) sensorimotor interaction. In this way, the agent will be physically grounded, hence, it will be situated and embodied. The first and pioneered attempt toward this direction came from Brooks (1986, 1993), who introduced the subsumption architecture. There is no need to analyze the specific architecture, as it is well-known for its merits and for its disadvantages (see e.g., Emmeche, 2001; Christensen & Hooker, 2004), but some things relevant to its allegedly emergent functionality should be put under consideration.

The main concern of Brooks was to design an agent who would be able to interact with its environment in real-time, so that it will be able to confront real-life situations. The dominant computational approach, strongly influenced by the computer-based metaphor of the mind, requires that an agent will first sense its environment, it will then think and at the end it will act. This approach demands an a-priori determined and imposed representational model of the world, which will guide the central processing unit of the system. Such an architecture cannot cope with the enormous variety of a real-life environment, hence, something else is needed.

Brooks proposed the subsumption architecture as an alternative to the representational/computational model of the mind. The subsumption architecture has no central controller, but on the contrary, global control emerges out of the interaction of hierarchically organized behavioral units of the system. For example, the control of a simple robot wandering around a room trying to avoid certain obstacles emerges out of one behavioral unit that makes the robot to move forward and from a second unit, which, every time the robot meets an obstacle, subsumes the first unit and makes the robot to turn towards another direction. The subsumption architecture begins with simple functional units supporting fundamental activities of the agent, the interactive capacity of which increases with the addition of other more elaborated levels of action. Such an artificial agent presents the following characteristics: distributed control, direct coupling between perception and action, cohesion between multiple hierarchically organized functional modules, interaction based on its own functionality and not through some abstract and ungrounded representations, action through the maintenance of the functional cohesion and taking under consideration its aims and goals, dynamic interaction with the environment and of course, situatedness and embodiment (physical grounding).

Considering the list with the characteristics of such an artificial agent in comparison with the properties of an autonomous agent sketched in section 2, one could assume that this is a genuine autonomous agent. Of course, this is not the case. An agent with the subsumption architecture exhibits no central control and this is something that reminds us of the self-organizing and autopoietic systems, where all the functional processes of the system are responsible for the emergence of novel organizations, hence, of emergent functionality. Additionally, such artificial systems make no use of representations, since their interaction is directly guided by the functionality of the respective modules engaging in the interaction. This is also something that pertains to the characteristics of second-order cybernetic systems, which ascribe the existence of representation in the eye of the observer. Therefore, such an artificial agent presents a direct coupling between perception and action, which results in a kind of weak structural coupling with its environment. This directness, which comes as a result of the agent's physical grounding, practically vanishes the symbol-grounding problem. The agent uses its functionally integrated meaning to guide its interaction and this guidance supports the cohesion of its functional levels in accordance with its goal. Based on the analysis of 2.2 it could be said that these characteristics are just the results of an emergent functionality via process closure, which results in a cohesion maintained by the interrelations of the functional modules. The closure of the process of each module will either be satisfied (will not loop forever and it will pass execution on another module) in the same module or in another module in case a subsumed module takes control. In this perspective, the most important module of the system can be considered as the initiator of a downward causation which also propagates through several lower levels.

So far so good for the subsumption architecture, but there are no more good news. The exhibited cohesion is not genuinely emergent as most of the respective functionality is the result of an external design. Even if someone leaves aside this "small" detail, the respective cohesion exhibits very strong and local bonds, which do not provide the possibility for a great variety of actions. This is apparent in such an autonomous agent who resembles mostly an action-reaction system (as almost all systems that cannot surpass the level of autopoiesis or of metabolic autonomy). Additionally, and due to the rigidness of its cohesion, as well as due to the absoluteness of its boundaries (i.e. the rule-based and automata-driven input-output units of each module) such an artificial agent cannot scale on its own, unless new functional modules are added. Of course, one should not leave aside the fact that the building plan/organizational code of an agent designed based on the subsumption architecture belongs to its designer and not to the agent itself. Therefore, the goal of the system under which this functional cohesion is maintained does not belong to the system. Considering that derivative intentionality results in derivative meaning, the symbol-grounding problem is not solved, rather it is postponed until the time when the designer will decide about the functional modules of the system based on his anticipations.

3.3.2 Emergence in Agents With Artificial Nervous Systems

Researchers in autonomous and cognitive robotics and in adaptive systems have, in a way, tried to achieve a greater functional flexibility than the one presented in the rigid functional cohesion of the subsumption architecture by designing self-organizing artificial nervous systems. A prominent work is the one of Ziemke and Thieme (2002), where they use multiple recurrent neural networks (RNNs) with a second-order feedback, in order to simulate the sensorimotor system of a simple robot. Specifically, what they are trying to model is von Foerster's notion of double closure between the senso-motoric and inner-secretoric-neuronal circuits (see Fig. 2). The authors argue that with the suggested architecture the sensorimotor mapping changes dynamically with the internal state of the agent. In other words, the artificial nervous system changes its modus operandi. Ziemke (2005) has already make the connection between their design suggestion and von Foerster's double closure, but let's take a closer look to the allegedly emergent characteristics of such an artificial system.

What Ziemke and Thieme have tried to do is to design a cohesion closer to the one which emerges in genuine self-organizing systems. In particular, by functionally implementing a second-order feedback between the RNNs they acquire greater flexibility and a greater variety of interrelations between different organizational levels (i.e. input-output and the hidden units representing context). In this way various interrelations between different time scales can take place, driving the system's action in a somehow, non-derivative way. The closure conditions achieved through this setting resembles the closure conditions that a natural nervous system exhibits. For this to be done, the logical structure of the respective artificial nervous system is analogous to the functionally interrelated structure between the sensorimotor system and the inner-secretoric-neuronal system. One has to admit that this is a type of cohesion which is closer to the one of natural self-organizing systems than the cohesion achieved in the subsumption architecture. Actually, Ziemke argues that the respective architecture result in the self-organization of the sensorimotor system of the robot. The interesting part would be to see if this new cohesion, which results from this kind of self-organization, offers any genuine emergence or any emergence at all.

First of all, it cannot be asserted that the respective artificial nervous system truly exhibit genuine self-organization. Collier, (2004a, p. 162) suggests up to six important characteristics of self-organizing systems, and mostly all of them are energetic characteristics, such as exportation of entropy, minimization of local entropy production, maximization of the efficiency of energy throughput under force, free energy source, phase separation and promotion of microscopic fluctuations to macroscopic order. It seems that what happens to the artificial nervous system which is simulated by RNNs is closer to re-organization that to self-organization. Practically, this means that the artificial nervous system does not emerge functional norms (see section 2.3), and how could have done this since it has been evolved independently of the robot's body. Hence, the nervous system alters its organization (although mostly in a resetting and recombining mode), but in which purpose and for the benefit of who? Certainly not for itself, because, first of all, the respective functionality (i.e. the selection of the RNNs and their functional interrelation, at least in the dimension of different levels), has been externally imposed. Secondly, and equally interestingly, because, even though the respective artificial nervous system exhibits an interesting process closure, which results in a certainly interesting cohesion, it cannot achieve the required interaction closure with its environment in an open-ended way. Hence, based on the analysis of section 2.3 and 2.4, this system cannot emerge functional norms and as such, it cannot emerge genuine representations. Although its coherence is an interesting one, its functional support results in the lack of normativity in the artificial agent. In other words, closure is necessary for functional emergence, but the endogenous evolution of closure is necessary for normative emergence and for the emergence of meaning for the system itself.

Normativity is a crucial issue for understanding the meaning processes in autonomous agents but it is highly neglected by the community of artificial systems research. Functional norms, in a way, attribute values of true or false, and they are emergent in system's interactions with the environment. Emmeche, rightly points out that a perceived sign may be the carrier of some general type, as danger, "but it has always also an aspect of being a tone, that is being qualitatively felt in some way (e.g., unpleasant)" (Emmeche, 2001, p. 680). The acceptance/understanding of such an unpleasant feeling and its consequent interpretation is probably the result of a normative functionality of an autonomous agent and of the respective anticipations with their representational content. For the moment, this is something that cannot be exhibited in silicon-based systems due to their dyadic nature, which first of all does not permit the emergence of complex and dynamically interactive boundaries, between the different functional levels of an artificial system and between the system and its environment. Normativity is indirectly related to downward causation in an autonomous agent. Process and interaction closure in a self-maintained cohesion may require that low-level open issues will achieve closure in higher levels. On the other hand, the higher the autonomy and agency of a system, the higher the degree of abstraction of the concepts/meanings to which some of its norms can be related. In this case, the system should interact with the environment based on its anticipations, but for closure to be achieved, the emergent organizational level should functionally determine the lower level associated with the respective norm. It is obvious that this cannot happen with any self-organizing artificial nervous system which cannot at least exhibit the kind of cohesion that will functionally provide the conditions for the emergence of process and interaction closure. In this perspective, a robot with such an artificial nervous system is not much more than a rock with wheels.

3.3.3   Emergence in *Self-organizing* and *Evolutionary* Artificial Agents
There is a great deal of research in the design and development of the so-called self-organizing agents that achieve an evolutionary adaptation with their environments. These attempts are characterized by self-organizing and evolution of robots bodies and controllers (see e.g., Nolfi & Floreano, 2000), and/or the so called self-organizing communication and evolution of languages (see e.g., Vogt, 2005). But again, all these works are falling under the same problems as those described in the previous section. Self-organization needs a self to organize (Collier, 2004b) and in all these cases, there is no self, at all. Imposed functionality in the form of an artificial ontogeny cannot create a genuinely autonomous system, as any kind of artificial ontogeny will result in the imposition of new functional norms, but not in their genuine emergence. As such, intentionality is still residing in the eye of the designer, or of the beholder. Imposed ontogeny which is not properly emerged cannot be functionally integrated with the building plan or the organizational code of the autonomous system, and as such, any structural emergence does not normatively serve the self-maintenance of the agent itself, but satisfies the emergent meaning that the designer himself associates with the aims that he has selected for its artificial agent.

The same goes for the allegedly emergent language and vocabularies in interacting robots. As it has been thoroughly analyzed in (Arnellos, Spyrou, & Darzentas, 2007b) communication between autonomous systems is crucial in order for an autonomous system to enhance its autonomy and consequently its cognitive capacities. For this to be done, the existence of inherent aims and goals, with a variable degree of definiteness, seems imperative, otherwise, the respective interactions will not have the respective emergent functional value, that is, new structures will be produced with no inherent grounding. Of course, ill-defined aims and goals, that is, higher-level anticipation emerges on the basis of endogenous and well-defined functional norms, which are grounded in the agent's self-maintenance. Contemporary artificial agents do not seem to exhibit such dispositions. At the end, all contemporary artificial agents are victims of their functionality in their attempt to overcome the symbol-grounding problem and to emerge new functional meaning.

4   Conclusions: Designing Representational Autonomous Agents

The critical review in section 4 is sure not an exhaustive one, but it is quite representative of the abilities of contemporary artificial agents and of their capacity for autonomous agency. The naturalistically emergent nature of agency (see Arnellos, Spyrou, & Darzentas, in press) does not allow for the partitioning of agency in *simpler problems* or the study of isolated cases of cognitive activity. Nevertheless, these phenomena are quite typical in the research of autonomous artificial agents. However, the notion of a simpler problem is always interpreted with respect to the theoretical framework upon which the design of the artificial agent relies.

In the more general domain of self-organization, where a systemically emergent perspective is adopted regarding the evolution of autonomous agency, the primary aim of an attempt to design an artificial autonomous agent is not to design an agent that will mimic in a great detail the activities of a human. Considering the analysis of section 2, this will probably demand the from scratch design and development of the extremely complex processes of life and of cognition combined with the evolution and the adaptation of the artificial agent. On the contrary, the aims of such research attempts should be the design of a complete artificial agent, that is, a design which will support, up to a certain satisfying level, the set of the fundamental and characteristic properties of autonomy, by maintaining its systemic and emergent nature in different types of dynamically changing environments. In this way, it is most probable that the design and development of an artificial agent that will tend to genuinely exhibit the emergent and interrelated properties of autonomy, intentionality, functionality and meaning will take a long time, but the respective trip will provide many interesting answers in a variety of really hard questions regarding the nature of an autonomous agent, while simultaneously will feedback and support the respective theoretical frameworks and models. The work of Ziemke (2005) is a work towards this direction, but it is still very difficult for the community of researchers to keep with the theoretical complexity and rigidity of the respective naturalized frameworks.

Considering the analysis of section 2, one may conclude that the design of an artificial autonomous agent requires the design of genuinely emergent representational autonomy. Such a system should emerge a functional cohesion which will allow for process and interaction closure. Process and interaction closure will provide the agent with the respective openness so that it will be able to follow the whole interactive cycle of its anticipations. This will result in a continuous emergence of new functional norms, and in consequence, of new meanings. The emergence of the proper type of cohesion cannot take place in an agent with a sensorimotor system, no matter its artificial variety and perplexity, which is being functionally separated, in terms of its structural evolution, with the body that it supposes to activate. Additionally, this emergence should be guided by the functional norms that it produces, namely, the functional requirement that every interaction of the system with its environment will be evaluated on the basis of its self-maintenance. This is a process of emergent functionality and of emergent meaning, which creates new functional organizations, which in turn are downwardly constraining or determining the respective functionality.

What should be made clear is that simple logical or/and formal co-evolution of body and mind is not enough, as it seems that the energetic characteristics of self-organization proper are crucial for the emergence of the required functional normativity. Moreno and Etxeberria (2005) are right to argue that one cannot leave the energetic aspects aside and solely try to build sensorimotor autonomy instead of basic autonomy. As they suggest, the problem is not that computer power is still not enough, or that the mathematics should be reformulated, but that "The difficulty is in the deep and radical interrelation between forms of organization and materiality" (Moreno & Etxeberria, 2005, p. 173).

The need for different materiality should not come as a surprise, as it is something that other researchers, either intuitively (e.g. von Neuman, 1966), or quite thoroughly (e.g. Emmeche, 1992, 2001), Collier (1999, 2007) have also suggested. Indeed, to design an autonomous artificial agent is to design an artificial agent that is able to engage in design processes for itself and this is a genuine semiotic phenomenon (Arnellos, Spyrou, & Darzentas, 2007a), which demands the coevolution of the autonomous system with the mediators of the signs with which it interacts (Arnellos, Spyrou, & Darzentas, 2006). It is highly likely that silicon-based systems cannot support this requirement, but a carbon-based biology is needed. In any other case, the emergence of intentional behavior seems, for the moment, really impossible. However, a symbolically grounded agent is a genuinely emergent autonomous agent.

References

Arnellos, A., Spyrou, T., & Darzentas, J. (2007a). Exploring creativity in the design process: A systems-semiotic perspective. *Cybernetics & Human Knowing, 14* (1), 37-64.

Arnellos, A., Spyrou, T., & Darzentas, J. (2007b). Cybernetic Embodiment and the role of autonomy in the design process. *Kybernetes, 36* (9-10), 1207-1224.

Arnellos, A., Spyrou, T., & Darzentas, J. (2006). Dynamic interactions in artificial environments: Causal and non-causal aspects for the emergence of meaning. *Journal of Systemics, Cybernetics and Informatics*, 3 (1), 82-89.

Arnellos, A., Spyrou, T., & Darzentas, J.(in press). Towards the Naturalization of Agency based on an Interactivist Account of Autonomy. *New Ideas in Psychology*. (special issue on Interactivism)

Baas, N. A. (1994). Hyperstructures – a framework for emergents, hierarchies, evolution and complexity. In C. G. Langton (Ed.), *Artificial Life III, Santa Fe Studies in the Sciences of Complexity, Proc. Volume XVII* (pp. 515-537). Redwood City, CA: Addison-Wesley.

Bedau, M.A. (1997). Weak emergence. *Philosophical Perspectives, 11*, 375-399

Bedau, M.A. (2002). Downward causation and the autonomy of weak emergence. Special issue on "Emergences and downward causation," *Principia, 6*, 5-50,

Bickhard, M. H. (1993). Representational content in humans and machines. *Journal of Experimental and Theoretical Artificial Intelligence, 5*, 285-333.

Bickhard, M. H. (2000). Autonomy, function, and representation. *Communication and Cognition – Artificial Intelligence, 17*, (3-4), 111-131.

Bickhard, M. H. (2005). Consciousness and Reflective Consciousness. *Philosophical Psychology, 18*(2), 205-218.

Brooks, R. A. (1986). A robust layered control system for a mobile robot. *IEEE Journal of Robotics and Automation,* 2,14-23.

Brooks, R. A. (1993). The engineering of physical grounding. *Proceedings of the Fifteenth Annual Meeting of the Cognitive Science Society* (pp. 153-154). Hillsdale, NJ: Lawrence Erlbaum.

Cangelosi, A., Greco, A., & Harnad, S. (2000). From robotic toil to symbolic theft: Grounding transfer from entry-level to higher-level categories. *Connection Science, 12*, 143-162.

Cangelosi, A., & Harnad, S. (2000). The adaptive advantage of symbolic theft over sensorimotor toil: Grounding language perceptual categories. Special issue on "Grounding Language." *Evolution of Communication, 4,* 117-142.

Cariani, P. (1991). Emergence and artificial life. In C. G. Langton, C. Taylor, J. D. Farmer, & S. Rasmussen (Eds.), *Artificial Life II. Santa Fe Institute Studies in the Sciences of Complexity Proceedings Vol. X* (pp. 775-797). Redwood City, CA: Addison-Wesley.

Chalmers, D. (1992). Subsymbolic computation and the chinese room. In J. Dinsmore (Ed.), *The symbolic and connectionist paradigms: Closing the gap* (pp. 25-48). New York: Lawrence Erlbaum.

Christensen, W. D. & Hooker, C. A. (2002). Self-directed agents. In J. MacIntosh (Ed.), "Naturalism, evolution & intentionality," *Canadian Journal of Philosophy, Special Supplementary, 27,* 19-52.

Christensen, W. D., & Hooker, C. A. (2004). Representation and the meaning of life. In H. Clapin, P. Staines, P. Slezak, (Eds.), Representation in mind: New approaches to mental representation (pp. 41-70). Oxford: Elsevier.

Collier, J. (1988). Supervenience and reduction in biological hierarchies. In M. Matthen & B. Linsky (Eds.), "Philosophy and biology," *Canadian Journal of Philosophy Supplementary, 14* , 209-234.

Collier, J. (1999). Autonomy in anticipatory systems: Significance for functionality, intentionality and meaning. In D. M. Dubois (Ed.), *Computing Anticipatory Systems, CASYS'98 - Second International Conference, American Institute of Physics* (pp. 75-81). New York: Woodbury.

Collier, J. (2000). Autonomy and process closure as the basis for functionality. In J. L.R. Chandler and G. van de Vijver (Eds.), Closure: Emergent organizations and their dynamics. *The Annals of the New York Academy of Science, 901,* 280-291.

Collier, J. (2002). What is autonomy? *International Journal of Computing Anticipatory Systems, 12,* 212-221. (Partial Proceedings of CASYS'01: Fifth International Conference on Computing Anticipatory Systems)

Collier, J. (2004a). Fundamental properties of self-organization. In V. Arshinov & C. Fuchs (Eds.), *Causality, emergence, self-organisation* (pp. 150-166). Moscow: NIA-Piroda.

Collier, J. (2004b). Self-organisation, individuation and identity. *Revue Internationale de Philosophie, 59,* 151-172.

Collier, J. (2007). Simulating autonomous anticipation: The importance of Dubois' conjecture. *BioSystems, 91* (2) 346-354.

Collier, J., & Hooker C. A. (1999). Complexly organised dynamical systems. Open systems and information *Dynamics, 6,* 241-302.

Collier, J., & Muller, S. (1998). The dynamical basis of emergence in natural hierarchies. In G. Farre and T. Oksala, (Eds.), Emergence, Complexity, Hierarchy and Organization: ECHO III Conference, Acta Polytechnica Scandinavica, MA91 Espoo: Finnish Academy of Technology.

Coradeschi S.& Saffioti, A. (2003). An introduction to the anchoring problem. *Robotics and Autonomous Systems, 43,* 85-96.

Emmeche, C. (1992). Modeling life: A note on the semiotics of emergence and computation in artificial and natural systems. In T. A. Sebeok & J. Umiker-Sebeok, (Eds.), *Biosemiotics: The semiotic web 1991* (pp. 77-99). Berlin: Mouton de Gruyter Publishers.

Emmeche, C. (1994). *The garden in the machine: The emerging science of artificial life.* Princeton, NJ: Princeton University Press.

Emmeche, C. (2000). Closure, function, emergence, semiosis and life: The same idea? Reflections on the concrete and the abstract in theoretical biology. pp. 187-197 In J. L. R. Chandler & G. Van de Vijver (Eds.), *Closure: Emergent organizations and their dynamics. Annals of the New York Academy of Sciences, Volume 901* (pp. 187-197). New York: The New York Academy of Sciences.

Emmeche, C. (2001. Does a robot have an Umwelt? Reflections on the qualitative biosemiotics of Jakob von Uexküll. *Semiotica, 134* (1/4), 653-693.

Fodor, J. A. (1990). *A theory of content and other essays.* Cambridge, MA: The MIT Press.

Harnad, S. (1990). The symbol grounding problem. *Physica D 42,*335-346.

Harnad, S. (1993). Grounding symbols in the analog world with neural nets. *Think* 2(1) 12-78 (Special Issue on "Connectionism versus Symbolism" D.M.W. Powers & P. A. Flach, Eds.)

Harnad, S. (1995). Grounding symbolic capacity in robotic capacity. In L. Steels, & R. Brooks (Eds.), *The "artificial life" route to "artificial intelligence." Building situated embodied agents* (pp. 276-286). New Haven, CT: Lawrence Erlbaum.

Hexmoor, H., Castelfranchi, C., & Falcone, R. (Eds.) (2003). *Agent autonomy.* Boston: Kluwer Academic Publishers, Boston.

Hoffmeyer, J. (1998). Surfaces inside surfaces: On the origin of agency and life. *Cybernetics & Human Knowing, 5* (1), 33-42.

Kampis, G. (1991). *Self-modifying systems in biology and cognitive science.* Oxford: Pergamon Press.

Kampis, G. (1999). The natural history of agents. In L. Gulyás, G. Tatai, and J. Váncza (Eds.), *Agents everywhere* (pp. 24-48). Budapest: Springer.

Langton, C. G. (1989). Artificial Life. In C. G. Langton (Ed.), *Artificial life: Proceedings of the Santa Fe Institute Studies in the Sciences of Complexity,VI,* 1-47. Redwood City, CA.: Addison-Wesley.

Luisi, P. L. (2003). Autopoiesis: A review and a reappraisal. *Naturwissenschaften, 90,* 49-59.

Moreno, A., & Barandiaran, X. (2004). A naturalized account of the inside-outside dichotomy. *Philosophica, 73,* 11-26.

Moreno, A., & Etxeberria, A. (2005). Agency in natural and artificial systems. Almeida e Costa, F., Rocha, L. and Bedau. M. (Eds.) Special Issue on new robotics evolution and embodied cognition. *Artificial Life, 11* (1-2), 161-176.

Newell, A. (1980). Physical symbol systems. *Cognitive Science, 4*, 135-183.

Nolfi, S. & Floreano, D. (2000). Evolutionary robotics: The biology, intelligence, and technology of self-organizing machines. Cambridge, MA: The MIT Press.

Rocha, L. M. (1996). Eigenbehavior and symbols. *Systems Research, 13* (3), 371-384.

Ruiz-Mirazo, K., & Moreno, A. (2000). Searching for the roots of autonomy: The natural and artificial paradigms revisited. *Communication and Cognition – Artificial Intelligence, 17,* (3-4), 209-228.

Ruiz-Mirazo, K., & Moreno, A. (2004). Basic autonomy as a fundamental step in the synthesis of life. *Artificial Life, 10*, 235-259.

Searle, J. (1980). Minds, brains, and programs. *Behavioral and Brain Sciences, 3*, 417-424.

Taddeo, M. & Floridi, L. (2005). The symbol grounding problem: A critical review of fifteen years of research. *Journal of Experimental and Theoretical Artificial Intelligence, 17*(4), 419 - 445.

Varela, F. (1979). *Principles of biological autonomy.* New York: Elsevier.

Varela, F., & Bourgine, P. (1992). Introduction: Towards a practice of autonomous systems. In F. Varela & P. Bourgine (Eds.), *Towards a practice of autonomous systems. Proceedings of the first european conference on artificial life,* (pp. xi-xvi). Cambridge, MA: The MIT Press.

Vogt, P. (2005). The emergence of compositional structures in perceptually grounded language games. *Artificial Intelligence, 167* (1-2), 206-242.

von Foerster, H. (1960/2003). On self-organizing systems and their environments. In *Understanding understanding: Essays on cybernetics and cognition* (pp. 1-19). New York: Springer-Verlag. (Originally published in M.C. Yvotis & S. Cameron (Eds.), Self-organizing Systems [pp. 31-50]. London: Pergamon, 1960)

von Foerster, H. (1976/2003). Objects: tokens for (eigen-) behaviors. In *Understanding understanding: Essays on cybernetics and cognition* (pp. 261-271). New York: Springer-Verlag. (originally published in *ASC Cybernetics Forum, 8* , 91-96, 1976)

von Foerster, H. (1981). *Observing systems.* Seaside, CA: Intersystems Publications.

von Foerster, H. (1988/2003). On Constructing a Reality. In *Understanding understanding: Essays on cybernetics and cognition* (pp. 211-228). New York: Springer-Verlag. (Originally published in *Adolescent Psychiatry, Developmental and Clinical Studies* [Vol. 15, pp. 77-95]. The University of Chicago Press, 1988)

von Neumann, J. (1966). *The theory of self-reproducing automata.* (A. W. Burks, Ed.). Urbana, IL: University of Illinois Press.

von Uexküll, J. (1982). The theory of meaning. *Semiotica, 42*(1):25-82.

Ziemke, T. (1999). Rethinking grounding. In A. Riegler, M. Peschl, & A von Stein (Eds.) *Understanding representation in the cognitive sciences* (pp. 177-190). New York: Plenum Press.

Ziemke, T. (2005). Cybernetics and embodied cognition: On the construction of realities in organisms and robots. *Kybernetes, 1/2*, 118-128.

Ziemke, T. & Sharkey, N. (2001) A stroll through the worlds of robots and animals: Applying Jakob von Uexküll's theory of meaning to adaptive robots and artificial life. *Semiotica, 134*(1- 4), pp. 701-746.

Ziemke, T. & Thieme, M. (2002) Neuromodulation of Reactive Sensorimotor Mappings as a Short-Term Memory Mechanism in Delayed Response Tasks. *Adaptive Behavior, 10*(3/4), pp. 175-199.

Forsythe, K. (2008). *Meditation 1* (detail). 15 cm x 22 cm, acrylic on canvas.

Cybernetics And Human Knowing. Vol. 15, nos. 3-4, pp. 42-49

Emergence of Autonomy in Contemporary Artificial Agents: Any Novelty?

Maria Eunice Quilici Gonzalez[1] & Osvaldo Pessoa Jr.[2]

The article by Arnellos, Spyrou and Darzentas discusses the question of whether an artificial system, such as a robot or artificial life, can be made genuinely autonomous. The negative answer that they present is sound, but seems to us to be a simple consequence of the definitions adopted. We argue that the theoretical considerations presented, based on the notions of functional emergence and meaning, need further explanation in order to give support for their argument. As it is presented so far, not very much novelty is added to the already existent research on autonomous and cognitive robotics and artificial life. Also, we would like to challenge the defenders of the "theory of self-referential systems" to set up conditions in which the theory would be considered falsified. The problem of whether life and autonomy could in principle be sustained with components other than carbon-based organic molecules seems to involve still unknown empirical aspects, and cannot be answered simply with theoretical considerations.

The main aim of the paper by Arnellos, Spyrou & Darzentas is to examine the possibility of emergence of autonomy in artificial agents, based on the principles of second-order cybernetics and on more recent theoretical developments in the area of evolutionary systems.

The authors begin by arguing that the concepts of autonomy, functionality, intentionality, and meaning play a fundamental role in the characterization of a natural agent. A detailed analysis of these concepts is provided, with special emphasis on the notion of emergence, which they argue constitutes "the ground for the theoretical evaluation of the autonomy of contemporary artificial agents with respect to the functional emergence of their capacities" (abstract, this issue, p. 15). They conclude by criticizing the claims made in the fields of artificial intelligence (AI), robotics, and artificial life (ALife), that ascribe too easily the notions of autonomy and agency to artificial systems, which, according to the authors, contain only basic abilities of interaction with their environment, and are not autonomous agents.

An *agent* is defined as a self-referential system that can take the initiative in its interactions with the environment in accordance with a purpose or goal. An *autonomous* agent is one that is relatively free from external controls or constraints, that is self-governing, that maintains itself, in a varying environment, based on its own resources.

1. Philosophy Dept., FFC, Universidade Estadual Paulista (UNESP) Av. Hygino Muzzi Filho, 737, 17525-900, Marília, SP, Brazil. Email: gonzalez@marilia.unesp.br
2. Philosophy Dept., FFLCH, Universidade de São Paulo (USP) Av. Prof. Luciano Gualberto, 315, 05508-900, São Paulo, SP, Brazil. Email: opessoa@usp.br

Inspired by von Foerster's (1960/2003, 1973/2003) second-order cybernetics, the authors describe autonomy as a property of self-referential systems exhibiting "a special form of functional organization that contributes to its own governance and uses this governance for its own maintenance in a variable environment" (this issue, p. 16). Autonomy, they claim, enhances the qualifications for agency.

Agency, in turn, is characterized as a capacity with a gradual and an evolutionary nature that calls for three features: *interactivity*, *intentionality*, and *autonomy*. The first involves the ability "to perceive and act upon its environment by taking the initiative." The second, intentionality, is defined as "the ability of an agent to effect a goal-oriented interaction by attributing purposes, beliefs and desires to its actions", and autonomy, as mentioned, is the system's ability to operate "intentionally and interactively based on its own resources" (this issue, p. 16).

In the case of living agents, two other properties are considered essential – *functionality* and *meaning*. The first refers to the network of causal properties, within an agent, that ensures the maintenance of the system, while *meaning* is initially loosely considered as a prerequisite for the maintenance of a system's autonomy. As a consequence of the definitions adopted, the authors stress the limitations that plague the attempts of robotics and AI projects, in general, for designing artificial systems that allow for the emergence of genuine autonomy.

It seems to us that from the very way that the concepts are defined, questions concerning the possibility of building an autonomous system would receive a negative answer – robots (or any other artificial system) cannot be autonomous agents –, simply because they are not, strictly speaking, agents, since they have no true purpose. They seem to act in a goal-oriented way because they were programmed to do so by the engineers that built them, but they don't have intentions or goals.

This solution would trivialize the discussion and end it prematurely, so let us adopt a looser definition of *agent*, as a system that has a purpose or behaves *as if* it had a purpose. A robot may then be considered an agent, but is it an autonomous agent? Is it free from external controls? Well, its basic structure and rules are (so far) established by human beings, even if part of them may be modified due to the system's interaction with the environment, so, roughly speaking, at the end of story, human beings are responsible for its agency. Therefore, robots (or other artificially built systems) cannot be autonomous agents, even if they eventually become uncontrollable for human beings.

This is a simplified version of the argument initially presented by Arnellos, Spyrou & Darzentas, and we consider it basically sound. The authors, however, go further and provide a good survey of the literature on the subject, emphasizing a general theoretical viewpoint that might be called the "theory of self-referential systems," in which the notions of *cohesion*, *emergence* and *downward causation* play a central role.

Cohesion is characterized as the correlation of the whole and the parts that emerges in a highly dynamic and reciprocal way. In the case of living self-referential systems, they stress that "the internal productive interrelations acquire a cohesive functional meaning in a collective way, since they contribute to the overall maintenance of the system" (this issue, p. 23).

Emergence, roughly speaking, is the appearance of a novel collective property of a system, in a way that is rather unexpected if only the more microscopic elements are considered. There are weaker and stronger concepts of emergence, and which of them apply to living beings is an open question. *Downward causation* is a controversial concept associated with a strong notion of emergence, and can be generally characterized as an emergent macroscopic cause which exerts an effect at the more microscopic level, in a way that cannot be accounted for solely with causes at the microscopic level.

The authors then proceed to examine in more detail additional emergent properties within the self-referential theoretical framework presented. One first concept is process closure that leads to the emergence of cohesion, which should bring in a holistic aspect to the system, precluding reductionism, or the possibility of analyzing the system in separate elements which interact according to the fields of classical physics. As they stress, "cohesion via process closure is a necessary but not a sufficient condition for genuine autonomy and agency" (this issue, p. 25). Another process is the emergence of normative functionality, which is the capacity that an autonomous agent has to change its internal functionality in order to adapt to changes in the environment. And finally, the emergence of *representations* is mentioned, which together with the capacity for anticipation would lead to the appearance of *meaning*.

With these more sophisticated theoretical considerations, the authors conclude that ALife systems, robots, such as those with the subsumption architecture (Brooks, 1986, 1993), and self-organizing artificial nervous systems developed in the area of autonomous and cognitive robotics (Ziemke & Sharkey, 2001; Ziemke & Thieme, 2002; Ziemke, 2005) cannot be autonomous agents. With reference to ALife systems, they stress that "computational emergence is in no way a genuine functional emergence, and on a basic level, it is not significantly different from any other kind of computationalism" (this issue, p. 33).

In the case of robots with the subsumption architecture, Arnellos, Spyrou & Darzentas argue that they have no genuine emergency given that their functionality is the result of an external design, and that their rigid cohesion and local bonds do not allow for a great variety of options. They also stress that "the building plan/ organizational code of an agent designed based on the subsumption architecture belongs to its designer and not to the agent itself. Therefore, the goal of the system under which this functional cohesion is maintained does not belong to the system" (this issue, p. 35).

As for the self-organizing artificial nervous systems proposed by Ziemke & Thieme, it is acknowledged that there is cohesion closer to the one which emerges in genuine living self-organizing systems. They admit that: "In particular, by functionally implementing a second-order feedback between the RNNs [recurrent neural networks] they acquire greater flexibility and a greater variety of interrelations between different organizational levels ... In this way various interrelations between different time scales can take place, driving the system's action in a somehow, non-derivative way" (this issue, p. 35). However, they question Ziemke's hypothesis that the emergent architecture of artificial nervous systems results in the self-organization of the sensorimotor system of the robot, arguing that neither genuine emergence nor self-organization are present in this kind of architecture.

The claim that genuine self-organization is not present in the mentioned artificial nervous system is based upon Collier's (2004) classification of the six main characteristics of self-organizing systems: "exportation of entropy, minimization of local entropy production, maximization of the efficiency of energy throughput under force, free energy source, phase separation and promotion of microscopic fluctuations to macroscopic order" (this issue, p. 36). Without explaining in detail why the artificial nervous system does not fulfill these characteristics, Arnellos, Spyrou & Darzentas suggest that its behavior is rather closer to re-organization, involving resetting and recombining modes, than to self-organization. Their conclusion is that no meaning and no functional norms emerge in such a system, and we can only agree that it could not have done this since "it has been evolved independently of the robot's body" (this issue, p. 36).

What we would like to discuss now is to what extent Arnellos, Spyrou & Darzentas' theoretical framework is essential for the argument they develop, and to what extent it is a good theory, after all. As we are going to argue, their supposition in relation to the emergence of meaning in living systems needs further explanation, given that it plays a fundamental role in their main claim, and also in the classical debate concerning the mechanistic/non-mechanistic opposition in discussions on the ontological nature of cognitive systems.

To start with, considering that life evolved on Earth from inorganic molecules, then it is reasonable to admit that the condition of being an agent must have appeared gradually in the evolution of its ancestors. What is the set of properties that is sufficient for characterizing mammals and their earlier ancestors as an agents?

One notices that scarce emphasis is given to two essential concepts related to the evolution of self-organizing systems: natural selection and noise (or fluctuations). Certain circular explanations are offered by the authors, which might be adequate for systems having negative feedback loops, but at times such circular explanations seem to presuppose the point that must be explained. There seems to be no interest in explaining how teleological or intentional behavior can arise in previously non-teleological and non-intentional systems. Thus, for example, they maintain that "normative functions emerge as a contribution for the autonomy of the agent, and with the goal of satisfying the respective functional norms" (this issue, p. 27). It is as if normative functions arise due to a purpose, which is to give a purpose to the system.

Other ambiguities have also been noted. On the one hand, the authors present a simple and artificial network due to von Foerster as an example of emergent functionality and downward causation. But afterwards, they attribute autonomous self-organization and autopoiesis only to living agents.

It is reasonable to consider all the features suggested by the authors as essential to agency, but the basic problem is how these features arise in phylogenesis: what is the theory that explains the emergence of such properties? They claim that "the foundations of such a functional emergence have been established in the systems-theoretic framework of second-order cybernetics" (this issue, pp. 18-19), which includes especially the theory of self-organization of von Foerster (1960/2003, 1973/2003) and the theory of autopoiesis (Varela, 1979; Varela & Bourgine, 1992; Maturana & Varela, 1980). One must stress, however, that second-order cybernetics is also consistent with a reductionist approach, exemplified perhaps by the works of Ashby (1962) and Debrun (1996). The more holistic approaches of von Foerster, Maturana, and Varela, and the authors of the present article, can be grouped under the name "theory of self-referential systems."

One should point out that many authors within the framework of self-referential systems are constructivists, as opposed to realists. Although Arnellos et al. do not assume an explicit position on this issue, it seems to us that they could be classified as constructivists. One inspiration to this philosophical worldview is the work of Jakob von Uexküll (1940/1982), mentioned in the article being reviewed, but a phrase quoted from von Foerster summarizes the thesis that what we call reality is only a construction: "The nervous system is organized (or organizes itself) so that it computes a stable reality" (this issue, p. 22). This thesis, however, can be translated into a realist view, replacing the final object with a stable *representation* of reality. It is usually easy to translate from a constructivist language to a realist one, but the converse is not so simple. For example, the authors mention that "the autonomous system is able to perceive and act in its environment by internally creating meaningful information about its external environment" (this issue, p. 22). What is the status of this external environment? Does it exist in reality or is it also a construction?

All these questions are philosophically relevant, and the paper invites the reader to think about them. However, the more polemical question at issue is the considerable divergence between AI researchers and Arnellos, Spyrou & Darzentas' perspectives on the possibility of building up autonomous artificial systems that deal with meaning. Although they do not offer any explicit definition of meaning, they regard it as a prerequisite for the maintenance of a system's autonomy during its purposeful interaction with the environment. As they clearly do not want to consider meaning as an ascription of an external observer, they claim that it should emerge with the functional structures of biological autonomous agents:

> One should always keep in mind that in such an autonomous system, intentionality is not reducible to the processing of meanings, nor are the combinations of meanings bringing forth any "aboutness." On the contrary, meaning and its functional substratum are properties that may emerge when an autonomous agent acts intentionally. In other words, an autonomous system may act intentionally if its actions are mediated by meaning. (this issue, p. 18)

The hypothesis that meaning and its functional substratum are the emergent properties of an autonomous agent in interaction with the environment would be really worth developing, if it wasn't mixed up with their problematic *internalist representational* conjectures. In agreement with the great majority of philosophers who wish to avoid either extreme ontological positions concerning dualism or eliminative materialism, they seem to take for granted the notion of meaning, adding to it presuppositions of the traditional representationalist paradigm, according to which perception/action is always mediated by internal representations about the external world.

From this representational perspective (with all its well known difficulties regarding the infinite regress and the homunculi problems), the authors articulate their view on the internal mechanisms of meaning production, claiming (in a loose way) that in a self-organized system "internal productive interrelations acquire a cohesive functional meaning in a collective way, since they contribute to the overall maintenance of the system" (this issue, p. 23). However, it is not clear at all how these productive interrelations acquire a cohesive functional meaning.

In the case of organisms possessing a nervous system, they argue that "a new functional meaning ... emerges out of the self-organizing activity of the sensorimotor system with the activity of the neurohypophysis that produces steroids and releases them in the synaptic gaps" (this issue, p. 22). But, would it be acceptable to conceive the emergence of meaning in "simple" self-organizing systems that do not have a nervous system? Or is it that only brain owners could entertain meaningful experiences?

Although they try to explain the construction of meaning by means of emergence and downward causation in biological self-organizing systems, it remains unexplained how physical, chemical and biological systems acquire meaning in their evolutionary path. The stress on downward causation and the emergent functionality that structure neural systems may help, and could be included in the list of necessary conditions for the structuring of meaningful events, but it does not explain how, from "closure, and the self-reference of an observation emerges meaning inside the cognitive system, which is used as a model for further observations in order to compensate for external complexity" (this issue, p. 19).

Given that emergence and downward causation may be present in several forms of self-organization that display no sign of dealing with meaningful information, we would like to understand how it is that material stimuli existing in the physical and biological world become "meaningful." Maybe a further explanation on the mentioned interdependence between self-organization, autonomy, functionality and meaning could somehow elucidate this difficult topic. In particular, *communication with others* and *learning abilities* should be included amongst the important characteristics of secondary self-organizing systems that could acquire meaning in *their* evolutionary path, but curiously these characteristics are not mentioned in the article.

As originally proposed by Ashby (1962), and developed by Debrun (1996), Gonzalez & Haselager (2003) amongst others, learning mechanisms are crucial to the structural development of a secondary form of self-organization: a process that allows the spontaneous emergence of more complex forms of organization by means of training and refined resources of adjustment between its components. In addition to learning abilities and circular feedback, the secondary process of self-organization involves communication with other systems, cooperation and competition among its components, all vital to the development and stability of the system in focus.

Differently from unstable primary forms of self-organization (that require no a priori form of organization and result mainly from the exclusive spontaneous dynamics of interaction between its originally independent elements), the secondary self-organization shows an intriguing property according to which mechanisms of adjustment and learning in the communication process with others seem to give place to certain criteria of relevance. Once created, criteria of relevance delimit and guide the communicative trajectories of the system, allowing the evaluation and correction of errors in its interaction with the external world (including the rich variety of other self organizing systems). It seems to be the existence of an evaluative criterion of relevance – emergent from the communication with others – that gives place to the manifestation of meaning in the behavior of secondary self-organizing systems, distinguishing their learning abilities from mere reactive habits. Without a criterion of relevance, physical stimuli would lack any meaning and, as Bateson (1972, 1980) stresses, differences would make no difference to the system.

From this very sketchy perspective of the dynamics of secondary self-organization, the main question under discussion could now be rephrased: to what extent the emergence of a criterion of relevance (with its possible development into meaningful information and abilities) is an exclusive privilege of evolved living beings? Could artificial systems evolve in such a way that they would autonomously acquire learning mechanisms with indicators (Dretske, 1997, Gonzalez, 2005) of relevant information in their selective interaction with the external world? It seems to us that the answer to this question involves empirical aspects, and cannot be properly responded simply using theoretical considerations.

Arnellos, Spyrou and Darzentas conclude the article stating that "the design and development of an artificial agent that will tend to genuinely exhibit the emergent and interrelated properties of autonomy, intentionality, functionality and meaning will take a long time" (this issue, p. 38). This apparently negative conclusion, however, could in fact be optimistic, since it suggests that the task of creating artificial autonomous agents is, in principle, feasible. Nevertheless, a really negative conclusion is provided, from Harnad (1990), according to which artificial agents will never be able to grasp the meaning of the symbols they manipulate, so they can never be autonomous.

We do agree that there is an open problem related to the materiality of living systems, which is the question of whether life and/or meaningful abilities could in principle be sustained with components other than carbon-based organic molecules; for example, with silicon-based components used in present-day computers. But, the crucial question is whether artificial systems are capable of communicating meaningfully with their neighbors. Again, the answer to this question seems to involve empirical aspects and, above all, a better understanding about our collective communication abilities that direct our actions.

In summary, the article by Arnellos, Spyrou and Darzentas discusses the question of whether an artificial system, such as a robot or ALife, can be made genuinely autonomous. The negative answer that they present is sound, but seems to us to be a simple consequence of the definitions adopted. We argued that the theoretical considerations presented, based on the notions of functional emergence and meaning, need further explanation in order to give support for their argument. As it is presented so far, little novelty is added to the already existent research on autonomous and cognitive robotics and ALife. Also, we would like to challenge the defenders of the "theory of self-referential systems" to set up conditions in which the theory would be considered falsified. If, as we suspect, the theory is not falsifiable, then it becomes difficult to see its pragmatic and explanatory value for AI research.

In spite of these criticisms, we consider that the authors have provided a far-reaching and inspiring source of reflection on the important and yet mysterious main characteristics of living systems.

References

Ashby, W. R. (1962). Principles of the self-organizing system. In H. von Foerster & G. W. Hopf, Jr. (Eds.), *Principles of self-organization* (pp. 255-278). Oxford: Pergamon.

Bateson, G. (1972). *Steps to an ecology of mind. Collected essays in anthropology, psychiatry, evolution, and epistemology.* Chicago: University of Chicago Press.

Bateson, G. (1980). *Mind and nature: A necessary unity.* Bantam: New York.

Brooks, R. A. (1986). A robust layered control system for a mobile robot. *IEEE Journal of Robotics and Automation, 2,* 14-23.

Brooks, R. A. (1993). The engineering of physical grounding. *Proceedings of the Fifteenth Annual Meeting of the Cognitive Science Society* (pp. 153-154). Hillsdale, NJ: Lawrence Erlbaum.

Collier, J. (2004). Fundamental Properties of Self-Organization. In V. Arshinov & C. Fuchs (Eds.), *Causality, emergence, self-organisation* (pp. 150-166). Moscow: NIA-Prioda.

Debrun, M.A. (1996). A idéia de auto-organização. In M. Debrun, M. E. Q. Gonzalez & O. Pessoa, Jr. (Eds.), *Auto-organização: Estudos interdisciplinares* (Coleção CLE, vol. 18, pp. 1-23). Campinas, Brazil: Centro de Lógica e Epistemologia, Unicamp.

Dretske, F. I. (1995). *Naturalizing the mind.* Cambridge: The MIT Press.

Gonzalez, M. E. Q. (2005). Information and mechanical models of intelligence. *Pragmatics & Cognition, 13,* 565-582.

Gonzalez, M. E. Q. & Haselager, W. F. G. (2003). Creativity and self-organization: Contributions from cognitive science and semiotics. *S.E.E.D. Journal – Semiotics, Evolution, Energy, and Development, 3,* 61-70.

Harnad, S. (1990). The symbol grounding problem. *Physica D, 42,* 335-346.

Maturana, H. R. & Varela, F. J. (1980), *Autopoiesis and cognition.* Dordrecht: Reidel.

Varela, F. J. (1979). *Principles of biological autonomy.* New York: Elsevier.

Varela, F. J. & Bourgine, P. (1992). Towards a practice of autonomous systems. Introduction to *Towards a Practice of Autonomous Systems: Proceedings of the First European Conference on Artificial Life* (pp. xi–xvi). Cambridge, MA: The MIT Press.

von Foerster, H. (1960/2003). On self-organizing systems and their environments. In *Understanding understanding: Essays on cybernetics and cognition* (pp. 1-19). New York: Springer-Verlag. (Originally published in M.C. Yvotis & S. Cameron (Eds.), Self-organizing Systems [pp. 31-50]. London: Pergamon, 1960)

von Foerster, H. (1973/2003). On constructing a reality. In *Understanding understanding: Essays on cybernetics and cognition* (pp. 211-228). New York: Springer-Verlag. (Originally published in F. E. Preiser (Ed.), *Environmental design and research* [vol. 2, pp. 35-46]. Stroudsberg: Dowden, Hutchinson and Ross, 1973)

von Uexküll, J. (1940/1982). The theory of meaning (T. von Uexküll,Trans.). *Semiotica, 42(1):* 25-82. (Originally published as *Bedeutungslehre.* Leipzig: Barth, 1940)

Ziemke, T. (2005). Cybernetics and embodied cognition: On the construction of realities in organisms and robots. *Kybernetes, 34* (1/2), 118–128.

Ziemke, T. & Sharkey, N. (2001). A stroll through the worlds of robots and animals: Applying Jakob von Uexküll's theory of meaning to adaptive robots and artificial life. *Semiotica, 134* (1/4), 701-746.

Ziemke, T. & Thieme, M. (2002). Neuromodulation of reactive sensorimotor mappings as a short-term memory mechanism in delayed response tasks. *Adaptive Behavior, 10* (3/4), 185-199.

Cybernetics And Human Knowing. Vol. 15, nos. 3-4, pp. 50-56

Meaning Needs Functional Emergence:
Shedding Novel Light onto Difficult Problems

Argyris Arnellos, Thomas Spyrou, John Darzentas[1]

1 Introduction

We would like to begin by thanking Gonzalez and Pessoa (this issue) for their interesting commentary. Of course, a critical commentary always needs the adoption of a perspective, and an improper perspective could lead to mistakes and misunderstandings. In this paper we will attempt to provide some explanations in order to better clarify our theoretical theses and overcome those misunderstandings.

Gonzalez and Pessoa's main argument is that "from the very way that the concepts are defined, questions concerning the possibility of building an autonomous system would receive a negative answer" (this issue, p. 43), with respect to whether robots or any artificial system can be considered as an autonomous agent. In the light of this perspective, they conclude that this is a simple consequence of the definitions adopted and as such, little novelty is added to the already existent research on autonomous and cognitive robotics and ALife.

A thorough reply to their remarks would probably be too long for the purposes of a paper, but let's start by trying to indicate the basis of their commentary.

2 Agency is a Systemic Capacity

In Arnellos, Spyrou, Darzentas (in press) it is made clear that agency is a systemic capacity. Moreover the relevant notions/properties of an agent cannot just be added together in an arbitrary manner. As such, the concepts of autonomy, functionality, intentionality and meaning do play a fundamental role in the characterization of a natural agent, but these notions are unjustifiable on their own. In the same way, interactivity is also a fundamental notion, but truly useless and difficult to be handled (either theoretically or experimentally) on its own. One would think that the notion of goal, goal-orientation and purpose in general would solve, at least the theoretical problems, but again, where is this goal or purpose coming from and where does it go?

Then, one is willing to dig in another resolution and to mention issues of self-organisation, self-reference, cohesion, organizational, process and interaction closure, normative functionality and the respective representations, and so forth. But still, the problem of how to handle these difficult and philosophically loaded notions has not so far attempted to be answered.

---

1. Department of Product and Systems Design Engineering, University of the Aegean, 84100, Syros, Greece.
    Email: arar@aegean.gr, tsp@aegean.gr, idarz@aegean.gr

It is this point that Gonzalez and Pessoa seem to neglect in their commentary. The work of Arnellos, Spyrou, Darzentas (this issue) is exactly on this track, as it is an attempt to provide a framework where all these theoretical notions can find a justifiable way to be integrated so that their emergence is naturalistically acceptable. Moreover, the second part of Arnellos, Spyrou, Darzentas (this issue) work tries to indicate and map these properties and their explicit or implicit consequences in the certain technical solutions being applied in the design of artificial agents.

Having said that and keeping in mind that we are aiming at a naturalized analysis of agency and of the emergence of agential capacities, it is very difficult that our thesis will not be shown as being prejudiced regarding a negative answer on the autonomy of contemporary artificial agents. However, the goal of Arnellos, Spyrou, Darzentas' work (this issue) is to provide a theoretical framework regarding the functional emergence of autonomy in an agent, to detect the gap between theoretical and practical aspects of analyzing and building autonomous agents and to provide some possible design guidelines.

As it was expected due to the theoretical emphasis of the paper, Gonzalez and Pessoa are criticizing whether the theoretical framework is essential for the arguments that are being developed. Certain disagreements are mentioned in their commentary. We will discuss each in turn.

3 Normativity via Functional Norms Precedes Intentional Behavior

Gonzalez and Pessoa argue that in our theoretical framework "there seems to be no interest in explaining how teleological or intentional behavior can arise in previously non-teleological and non-intentional systems" (this issue, p. 45). In this case, the explanation for the emergence of normative function seems circular.

But this is not the case. In section 2.2 we specifically mention that the emergence of cohesion in a self-organising system is primarily solely due to its organizational (functional) dynamics. This cohesion, at least at this fundamental level, can only be explained with respect to the causal roles of the constituents and the relations among them. However, as it is also suggested in section 2.2, there are certain kinds of cohesion, with different types of correlations between the respective functional processes, and not all of this kinds of cohesion will provide a genuine autonomy for a system. One of these cases is the case of self-maintenant systems, which do not need to be living systems, but just non-living self-maintaining far-from-equilibrium systems, such as a candle, a flame, a tornado, and so forth. As Vehkavaara (2003, pp. 565-566) soundly states,

> these systems are serving their self-interest and, as a consequence, are 'staying alive' (without being living), they are nevertheless not *trying* to serve it. Their self-interest is not *forcing* or 'suggesting' them to do anything. They are not *seeking* how they can survive, but they just *happen* to have such a structure that fulfills their sole self-interest and existential precondition for some period. There self-maintenance does not yet give birth to any real growth or increase in complexity." (Vehkavaara, 2003, pp. 565-566, emphasis in the original).

Vehkavaara's suggestion is in accordance with our argument that for a self-maintaining system this is the phase where constructive processes dominate the system through process closure. The result is a functionality which is unbreakably related to the maintenance of the systemic cohesion and in consequence, of its self-organisational dynamics. This is not a genuinely autonomous system, it is non-teleological and non-intentional and it is neither living nor representative one. However, this asymmetric functionality (between system and environment), which results in unintentional self-maintenance provides functional norms (i.e. primitive/fundamental normativity), which forms the basis for the emergence of other more developed normative functions in the representative/interpretive phase of a system. But this organizational level will not come until life comes about. As it is thoroughly explained in section 2.3, this will not happen until the unintentional self-constructive processes are complemented with interactive processes forming an interpretive asymmetry, which also provides the capacity for "meaningful critique regarding the functional and the dysfunctional with respect to the maintenance of the system" (this issue, p. 26). This capacity is a normative one and such systems are truly autonomous. In this perspective, that case where "normative functions emerge as a contribution for the autonomy of the agent, and with the goal of satisfying the respective functional norms" (this issue, p. 27) cannot be considered as circular, but as vital for the maintenance and further enhancement of the autonomy of the system.

We are closing this remark by noting that the aspects of this section are highly related to the notions of *purpose* and to certain aspects of the *materiality* of the system under consideration. These aspects will be discussed in following sections.

4 Interaction Based on Thermodynamics Leaves no Room for non-Pragmatical Considerations

Gonzalez and Pessoa agree that all the features we suggest in Arnellos, Spyrou, Darzentas (this issue) are essential to agency, but they are wondering if the emergence of such properties can be explained by a system's theoretic framework of second-order cybernetics, while on the same time, they are posing questions related to whether our view is a constructivistic or a realistic one.

This is a considerable remark by Gonzalez and Pessoa, which is difficult to be answered if one decides to stay merely in the constructivist camp. However, we have adopted a different view, where interaction complements the constructive dimension providing interpretive constitution to our theoretical framework (Arnellos, Spyrou, Darzentas, in press). That said, we have no problem translating from a constructivist language to a realist one, since in accordance with our theoretic framework, a nervous system organizes itself so that it computes a stable representation of reality as this representation emerges in the interaction of the system with its environment.

In this perspective, it seems that it cannot exist as a merely constructivist or realist view, since any construction should be able to be tested in the system and by the system itself, the possible representational error should be functionally available in the system itself (Bickhard, 1993, 2000; Arnellos, Spyrou, Darzentas, in press) and the test will take place at the system's interaction with the environment. In other words, whatever the status of the external environment, the results of the interaction should be internally and functionally available.

However, Gonzalez and Pessoa continue their criticism by asking how we come to attribute autonomous self-organization and autopoiesis only to living agents, while we are also presenting the double closure of the sensorimotor system as a case of emergence and downward causation. First of all, this is not an artificial network, but a part of a greater living network of organizational processes, which cannot exist outside of it. This is the reason why Ziemke and Thieme's (2002) model cannot emerge on its own and it does not scale to greater levels of complexity. Again, Gonzalez and Pessoa ask about the means with which the kind of features being supported by such organizational networks may arise in phylogenesis and they are also asking why the artificial network suggested by Ziemke and Thieme's (2002) does not fulfill the characteristics for self-organization indicated by Collier (2004a).

We will try to answer these two comments using as a basis the criticism from Gonzalez and Pessoa on (this issue, p. 45), stating that our theoretical framework gives no emphasis to the concepts of *natural selection* and *noise*, as two essential concepts regarding the evolution of self-organising systems. Well, natural selection has many problems related to normative functionality (see e.g., Collier, 2004b), as this is defined and described in Arnellos, Spyrou, Darzentas (in press, this issue). The main problem is that in its abstract and disembodied version seems to be a possible solution to the problems discussed in the present paper, but once studied in its embodied version, the picture seems to turn upside down. Specifically, natural selection is not an abstract/formal process but an energetic/thermodynamic one. Its thermodynamic aspect is being taken care by the constructive/interactive processes of the system itself and as such, each noise triggering the self-organisation of the system is integrated into the respective functional processes, sometimes successfully and sometimes not. In either case, the phylogenetic aspects of such evolution are bounded to the materiality of the system and as Deacon (2006) suggests, in living systems selection is directly depended on the energetical aspects of the respective materiality.

Of course, the exact mechanisms are still unknown, but we have tried to provide some hints towards this direction by suggesting some logical features and conditions based on which such evolution could be started or even better, based on which a system can be said that it evolves while its interaction with the environment. However, the problem of the materiality of the system that would be able to support such features (process, interaction closure, formation of asymmetries that will result in the internal construction of new functions, etc.) remains. Nevertheless, we think that researchers of A-life should consider these features and conditions while trying to build systems that will develop intentions out of non-intentional dynamics.

5 Meaning is Emergent and has a Functional Substratum

Gonzalez and Pessoa agree that meaning should have a functional substratum and that the respective functionality should be emergent in the interaction with the environment. But they seem to strongly criticize the suggested framework as being mixed up with problematic *internalist representational* conjectures (this issue, p. 47). Well, we think that this is due to a misunderstanding due to their missing out the descriptive and explanatory power of the notion of interaction, as well as of the feature of normativity. Let us start from the latter.

Although we do say that "internal productive interrelations acquire a cohesive functional meaning in a collective way, since they contribute to the overall maintenance of the system" (this issue, p. 23), we do not adopt a pansemiotic position. As it is thoroughly explained in Arnellos, Spyrou, Darzentas, meaning is expressed through the choice of a certain function in the light of several possible choices and with respect to a purpose of the system. In this perspective, any cohesive system at the level of self-maintenance cannot be said to express meaning other than the one defined at the level of its respective functional norms (see section 3). This should be a satisfying answer to what happens in "simple" self-organizing systems that do not have a nervous system.

And now let's turn to the issue of the *internalist representational* conjectures. Bickhard's interactivist model, which we have tried to integrate in the suggested framework regards recursively self-maintaining systems – systems with more than one function at their disposal and systems which have already a functional substratum – as exhibiting certain functional norms. In general, each interaction of such systems with their environments will result in a specific internal outcome for the set of subsystems engaging in the specific interaction. We have specifically stated in section 2.4 that these outcomes depend both on the functional organization of the subsystems and on the environment. These outcomes create a differentiation in a way that they predicate the existence of a certain type of environment. So, either constructively or realistically, this differentiation is the only epistemic contact of the system with its environment.

But this differentiation does not provide any representational content as it is not considered as a representation in the suggested framework. So, there is not any internalistic representational conjecture. On the contrary, what we really have at this case is a functional state of the respective subsystems which is evolutionary connected to other functional processes of the system. These processes are forming a functional cohesion since we consider a recursively self-maintaining system. According to what has been mentioned in section 3 (this paper) this integrated functionality serves some purposes, in spite of their unintentional basis. These purposes may just be of the kind with which the system maintains itself, or as Bickhard (1993, 2000) suggests, it may be a simple goal system where a certain process, whose conditions of operation are driven by the environment, may direct the flow of operation to another process, which may either redirect the flow to the former process or outside the system. This is the simplest type of a goal-oriented system and it can be found in living and in non-living systems. What needs to be clearly understood is that the possibility of this redirection of operation between these two processes, or between many more processes in more evolved systems creates a *representational content* which emerges in the system's interaction with the environment.

The representations that will emerge depend both on the system and on the environment. Moreover, these representations should be considered as the anticipation of the system regarding its interactive capabilities towards the respective environment. As the system develops new representations, it further develops new anticipations and hence, normative functionality emerges. Therefore, it is totally wrong and misleading to consider a continuous modulation of action, taking place in a context of downward causation and based on any interactive context, while being driven by the system's norms, as an internalist representation.

At this point one should note that in the pragmatic context, a representation could be wrong. This is true and at this point Gonzalez and Pessoa are right to argue in favor of the adoption of mechanisms of learning. We have deliberately leaved learning out of the picture, as it was implicitly assumed when we mentioned that the interactive capabilities of the system, that is its anticipation may be inappropriate and this is an error which should be detectable by the system itself. So, we agree with Gonzalez and Pessoa that learning is necessary, as we have extensively mention elsewhere (Arnellos, Spyrou, & Darzentas, 2007, in press). But there can be no learning unless the system has a functional organization where any representational error would be internally detected and also available to the system itself. In this perspective, any kind of learning, (via communication with others, training, etc.) requires a capacity of constructing anticipations and representational content with a reference to a certain purpose. In other words, it requires a communication via meaning though the respective functional structures (Arnellos, Spyrou, & Darzentas, 2007).

At this point we are ready to answer to the last question posed by Gonzalez and Pessoa, namely whether "artificial systems could evolve in such a way that they would autonomously acquire learning mechanisms with indicators of relevant information in their selective interaction with the external world?" (this issue, p. 48). As we mentioned in section 3, the emergence of normativity takes place on the basis of primitive functional norms, which may even correspond to the fundamental purpose of self-maintenance, which in turn may be purely unintentional and based solely on the properties of the physical system under consideration. Nevertheless, according to the suggested framework, this is the functional norm upon which the emergence of other more developed norms will take place. As such, it seems that the condition to be satisfied is the evolution of newer purposes on the basis of a purpose denoting *self-interest*, independently whether it is a living or a non-living system.

A characteristic example of such a system is the "Big-Dog" (http:// www.bostondynamics.com/content/sec.php?section=BigDog). Although not the result of endogenous evolution, this can be considered as an artificial agent that serves the self-interest of not falling down. Is this enough in order to be characterized as autonomous? The answer is negative based on our framework, but its functional norm could be the basis for the development of an autonomous agent if there could be a way of evolving emergent capacities which would be functionally integrated on this norm. Again, materiality is the key to this question.

6 Conclusions

There is a significant difference between primitive functional norms and any further developed normative functionality. The suggested theoretical framework aims in providing directions for research in AI and is not meant to be an absolute theory for building autonomous artificial systems capable of evolving new meanings based on new functions. As such, the conditions for its falsification could not be other than the arguments that will render the framework as being non-naturalised as possible. But we all know that this is the case by default. However, the commentary of Gonzalez and Pessoa has by no means been directed towards the indication of architectures that are trying to support at least one of the features/aspects being mentioned by our framework.

Therefore, AI does not move towards such a direction, but in our humble opinion, AI is tinkering at the moment and this is something that should make even more evident the power of an interactivist framework of building autonomous artificial agents, as well as the importance of materiality. All these aspects should probably make our judgment, regarding the possibility of the existence of autonomous artificial agents, much more easier, but we also think that the analysis of our theoretical framework combined with the evaluation of the several attempts so far (at the technical level), are shedding new light in this very difficult problem.

References

Arnellos, A., Spyrou, T., & Darzentas, J. (2007). Cybernetic embodiment and the role of autonomy in the design process. *Kybernetes, 36* (9/10), 1207-1224.

Arnellos, A., Spyrou, T., & Darzentas, J. (in press). Towards the naturalization of agency based on an interactivist account of autonomy. *New Ideas in Psychology*.

Bickhard, M. H. (1993). Representational content in humans and machines. *Journal of Experimental and Theoretical Artificial Intelligence, 5*, 285-333.

Bickhard, M. H. (2000). Autonomy, function, and representation. *Communication and Cognition — Artificial Intelligence, 17,* (3-4), 111-131.

Collier, J. (2004a). Fundamental properties of self-organization. In V. Arshinov & C. Fuchs (Eds.), *Causality, emergence, self-organisation* (pp. 150-166). Moscow: NIA-Piroda.

Collier, J. (2004b) Self-organisation, individuation and identity. *Revue Internationale de Philosophie, 59*, 151-172.

Deacon W. T. (2006) Reciprocal linkage between self-organizing processes is sufficient for self-reproduction and evolvability. *Biological Theory, 1* (2), 136-149.

Vehkavaara, T. (2003). Natural self-interest, interactive representation, and the emergence of objects and *Umwelt*: An outline of basic semiotic concepts for biosemiotics. *Sign Systems Studies, 31*(2), 547-587.

Ziemke, T. & Thieme, M. (2002) Neuromodulation of reactive sensorimotor mappings as a short-term memory mechanism in delayed response tasks. *Adaptive Behavior, 10* (3/4), 175-199.

Cybernetics And Human Knowing. Vol. 15, nos. 3-4, pp. 57-63

Emergence: Process Organization, not Particle Configuration

Mark H. Bickhard[1]

The intuition of emergence is that new properties, properties that make a causal difference in the world, can emerge in higher level organization. A realm of issues in which the metaphysical possibility (or impossibility) of emergence is focal is the realm of mental phenomena. Are minds – in particular, yours and mine – genuine emergents, with causal power in the world, or are they at best epiphenomena, with no consequence? I will argue that the simple intuition of emergence is roughly correct, but that it requires a very non-simple shift in underlying metaphysical framework in order to make sense of it. In particular, it requires a rejection of standard particle or substance metaphysical frameworks in favor of a process metaphysics.

A Short History

I begin by looking at some of the history – a very short history – of the metaphysical frameworks that, so I will argue, make emergence so much of a mystery. The story begins with the Pre-Socratics: An argument was generated whose outcome has dominated Western thought since.

Heraclitus, famously, argued that all is flux, everything is process (Graham, 2006). Parmenides countered that change is not even possible: In order for change to occur, in order for A to change into B, for example, A would have to disappear into nothingness and B would have to appear (emerge)[2] out of nothingness. But nothingness cannot exist, therefore change cannot occur. The appearance of change in the world is mere appearance, not genuine.

The nothingness that Parmenides was alluding to was a metaphysical nothingness (a vacuum, for example, is not nothingness in this sense). A contemporary parallel might be something like "the nothingness" that "exists" outside of the universe. It is not clear that such a notion makes any sense at all, and similarly for Parmenides and his Greek readers. Furthermore, to talk about or think about something was, for the ancient Greeks, akin to pointing to it, and nothingness cannot be pointed to. A contemporary parallel for this point can be explored in the difficulties that Russell and Fodor (and many others) have had in trying to account for representations of non-existents or falsehoods.

In any case, the Parmenidean arguments were taken seriously, and responses attempted. Empedocles proposed that earth, air, fire, and water were the basic substances out of which everything is composed. These substances did not change, and, thus, satisfied the Parmenidean constraint. Apparent change is constituted in

---

1. Email: mark@bickhard.name; Website: http://www.bickhard.ws/
2. Not to imply that any notion of emergence was available.

changing mixtures of the substances. Similarly, Democritus proposed indivisible atoms as unchanging Parmenidean wholes, with apparent change being constituted by alterations in the configurations of these atoms.

Aristotle, among others, also took these issues quite seriously, and developed his own earth, air, fire, and water framework. This was much more sophisticated than that of Empedocles, and change was possible from one into another, but there was still a Parmenidean-satisfying base of unchanging prime matter (Bickhard, forthcoming, in preparation; Campbell, 1992; Gill, 1989; Guthrie, 1965; Taylor, 1997; Wright, 1997). This is the heritage from which the Western tradition of substance and particle derives.

Problems

This tradition appears to resolve the problems that Parmenides introduced, but, unfortunately, it introduces problems of its own that have perplexed or perniciously guided many since then. Three of them are:

1. Stasis or stability is the default. Change requires explanation, and self-movers are not possible.
2. Emergence is not possible. Earth, air, fire, and water can mix, but there is no possibility of generating a fifth substance.
3. A metaphysical realm of substance or atom is created. This realm might also involve cause and fact, but it does not include normativity, intentionality, or modality. These are split off into their own second realm, leaving the relationships to the first problematic.

Given the apparent necessity of a substance or particle metaphysics to satisfy the Parmenidean argument, and the resultant metaphysical split, there are only three general possibilities. Two distinct realms could be explicitly proposed, and the metaphysics of the world addressed from within such a two realm framework. Aristotle's substance and form, Descartes' two kinds of substances, Kant's two realms, and analytic philosophy's realm of scientific fact set off from that of linguistic normativity and modality would all be examples. A second possibility would be to attempt to account for everything in terms of the intentional realm alone, resulting in some sort of idealism, such as those of Hegel, Green, or Bradley. And, finally, one could attempt to account for the world just in terms of the physicalistic realm, as with Hobbes, Hume (on most interpretations), Quine, and most of contemporary philosophy and science.

There is, of course, a temptation to try to account for mental phenomena as emergents from a non-normative, non-intentional, realm, but that is precisely one of the conceptual possibilities that is precluded by the metaphysics that generates the split in the first place.

Hume

This framework has been explored and elaborated in many ways. One that I will address, that has had a major influence in subsequent centuries, is Hume's argument against being able to derive norms from facts (Hume, 1978). As standardly interpreted (Hume didn't actually elaborate the argument), Hume concludes that any valid reasoning containing only factual terms in the premises can have only factual terms in the conclusion. The argument is that any new terms that might be introduced in the course of the reasoning must be defined using the terms in the premises together with any terms previously defined. Any new terms, therefore, can always in principle be back-translated through their definitions – substituting the defining phrase or clause for the defined term – ultimately ending up with only terms that were in the original premises. Any valid conclusion, therefore, can always be stated using only factual terms, and will thus be a factual, not a normative, conclusion.

But Hume's argument turns on the assumption that all legitimate forms of definition permit back-translation, and that assumption is false. In particular, implicit definition does not. Implicit definition was most forcefully proposed by Hilbert in his implicit definitional axiomatization of geometry (Chang & Keisler, 1990; Doyle, 1985; Hale & Wright, 2000; Hilbert, 1971; Kneale & Kneale, 1986; Kolaitis, 1990; Otero, 1970; Quine, 1966). The basic idea is that the relations in the axioms define the class of models that would satisfy those axioms (though model theory per se took some further decades to develop). More generally, implicit definitions are definitions in terms of such classes of satisfiers of relational criteria.

Most importantly for current purposes is that implicit definitions are legitimate, and they do not permit back-translation. Hume's argument, therefore, is unsound.

Note that, in its general form, Hume's argument precludes any valid reasoning from arriving at anything other than certain re-arrangements of the original terms in the premises. In this form, it not only excludes deriving norms, it excludes deriving anything new: It is an argument against emergence. It expresses a term-level version of the substance/particle assumption that the only possibilities are just rearrangements of what is already there. Because the argument is unsound, however, this block to emergence is eliminated.

Jaegwon Kim

A second elaboration of the underlying framework that I will address is that of Jaegwon Kim. Kim argues that any apparent causal regularities manifest by a higher level configuration will be epiphenomenal relative to the causality of the particles making up that configuration. Therefore, although it may be that new causal *regularities* may appear, they will simply be the working out of the causal interactions among the constituent particles within that configuration, and no new genuine causal *powers* will appear.

His primary argument for this is the preemption argument. Either higher level causal regularities are in fact new and non-epiphenomenal, in which case the micro-physical "world" is not causally closed and we have some sort of dualism – or, perhaps, one of the British emergentists notion of emergence (McLaughlin, 1992) – or else the particle level causal interactions suffice for the manifest regularities, in which case it is superfluous to posit any additional causality beyond them. The particle level causality preempts any purported higher level causality (Kim, 1991). Configurations, then – unless we abandon the causal closure of the micro-physical world – are just the stage settings within which the genuine causal interactions of the particles take place. Everything else is causally epiphenomenal appearance.[3]

This is a powerful argument, but there is a basic flaw. It assumes a particle framework, that physical causality is constituted as particle causality. The key here is that particles have no organization. They can participate in organization, they can be arranged in configurations, and work out their causal interactions accordingly, but they have no organization themselves. In this view, then, everything that does have causality does not have organization. Organization is delegitimated as a potential locus of causality by the metaphysical framework within which the argument is made. But, if organization cannot be a locus of causality, then emergent causality is not possible. The argument, at best, begs the question.

Worse, however, is that the particle framework assumed here is false. There are several lines of consideration that demonstrate that. First, a pure point particle metaphysics would yield a world in which nothing ever happens: particles have zero probability of ever hitting each other. Second, in what is perhaps the standard naïve view today, the world is constituted not only by particles, but also by fields in terms of which the particles interact. But fields, then, must have causal power, and fields have whatever causal power they do in virtue (in part) of their organization. So organization cannot be delegitimated as a locus of causality without removing causality from the world.

Third, and most serious, our best physics tells us that there are in fact no particles at all. The world is constituted of (interactions among) quantum fields, and quantum fields are processes – and fields (and processes in general) have whatever causality they have in virtue of their organization. So, again, organization cannot be delegitimated as a potential locus of causal power without eliminating causality altogether.

The apparent particle-like properties of quantum field interactions are due to the quantization of such interactions, and the conservations of (some of) such quantized properties (Aitchison, 1985; Aitchison & Hey, 1989; Bickhard, 2003; Brown & Harré,

---

3. In recent years, Kim has been exploring the possibilities opened up by excluding relations from the definitions of various kinds of bases – supervenience base, micro- macro base, and so on (Kim, 1998, 2005). This has led him to at times even endorse a kind of emergence (Kim, 1998, 2005). But such changes in stipulative definition cannot ultimately do any metaphysical work. I find his earlier argument against emergence to still be the strongest, and it overrides his subsequent flirtation with emergence – the earlier argument is not blocked by his later work (except for his definitions, which he gives no particular reasons for accepting), and so it can just be run against his adversions to emergence (Campbell & Bickhard, 2008).

1988; Cao, 1999; Clifton, 1996; Davies, 1984; Halverson & Clifton, 2002; Huggett, 2000; Kuhlman, Lyre, & Wayne, 2002; Ryder, 1985; Sciama, 1991; Weinberg, 1977; Weinberg, 1995; Zee, 2003). But this quantization is akin to the quantization of the number of wavelengths in a guitar string, and there are no particles in either case – there are no more physical particles than there are guitar sound particles.

Everything is (quantum field) process, all the way up and all the way down. Organization, therefore, *must* be a potential locus of causality, including, in particular, complexly hierarchically organized such organizations, such as, perhaps, you or me. Such causal manifestations of higher level organization, then, are not blocked from being possible emergents, emergents with causal consequence in the world.

Kim, in effect, has found a reductio of the classic particle and property metaphysics: Everything that we know is emergent. That is, nothing that we know of was present thirteen or fourteen billion years ago, but those phenomena do exist now. Therefore, they have to have emerged. If some metaphysical framework precludes emergence, then it is refuted by the emergence of the universe as we know it.

A rejoinder might be to claim that "all that we know" is in fact epiphenomenal because all causality is resident in basic particles and that those particles (whatever physics ultimately finds them to be) have been in existence since the Big Bang. But this reversion to particles encounters the points made above: 1) nothing but particles yields a universe empty of phenomena, 2) fields are required for particles to interact, and fields already legitimize causally efficacious organization, and 3) quantum field theory shows that particles do not exist, and that, among other consequences, it is not the case that some basic set of particles has been in existence since the Big Bang.

A last attempt at a rejoinder might be to point out that contemporary physics is incomplete and certain to be wrong in at least some respects. This is correct, but any conclusion that there is a possibility of a reversion to particles fails. We still need fields of some sort, and, so, we need causally efficacious organization. And there are multiple strongly empirically supported phenomena that violate the assumed local independence and non-relational existence of anything like a particle model.[4] Particles are gone, and gone for good. The Empodoclean/Democritean heritage has run out. We must return to process – to Heraclitus, if you wish.

Reversing the Metaphysical Split

If we adopt a process metaphysics, we reverse all three of the central consequences of the substance/particle metaphysics:

1. Change becomes the default, and stability, should it occur, requires explanation.
2. New organization is a candidate for emergent causal power – the possibility of emergence is not precluded.

---

4. Such as the exclusion principle, the Casimir effect, Rindler and related quanta, virtual "particles", and so on, and on (e.g., Bickhard, 2003; Cao, 1999; Halverson & Clifton, 2002; Sciama, 1991).

3. And the possibility is available that normativity, intentionality, and other mental phenomena are emergent from non-normative, non-intentional phenomena.

These reversals open up possibilities that had been blocked. They do not tell us how such emergent phenomena are to be modeled. They only make it metaphysically sensible to assume that such phenomena might be emergent, and might be understandable as such. In particular, they make it sensible that emergence can occur in (higher level) organizations of process, but not in configurations of particles.[5]

Conclusion

The substance and particle tradition began in Western thought with the earliest beginnings of the differentiation of naturalistic explanation from myth and religion (Graham, 2006). It has been an extremely powerful metaphysical framework that has borne scientific and conceptual fruit for over 2500 years. Nevertheless, so I argue, it is false and it generates insurmountable conceptual problems in attempting to understand the world. In particular, it elevates stasis to a default condition, it makes genuine emergence impossible, and it splits a metaphysical realm of substance, particle, fact, and cause from that of normativity, intentionality, and modality.

This aporetic nest of issues has its strongest contemporary focus with respect to mind and mental phenomena: are they part of the natural world, or do they involve some sort of special non-natural realm or substance or property? They cannot be understood as part of the natural world so long as that world is understood to be constituted in substances or particles. That is the metaphysical framework that generates the split in the first place. But shifting to a process metaphysical framework is not only conceptually and scientifically advisable, it also dissolves all three of the basic sources of that split. Removing these metaphysical barriers does not in itself provide explanatory models of such phenomena as intentionality or normativity, but it does make the project of attempting such models no longer pointless. It makes emergence metaphysically possible, no longer mysterious, and even ubiquitous.

References

Aitchison, I. J. R. (1985). Nothing's plenty: The vacuum in modern quantum field theory. *Contemporary Physics, 26*(4), 333-391.

Aitchison, I. J. R.,& Hey, A. J. G. (1989). *Gauge theories in particle physics.* Bristol, England: Adam Hilger.

Bickhard, M. H. (2003). Variations in variation and selection: The ubiquity of the variation-and-selective retention ratchet in emergent organizational complexity, Part II: Quantum field theory. *Foundations of Science, 8*(3), 283-293.

Bickhard, M. H. (2004). Process and emergence: Normative function and representation. *Axiomathes – An International Journal in Ontology and Cognitive Systems, 14*, 135-169. (Reprinted from: Bickhard, M. H. [2003]. Process and Emergence: Normative Function and Representation. In: J. Seibt [Ed.], *Process theories: Crossdisciplinary studies in dynamic categories* [pp. 121-155]. Dordrecht: Kluwer Academic.)

Bickhard, M. H. (in press-a). Interactive Knowing: The Metaphysics of Intentionality. In R. Poli, J. Seibt, J. Symons (Eds.), *Theory and applications of ontology.* Dordrecht: Kluwer

5. For an attempted account of emergent normative phenomena – in particular, normative function and representation – see Bickhard (2004, in press-a, in press-b, 2008).

Bickhard, M. H. (in press-b). The interactivist model. *Synthese*.

Bickhard, M. H. (2008). *The whole person: Toward a naturalism of persons – Contributions to an ontological psychology*. Manuscript in preparation.

Brown, H. R., & Harré, R. (1988). *Philosophical foundations of quantum field theory*. Oxford: Oxford University Press.

Campbell, R. J. (1992). *Truth and historicity*. Oxford: Oxford University Press.

Campbell, R. J., Bickhard, M. H. (2008). *Physicalism, emergence, and downward causation*. Manuscript in preparation.

Cao, T. Y. (1999). *Conceptual foundations of quantum field theory*. Cambridge: U. of Cambridge Press.

Chang, C. C., & Keisler, H. J. (1990). *Model theory*. Amsterdam: North Holland.

Clifton, R. (1996). *Perspectives on quantum reality*. Dordrecht: Kluwer Academic.

Davies, P. C. W. (1984). Particles do not exist. In S. M. Christensen (Ed.), *Quantum theory of gravity* (pp. 66-77). Bristol, England: Adam Hilger.

Doyle, J. (1985). Circumscription and implicit definability. *Journal of Automated Reasoning, 1*, 391-405.

Gill, M-L. (1989). *Aristotle on substance*. Princeton, NJ: Princeton University Press.

Graham, D. W. (2006). *Explaining the cosmos*. Princeton, NJ: Princeton University Press.

Guthrie, W. K. C. (1965). *A history of Greek philosophy, Vol. II: The Presocratic tradition from Parmenides to Democritus*. Cambridge: Cambridge University Press.

Hale, B., & Wright, C. (2000). Implicit definition and the a priori. In P. Boghossian & C. Peacocke (Eds.), *New essays on the a priori* (pp. 286-319). Oxford: Oxford University Press.

Halvorson, H., & Clifton, R. (2002). No place for particles in relativistic quantum theories? *Philosophy of Science, 69*(1), 1-28.

Hilbert, D. (1971). *The foundations of geometry*. La Salle, IL: Open Court.

Huggett, N. (2000). Philosophical foundations of quantum field theory. *The British Journal for the Philosophy of Science, 51*(supplement), 617-637.

Hume, D. (1978). *A treatise of human nature* (Index by L. A. Selby-Bigge; Notes by P. H. Nidditch). Oxford: Oxford University Press.

Kim, J. (1991). Epiphenomenal and supervenient causation. In D. M. Rosenthal (Ed.), *The nature of mind* (pp. 257-265). Oxford: Oxford University Press.

Kim, J. (1998). *Mind in a physical world*. Cambridge, MA: The MIT Press.

Kim, J. (2005). *Physicalism, or something near enough*. Princeton, NJ: Princeton University Press.

Kneale, W., Kneale, M. (1986). *The development of logic*. Oxford: Clarendon.

Kolaitis, P. G. (1990). Implicit definability on finite structures and unambiguous computations. *Proc. 5th IEEE LICS*, 168-180. Conference held in Philadelphia, PA, 4-7 June, 1990.

Kuhlmann, M., Lyre, H., & Wayne, A. (2002). *Ontological aspects of quantum field theory*. River Edge, NJ: World Scientific.

McLaughlin, B. P. (1992). The rise and fall of British emergentism. In A. Beckermann, H. Flohr, & J. Kim (Eds.), *Emergence or reduction? Essays on the prospects of nonreductive physicalism* (pp. 49-93). Berlin: Walter de Gruyter.

Otero, M. H. (1970). Gergonne on Implicit Definition. *Philosophy and Phenomenological Research, 30*(4), 596-599.

Quine, W. V. O. (1966). Implicit definition sustained. In W. V. O. Quine (Ed.) *The ways of paradox* (pp. 195-198). New York: Random House.

Ryder, L. H. (1985). *Quantum field theory*. Cambridge: Cambridge University Press.

Sciama, D. W. (1991). The physical significance of the vacuum state of a quantum field. In S. Saunders & H. R. Brown (Eds.), *The philosophy of vacuum* (pp. 137-158) Oxford: Clarendon.

Taylor, C. C. W. (1997). Anaxagoras and the atomists. In C. C. W. Taylor (Ed.), *From the beginning to Plato*, (pp. 208-243). London: Routledge.

Weinberg, S. (1977). The search for unity: Notes for a history of quantum field theory. *Daedalus, 106*(4), 17-35.

Weinberg, S. (1995). *The quantum theory of fields. Vol. 1: Foundations*. Cambridge: Cambridge University Press.

Wright, M. R. (1997). Empedocles. In C. C. W. Taylor (Ed.) *From the beginning to Plato* (175-207). London: Routledge.

Zee, A. (2003). *Quantum field theory in a nutshell*. Princeton: Princeton University Press.

Forsythe, K. (2008). *Meditation 3* (detail). 15 cm x 22cm, acrylic on canvas.

Cybernetics And Human Knowing. Vol. 15, nos. 3-4, pp. 64-70

Some Remarks on Bickhard and Process Metaphysics

João Queiroz[1] and Floyd Merrell[2]

C. S. Peirce developed a process metaphysics based on the notion of indetermination, continuity and chance. His process metaphysics afforded him the wherewithal for creating a general theory of meaning that radically differs from the most standard view developed in philosophy of language, theoretical linguistics and cognitive science. The premises behind Peirce's concept of meaning support Bickhard's argument and can be summarized thus: The concept of a substantive-particulate nature of the world and its offshoot, a deterministically oriented concept of meaning the ideal of which is closed, complete, and self-sufficient, goes against the grain of process metaphysics. Meaning, in Peirce's conception, is open, and inherently incomplete.

Some consequences of this argument will be explored here. (1) Meaning is neither in any correspondence between a sign and its reference, nor is it the case that meaning or sense (*Sinn*) determines reference (*Bedeutung*) (contra Frege); (2) Meaning is neither in the brain-mind (contra GOFAI) as an autonomous organism, nor is it in a synchronic slice of language as an autonomous entity (contra Saussure); (3) Meaning is not in the referent that "causes" stimulation within the brain-mind evoking a certain response to a sign (contra Kripke); (4) Meaning is in the entirety of contextualized bodymind inter-action, but it *is* not in the solicitation of relatively static schemes (contra Lakoff and Johnson).

I. Semiosis and process

A number of investigators maintain that semiosis (meaning process), and its metaphysical counterpart, must be considered in terms of complex emergent, self-organizing adaptive systems (see Port, in press; Bickhard 2007; Steels, 2003; Wagner et al., 2003; Christiansen & Kirby, 2003; Cangelosi & Turner, 2002; MacLennan, 2001; Vogt, 2002; Jung & Zelinsky, 2000; Merrell, 1997; Keller, 1994; Hutchins & Hazlehurst, 1995; Rosenthal, 1994). As Kelso (1995, p. 1) argues, "symbols, like the whirlpools in a river, may evince relatively stable patterns or structures that persist for a certain lapse of time, but actually they are neither static nor atemporal." In this light, we have theoretically and empirically explored diverse consequences of complex system simulation and modeling in terms of the concept of meaning as process (e.g.,

1. Graduate Studies Program in History, Philosophy, and Science Teaching, Federal University of Bahia (UFBA/UEFS), Brazil. Email: queirozj@ecomp.uefs.br
   Dept. of Computer Engineering and Industrial Automation, State University of Campinas (UNICAMP), Brazil. Email: queirozj@pq.cnpq.br
2. Department of Foreign Lang. & Lit., Purdue University, West Lafayette, IN, USA. fmerrell@purdue.edu

Ribeiro et al., 2007; Gomes et al., 2007; Queiroz & Merrell, 2006; Queiroz & El-Hani, 2006a). With this in mind, we argue here that an adequate concept of meaning must entail process metaphysics as its basic presupposition.

Peirce, as a process thinker, was representative of a philosophical tendency that treats processes as being more fundamental than substantive metaphysic based on fixed ontological categories (see Rescher, 1996). According to Peirce's pragmatic approach, *semiosis* (meaning process) is an interpreter-dependent process that cannot be dissociated from the notion of a situated (and actively distributed) communicational agent (potential or effective). It is an interpreter-dependent process in the sense that triadically connects sign (representation), object, and an effect on the interpreter (interpretant). The object is a habit (regularity, or a pattern of constraints) embodied as a constraining factor of interpretative behavior – a logically "would be" fact and its attendant response on the part of the interpreting agent.

For Peirce,[3] a sign is a medium for the communication of a form or habit embodied in the object to the interpretant, so as to constrain (in general) the interpreter's behavior:

> a Sign may be defined as a Medium for the communication of a Form. ... As a medium, the Sign is essentially in a triadic relation, to its Object which determines it, and to its Interpretant which it determines. ... That which is communicated from the Object through the Sign to the Interpretant is a Form; that is to say, it is nothing like an existent, but is a power, is the fact that something would happen under certain conditions. (MS 793, pp. 1-3. See EP 2.544, n.22, for a slightly different version).

The notion of semiosis as form communicated from object to interpreter through mediation of sign allows us to conceive meaning, and meaning change, in a processual (non-substantive) way, as a constraining factor of possible patterns of interpretative behavior through habit and change of habit.

When applying this general semiotic approach to biological and social systems, meaning will most often be an interpreter-dependent objective process. According to the pragmatic approach, meaning is not an infused concept, but a power to engender interpretants (effects on interpreters). According to Peirce's pragmatic model of the sign, meaning (semiosis) is a triadic, context-sensitive (situated), interpreter-dependent (dialogic), materially extended (embodied) dynamic process. It is a social-cognitive process, not merely a static, symbolic system. It emphasizes process and development. Peirce's emphasis rests not on content, essence, or substance, but, more properly, on dynamic relations. It is context-sensitive in the sense that it is determined by the network of communicative events within which the interpreting agents merge with signs, such that they cooperate with one another. It is both interpreter-dependent and objective because it triadically connects representamen or sign (O), semiotic

---

3. We shall follow the practice of citing from the *Collected Papers of Charles Sanders Peirce* (Peirce, 1931-35, 1958) by volume number and paragraph number, preceded by CP; the *Essential Peirce* by volume number and page number, preceded by EP. References to the microfilm edition of Peirce's papers (Harvard University) will be indicated by MS, followed by the manuscript number.

object (S), and an effect or interpretant (I), in the interpreter (who, along with the signs being interpreted, is invariably part of the semiotic process).

II. Semiosis and self-organization

Semiosis can be defined as a self-corrective process involving cooperative interaction between three components, S-O-I. For Peirce, semiosis and communication processes are defined in terms of the same basic theoretical relationships (Ransdell, 1977), that is, in terms of a self-corrective process whose structure exhibits an irreducible relation between the three elements mentioned above, S, O and I. In a communication process, "it is convenient to speak as if the sign originated with an utterer and determined its interpretant in the mind of an interpreter" (MS 318, p. 11). Consequently, *self-organization* is very compatible with Peirce's theory, especially with his communication model accompanied by habit change processes, its self-correcting dynamics, and the circular relations between interpreters and utterers.[4]

The class of systems we are focusing on can be regarded as the embodiment of this process, including what Fetzer (1988) calls semiotic systems. A semiotic system is a system that produces, transmits, receives, computes, and interprets signs of different kinds. Semiotic systems show, therefore, self-corrective behavior, or some kind of goal-directed activity (see Ransdell, 1977, p. 162). Semiotic systems are capable of using signs as media for the communication of a form or the transference of a habit embodied in the Object to interpreters so as to constrain their behavior. The instantiation of such triadic relationships depend on the handling of Signs by semiotic systems, in such a way that the system can go beyond the merely dyadic relation of a simple reaction to an Object. Examples can be found in the sciences of complexity, a set of interdisciplinary research fields that study the properties of living and mental systems by means of computer simulations and robotics techniques. Artificial Life, Animats, and Evolutionary Robotics are some of the areas involved in the synthetic design of self-organized semiotic systems.

III. Some implications of the Peircean processual theory of meaning

Peirce's theory, outlined here, is of the nature of processual becoming, from possibility (Firstness—of Peirce's three categories of organismic, mental and physical world processes) to actuality (Secondness) to potentiality (Thirdness) as one of the indeterminate number of possibilities, any of which could have been actualized in place of what was selected for actualization. In this sense, account is given of genuine triadic *semiosis*. Semiosis includes not merely signs of intellection (thought-signs) but also signs of feeling, of inter-dependent, inter-related inter-action (signs integrating

---

4.   Self-organization is a process that mainly occurs in complex systems composed of interacting entities that
     mutually affect each other's process, leading the system to an "ordered" and provisionally stable state, i.e. a state
     of reduced variability and ambiguity, with increased redundancy.

body and mind into one process, *bodymind*). In this respect, Lakoff and Johnson warrant a favorable nod.

But there is more to this story. It bears on the notion that whatever logic there may be, it cannot be other than multi-valued. And above all, as illustrated in the previous paragraphs, it must include time. The notion of meaning must be non-linearly applied, and change must be allowed. What is meaningful in one space-time slice can become meaningless in another one, and what is meaningful within one space-time slice can have emerged from what was meaningful within a previous space-time slice but has become meaningless within the present space-time slice. Hence the notion of *becoming* is all-important. What *is becoming* does so in the process of present becoming, which was past becoming and will have been future becoming. Atoms as solid spheres eventually became atoms as largely vacuous, and those in their own turn became cloud-like wave amplitudes. The concept of becoming is imperative, because all that is semiosis, is flux.

IV. Abduction, semiosis, firstness

Induction and deduction can effectively account for (1) stasis as default, (2) the infeasibility of emergence, and (3) the substance and particulate nature of physical reality—following the Newtonian-Cartesian corpuscular-kinetic (mechanistic) model of the world. It is as if the subject, the observer, the knower, were capable of a "view from nowhere," a detached "God's-eye view," and as if the view from nowhere were of a fixed substance world of particulate nature. This account does not allow for emergence, for process. In contrast, Charles S. Peirce, in an attempt to free this mechanistic world-view of its static conception of the world, introduces *abduction*—a third term complementing induction and abduction. Abduction requires someone who experiences something – an object, act, or fact – that should not have occurred, and she or he is absorbed by the unexpected happening as if merges with her or him.

It bears mentioning that the fact of the unexpected happening is not entirely divorced from Heisenberg matrix mechanics or Schrödinger wave mechanics. The first consists of no more than a set of numbers accounting for what might possibly happen, and the second consists of a wave amplitude specifying what might possibly happen (both of which are comparable to Peirce's Firstness). Neither of them has anything to do with substantive, particulate existence; both of them are entangled with mind-body (as one, never dualistic in the sense of materialist metaphysics) of the possible observer (which can be via an instrument reading). When the wave function "collapses" into a substantive, particulate event (as Peircean Secondness), it involves the observer, and an irreversible act, such that what has happened might be a surprise, something new, something emergent, bringing about an abduction by the observer, which could not have occurred without that observer's *co-participation* with the world. This act of abduction regarding what might be the case, or Firstness, is then followed by a hypothetico-deductive conjecture, Thirdness, regarding the new happening, which can then be put to the test in the world of Secondness. This sequence is processual in nature. John Archibald Wheeler's (1980) interpretation of quantum reality accounts for this co-participatory happening, and Ilya Prigogine's (1980) dissipative structures account for the irreversibility of emergence, and the self-organization of novelty, of processual nature.

Wheeler offers a series of thought experiments in an effort to illustrate how it is that, to use a commonplace Niels Bohr (1963) phrase, no phenomenon is a phenomenon unless it is a registered (observed) phenomenon, which is to say that the physicist, through her instruments of detection, must be interrelated and interact with some aspect of the quantum world before it can gain genuine entry into what the physicist conceives as her physical world. Thus the physicist and the universe are co-participatory. In the Peircean semiotic sense, we can paraphrase Bohr's expression as: No sign is a genuine sign unless it has been interpreted (through creation of the sign's interpretant) by some co-participatory semiotic agent. Prigogine avails himself of physical world phenomena – Bénard cells, the Belosouv-Zabotinsky reaction, among others – to argue that, by way of dissipative structures that are capable of bringing order out of chaos, inorganic, and presumably nonliving matter can, under certain conditions, spontaneously self-organize so as to take on properties that were hitherto attributed solely to living organisms. Thus there is no absolute line of demarcation between living and nonliving matter. Along comparable lines, Peirce's philosophy tells us that signs are like living organisms: They grow, they can replenish themselves, and they pass away. Signs, in this manner, are capable of functioning like dissipative structures, breaking down the boundary between signs and living organisms.

Peirce's process philosophy, in light of Wheeler's co-participatory universe and Prigogine's self-organizing universe, help corroborate Bickhard's argument that everything is (quantum field) process, all the way up and all the way down, and that everything is complexly hierarchically organized.

V. Conclusion

(1) The meaning of a sign depends upon comparable past contexts of what is taken to be the same sign, in the present context, and in imagined, conjectured, or hypothetical future contexts; sign meaning is a time-bound process, beginning with context-dependent abductive possibilities of meaning, hypothetico-deductive inferences, and inductive inter-action in the arena of practical everyday affairs.

(2) Meaning, emerging from within this arena of practical everyday affairs bears on regularities with respect to inter-dependent, inter-action in the form of general modes of behavior guided by habit; habit forming is the consequence of multiple, everyday abductive, deductive and inductive acts.

(3) Meaning entails a process of imagination (abduction), consideration of possible consequences (deduction), and inter-action with particular aspects of the physical world (induction)—or mental worlds in terms of purely 'thought-signs'—in this sense it is most fundamental to Peirce's "realist" philosophy; this process is ongoing, which is to say that the emergence of sign meaning does not involve separate

abductive, deductive and inductive acts, but rather, they merge into one another. In this sense, as Bickhard argues: (i) change becomes the default, (ii) emergence is self-organizing, and (iii) mental phenomena can be emergent from non-normative, non-intentional phenomena, that is, from novel abductions.[5]

(4) Just as for Peirce it is impossible to think without signs, so also thought itself is impossible without the material incorporation of some aspect of the world, and meaning is impossible without co-participation of S, O, and I (CP 1.538, 2.253, 5.265, 5.314, 5.470). In this manner, and in addition to Bickhard's conclusions, process philosophy must include sign processes and the emergence of meaning within the creative advance of the world, which includes both mental processes and world processes.

Acknowledgement

J.Q. is indebted to the Brazilian National Research Council (CNPq) and the State of Bahia Foundation for Research Support (FAPESB).

References

Bickhard, M. (2007). Modern approaches to language. *New Ideas in Psychology, 25*, 67–69.

Bohr, N. (1963). Light and life revisited. In *Essays 1958-1962 on atomic physics and human knowledge* (pp. 23-28). Woodbridge, CT: Ox Bow Press.

Cangelosi, A & Turner, H. (2002). L'emergere del linguaggio. In A.M.Borghi & T. Iachini (Eds.), *Scienze della Mente* (pp.227-244). Bologna: Il Mulino.

Christiansen, M. H., & Kirby, S. (2003). Language evolution: Consensus and controversies. *Trends in Cognitive Sciences, 7* (7), 300-307.

Fetzer, J. H. (1988). Signs and minds: An introduction to the theory of semiotic systems. In Fetzer, J. H. (Ed.), *Aspects of artificial intelligence* (pp. 133–161). Dordrecht: Kluwer Academic Press.

Gomes, A., El-Hani, C., Gudwin, R., & Queiroz, J. (2007). Towards the emergence of meaning processes in computers from Peircean semiotics. *Mind & Society: Cognitive Studies in Economics and Social Sciences, 6*, 173-187.

Hutchins, E., & Hazlehurst, B. (1995). How to invent a lexicon: The development of shared symbols in interaction. In G. N. Gilbert & R. Conte (Eds.), *Artificial societies: The computer simulation of social life* (pp. 132-159). London: UCL Press.

Keller, R. (1994). *On language change: The invisible hand in language*. London: Routledge.

Kelso, S. (1995) *Dynamic Patterns: The Self-organization of brain and behavior*. Cambridge, MA: The MIT Press.

Jung, D. & Zelinsky, A. (2000). Grounded symbolic communication between heterogeneous cooperating robots. *Autonomous Robots journal, 8* (3), 269–292.

MacLennan. B. J. (2001). The emergence of communication through synthetic evolution. In M. Patel, V. Honavar, & K. Balakrishnan (Eds.), *Advances in the Evolutionary Synthesis of Intelligent Agents* (pp. 65-90). Cambridge, MA: The MIT Press.

Merrell, F. (1997). *Peirce, signs, and meaning*. Toronto: University of Toronto Press.

Peirce, C. S. (1967). *Annotated catalogue of the papers of Charles S. Peirce*. Robin, R. S. (Ed.). Amherst: University of Massachusetts Press. (Cited as MS, followed by the number of the manuscript.)

Peirce, C. S. (1994 [1866-1913]). *The collected papers of Charles S. Peirce*. Electronic edition, Vols. I-VI (Hartshorne, C. & Weiss, P. (Eds.) Cambridge: Harvard University, 1931-1935], Vols. VII-VIII (Burks, A. W. (Ed.) Cambridge: Harvard University, 1958]. Charlottesville: Intelex Corporation. (Cited as CP, followed by volume and paragraph number.)

Peirce, C. S. (1998 [1893-1913]). *The essential Peirce: Selected philosophical writings*. Vol. 2. Peirce Edition Project (Ed.). Bloomington, IN: Indiana University Press. (Cited as EP2, followed by page number.)

---

5. It bears mentioning that Peirce labels his philosophical posture "objective idealism." *Idealism* in view of the input of imagination as described above, and *objective* in terms of the sign's, interpretant's and interpreter's inter-dependence and inter-action with the object and the object reciprocally with them.

Prigogine, I. (1980). *From being to becoming: Time and complexity in the physical sciences.* New York: W. H. Freeman.
Port, R. (in press) Language and its two complex systems. *The Encyclopedia of Complexity and System Science.* Heidelberg: Springer-Verlag.
Queiroz, J. & El-Hani, C. N. (2006a). Semiosis as an emergent process. *Transactions of C. S.Peirce Society: A Quarterly Journal in American Philosophy, 42* (1), 78-116.
Queiroz, J. & El-Hani, C. N. (2006b). Towards a multi-level approach to the emergence of meaning processes in living systems. *Acta Biotheoretica, 54* (3), 174-206.
Queiroz, J. & Merrell, F. (2006). Semiosis and pragmatism: Toward a dynamic concept of meaning. *Sign System Studies, 34* (1), 37-66.
Ransdell, J. (1977). Some leading ideas of Peirce's Semiotic. *Semiotica, 19* (3/4), 157–178.
Rescher, N. (1996). *Process metaphysics: An introduction to process philosophy.* New York: SUNY Press.
Ribeiro, S., Loula, A., Araújo, I., Gudwin, R. & Queiroz, J. (2007). Symbols are not uniquely human. *Biosystems, 90,* 263-272.
Rosenthal, S. (1994). *Charles Peirce's pragmatic pluralism.* Albany, NY: State University of New York Press.
Steels, L. (2003) Evolving grounded communication for robots. *Trends in Cognitive Sciences, 7* (7), 308-312.
Vogt, P. (2002). The physical symbol grounding problem. *Cognitive Systems Research, 3* (3), 429–457.
Wagner, K., Reggia, J. A., Uriagereka, J., & Wilkinson, G. S. (2003). Progress in the simulation of emergent communication and language. *Adaptive Behavior, 11*(1), 37-69.
Wheeler, J. A. (1980). Beyond the black hole. In H. Wolff (Ed.), *Some strangeness in the proportion* (pp. 341-80). Reading, MA: Addison Wesley.

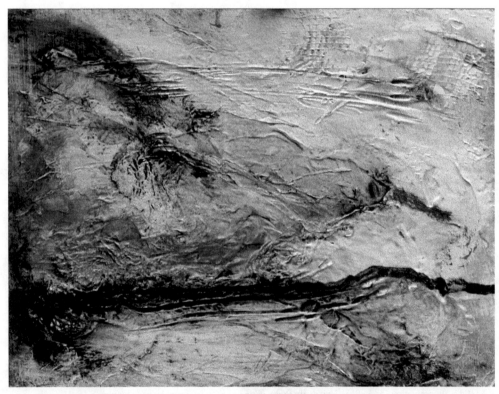

Forsythe, K. (2008). *Meditation 4* (detail). 15 cm x 22 cm, acrylic on canvas.

Cybernetics And Human Knowing. Vol. 15, nos. 3-4, pp. 71-74

Some Remarks on Process Metaphysics and Representation

Mark H. Bickhard[1]

In "Emergence: Process Organization, not Particle Configuration" (this issue) I argued that conceptual barriers to understanding emergence as a metaphysically real kind of phenomena trace back to the pre-Socratics – Parmenides and subsequent philosophers in particular – and that shifting to a process metaphysics dissolves these barriers, making emergence a natural and ubiquitous kind of phenomena rather than something mysterious or impossible. In their remarks, Queiroz and Merrell (this issue) show that Peirce's model of semiosis is deeply involved with his own process metaphysics, in this respect making some strong convergences with the process based emergence model that I outlined here, as well as with the interactivist model of representation that has been elaborated elsewhere (e.g., Bickhard, 2000, 2004, 2005, 2006, in press-a, 2008).

I am in full agreement that Peirce's process metaphysics is in general convergence with the considerations that I discussed in the paper, and, further, that there are similarities between the interactivist model of representation and Peirce's semiosis model, and would like to thank Queiroz and Merrell for introducing these points. I would like to take the opportunity to expand a little on these topics — in particular, with some comments on 1) some additional process metaphysical frameworks, 2) a few further consequences of a shift to a process metaphysics, and 3) some questions concerning Peirce's work.

Process Metaphysical Frameworks

Process metaphysics have been rare in Western thought, but such proposals do exist, some rather straightforwardly and some more partial or indirect (Rescher, 1996). Here I will mention just a few. Perhaps the earliest, of course, is Heraclitus, whose metaphysical proposals were arguably much more sophisticated than is sometimes appreciated (Graham, 2006). Parmenides work seems to have been an argument against Heraclitus, so the alternative conceptions were established as competing frameworks from very early on.

Leibniz and Hegel are two of the few subsequent Western philosophers to propose, at least in part, process metaphysics prior to the late 19th century. Perhaps triggered by Darwin's work, considerations of process metaphysics became more common, with Peirce, James, Bergson, and others being examples. Process philosophy became almost identified with Whitehead's work (Whitehead, 1979)

1.   Email: mark@bickhard.name Website: http://bickhard.ws/

throughout much of the 20th century, though I have some strong reservations in this regard: 1) Whitehead proposes something more akin to an event ontology rather than a process ontology, 2) Whitehead builds into his central notion of concrescence everything that he wants to get out of it, including various mental properties, 3) in this way, Whitehead "accounts" for mind in the universe, but at the cost of a pan-psychism, and thereby 4) avoids any commitment to ontological emergence. In fact, Whitehead rejects ontological emergence. His use of the term *emergence* is rare and refers to issues of complexity, not to the emergence of anything ontologically new.

In contemporary work, I would recommend that of Seibt (2003, in press). She shows how to construct a conceptual foundation of process that avoids the basic Aristotelian derived notions of fundamental particularity, and how to build on that a general process model that accounts for a wide range, potentially all, of our ordinary conceptions of the world.

I would suggest that among the strongest explanations for a more serious consideration of process metaphysics in the last century is not only Darwin and subsequent pragmatic and process frameworks, but also the development of quantum theory and quantum field theory in the 20th century. As Darwin introduced process and change into notions of species that had previously been static, fundamental physics progressively peeled away properties of particles and particulars, leaving little remaining beyond various quantization phenomena. One of the basic trends in the history of science has been the replacement of substance notions with process models: combustion instead of phlogiston for fire, random kinetic motion instead of caloric for heat, various kinds of self-organizing self-maintaining organizations of process instead of vital fluid, and so on. Evolutionary theory and quantum field theory are two further major developments of process conceptions. This trend in the history of science has had strong influences in the development of metaphysical thought, though phenomena of mind – for example, representation – are a vestigial hold-out against these general moves to process (Bickhard, 2004, 2006, in press-a, 2008).

A Few Further Consequences of Process Metaphysics

A shift to a process metaphysics changes the explanatory default to that of change, introduces the possibility of organizational emergence, and thereby opens the possibility to an emergent explanation of mental phenomena. But such a shift also has many additional consequences for our most familiar metaphysical presuppositions.

Consider a rock: it has a clear boundary, at least three, in fact – a boundary at which there is a phase shift from solid to gas, a boundary at which the rock can be pushed, and a boundary at which the rock can be isolated – and these three boundaries are coextensive. Such examples and properties frame our usual conceptions of the world. But now consider a candle flame: it has a phase shift boundary, in fact, more than one, at which the colors of light emitted change; it has no boundary at which it can be pushed; and it has no boundary at which it can be isolated – it is a necessarily open process organization, and to isolate it is to eliminate it. The notion of boundary, then, becomes much more problematic in a process view – what is the boundary of a vortex, a flame, and so on. And some phenomena do not have any natural boundary: in a field of clumps of crabgrass, how many individuals are there? Some of the clumps are still connected via runners while in other cases the runners have disappeared, and still others are in various intermediate states. Boundaries, and related notions of individuation, are *products* of process organizations, not inherent and necessary aspects of basic ontology. There can be more than one kind, or none at all, and in all cases their existence and nature is itself something to be explained, not assumed.

In similar manner, boundaries, principles of individuation, notions of supervenience, and multiple other ontological notions come into question within a process framework (Bickhard, 2006, 2008, in press-b). Just as substance and particle conceptions permeate our ontological intuitions, a shift to a process ontology involves many permeated changes in those conceptions.

Some Comments on Peirce

There are strong convergences between the process framework that I have argued for and Peirce's process metaphysics, and also between the model of representation that I base on an underlying process framework and Peirce's model of meaning (Rosenthal, 1983). More generally, the pragmatic movement has many aspects that are quite congenial to and convergent with the general model that I have been developing (Bickhard, 2004, 2006, in press-a, 2008).

There are, however, some differences. Rather than attempt to elaborate and argue these differences, which would require much more time and pages than are available here, I would like to just point to three issues concerning Peirce's work that suggest a less than complete convergence.

The first has to do with Peirce's process metaphysics in a broad sense. In particular, is there some way to extract Peirce's panpsychism from this metaphysics leaving a process framework that is more amenable to an emergentist model of mental phenomena such as representation? Second, Peirce's semiotics seems to address representational phenomena deriving from contact with the world: Is there a way to account within this framework for representation that is strictly counterfactual, hypothetical, modal, and other manners in which representation is not necessarily deployed with respect to environmental contact? And third, how can Peirce's model of semiotics account for phenomena of system-detectable representational error? Such system- or organism-detectable error is necessary to error guided behavior and to learning, but it is a criterion for models of representation that is rarely addressed in the literature (Bickhard, 2004, 2006, in press-a, 2008), and it is not clear to me how Peirce could satisfy it.[2]

Conclusion

The discussion of emergence, and the proposal that emergence can be understood within a process metaphysics, is a small part of a much larger web of issues. Queiroz and Merrell have introduced some further considerations about Peirce's process metaphysics and semiotic model, and I have taken the opportunity to elaborate yet a few further considerations that flow from investigating a basic process framework. I thank Queiroz and Merrell for introducing a crucially relevant consideration of one of the major process thinkers of the last century and a half. I think it worth commenting that we have barely touched upon the vast array of substance/particle metaphysical issues that ubiquitously permeate Western thought. Substance and particle thought has dominated and developed for over two millennia, while process thought has only become a more ongoing focus for less than two centuries: we have a long way to go.

References

Bickhard, M. H. (2000). Emergence. In P. B. Andersen, C. Emmeche, N. O. Finnemann, & P. V. Christiansen (Eds.), *Downward causation* (pp. 322-348). Aarhus, Denmark: University of Aarhus Press.

Bickhard, M. H. (2004). Process and emergence: Normative function and representation. *Axiomathes: An International Journal in Ontology and Cognitive Systems, 14*, 135-169. (Reprinted from Bickhard, M. H. (2003). Process and Emergence: Normative Function and Representation. In J. Seibt [Ed.], *Process theories: Crossdisciplinary studies in dynamic categories* [pp. 121-155]. Dordrecht: Kluwer Academic.)

Bickhard, M. H. (2005). Consciousness and reflective consciousness. *Philosophical Psychology, 18* (2), 205-218.

Bickhard, M. H. (2006). Developmental normativity and normative development. In L. Smith & J. Voneche (Eds.), *Norms in human development* (pp. 57-76). Cambridge: Cambridge University Press.

Bickhard, M. H. (2008). Issues in process metaphysics. *Ecological Psychology, 20* (3), 252-256.

Bickhard, M. H. (in press-a). The interactivist model. *Synthese.*

Bickhard, M. H. (in press-b). Systems and process metaphysics. In C. Hooker (Ed.), *Philosophy of complexity, chaos, and lon-linearity. Handbook of the philosophy of science, Vol. 16.* Amsterdam: Elsevier.

Bickhard, M. H. (2008). *The whole person: Toward a naturalism of persons – Contributions to an ontological psychology.* Manuscript in preparation.

Graham, D. W. (2006). *Explaining the cosmos.* Princeton, NJ: Princeton University Press.

Rescher, N. (1996). *Process metaphysics.* Albany: SUNY Press.

Rosenthal, S. B. (1983). Meaning as habit: Some systematic implications of Peirce's pragmatism. In E. Freeman (Ed.) *The relevance of Charles Peirce* (pp. 312-327). La Salle, IL: Monist.

Seibt, J. (2003). Free process theory: Towards a typology of occurings. In J. Seibt (Ed.) *Process theories: Crossdisciplinary studies in dynamic categories* (pp. 23-55). Dordrecht: Kluwer Academic.

Seibt, J. (in press). Forms of emergent interaction in general process theory. *Synthese.*

Whitehead, A. N. (1979). *Process and reality* (2nd Ed.). New York: Free Press.

---

2. There would seem to be an intuitive way in which Peirce's model of meaning (Rosenthal, 1983) could support violations of "expectations" that would ground the detection of error — and this is roughly the manner in which the interactivist model accounts for system detectable error — but Peirce's technical definitions make it unclear how to model both aboutness and error-in-that-aboutness in the same framework. Furthermore, those definitions do not seem to be amenable to any basic changes that would introduce such a distinction. In any case, it is at least an interesting question how Peirce's model could address this issue.

Cybernetics And Human Knowing. Vol. 15, nos. 3-4, pp. 75-86

A Dynamical Account of Emergence

John Collier[1]

Emergence has traditionally been described as satisfying specific properties, notably non-reducibility of the emergent object or properties to their substrate, novelty, and unpredictability from the properties of the substrate. Sometimes more mysterious properties such as independence from the substrate, separate substances and teleological properties are invoked. I will argue that the latter are both unnecessary and unwarranted. The descriptive properties can be analyzed in more detail in logical terms, but the logical conditions alone do not tell us how to identify the conditions through interactions with the world. In order to do that we need dynamical properties – properties that do something. This paper, then, will be directed at identifying the dynamical conditions necessary and sufficient for emergence. Emergent properties and objects all result or are maintained by dissipative and radically nonholonomic processes. Emergent properties are relatively common in physics, but have been ignored because of the predominant use of Hamiltonian methods assuming energy conservation. Emergent objects are all dissipative systems, which have been recognized as special only in the past fifty years or so. Of interest are autonomous systems, including living and thinking systems. They show functionality and are self governed.

1. Logical conditions for emergence

Emergence is usually attributed to things that have new properties not present in the phenomena from which they are formed. Some emergentists invoke notions of separate substances, causal independence and teleology that border on obscurantism. They believe that emergent properties must arise from but not be causally dependent on underlying or prior properties. Whether or not this position is coherent, it is certainly mysterious, and evidence in its favour is lacking. The only place in modern science that indeterminism is possibly supported is in quantum mechanics (even there the laws are deterministic). Otherwise, the evidence for determinism is very strong, certainly in the macroscopic domains where emergent phenomena occur. Furthermore, teleological causes are not known to work independently of the usual physical causes.

The metaphysical problems with explanatorily independent domains in a common world, together with the evidence for physical determination of all but the most fundamental properties justify the *principle of supervenience* (Kim, 1978; Rosenberg, 1978, 1985): If all of the (determinate) physical facts are determined, then all (determinate) facts are determined. Kim (1978) bases the principle on a general metaphysical position that the world is determined by its physical structure, whereas Kincaid (1987) suggests that the principle is empirically based. I believe that the metaphysical and empirical reasons are each sufficient independently, but combined they are stronger than either alone. Each answers certain doubts otherwise left open by

1. School of Philosophy and Ethics, University of KwaZulu-Natal, Durban 4041, South Africa
   Email:collierj@ukzn.ac.za   Website: Http://www.ukzn.ac.za/undphil/collier

the other. If emergence entails radical indeterminism the principle of supervenience rules it out. Nagel, however, (1961, p. 377) pointed out that although emergence is sometimes associated with radical indeterminism and/or teleological causation, this association is not essential. Let us assume that his usage, which follows C. D. Broad's (1925), is authoritative.

The major physicalist alternative to emergentism is ontological reductionism. Assuming physicalism and determinism, and a modest finitism implying the closure and self-sufficiency of objects on their composition (sometimes called *atomism*), ontological reduction is in principle always possible (Rosenberg, 1985, pp. 62-64). This sort of reduction requires peculiar physical properties and objects (sometimes called *logical constructs*), as well as an artificial consideration of systems as closed. If we reject finitism, closure and logical constructs as the figments of a logician's imagination, micro-reduction is not so easily justified.

Micro-reduction does not easily account for the organizing effect of higher level (more extended) entities (Campbell, 1974). The reductionist must hold that these capabilities were present at the lowest level all along, and that nothing new has been acquired. From the reductionist perspective, composition, far from creating new capabilities, places constraints on the system that eliminate certain possibilities. The reductionist is forced to reinterpret the appearance of new phenomena as the elimination of available possibilities. Aside from the awkwardness of this interpretation, reductionism must find some way to reconcile the elimination of possibilities through composition with the continued presence of the possibilities in the underlying microstructure. I will return to this issue in section 3 below.

a) Descriptive conditions for emergence

Aside from the mysterious attributes of emergent entities that I rejected above, emergent properties and objects generally are assumed not to be reducible to the binary relations among their components,[2] to be unpredictable from the properties of their compositional substrate, and to show new or novel properties that do not exist in their substrate. Any adequate account of emergence must account for these characteristics. The main problem with these qualitative characteristics is that they are hard to determine by observation alone and ignorance of details or confusion of epiphenomenal properties with real properties (the properties of the substrate on the reductionist view) can lead to mistaken evaluations of emergence. We need more precise characteristics at the very least.

---

2. If all relations including the dynamical organization of the parts were allowed, then one relation would just be the emergent entity. It would therefore be reduced to itself, and we would get nowhere. (See below on fusion.) If we allow binary relations, then we also allow all logical sums and products of these relations by that can be computed (sensu Church-Turing). My specific claim is that if an object is emergent, this set does not contain the emergent properties.

b) Computational conditions for emergence

A system is temporally predictable if and only if its time evolution can be calculated from its initial conditions specified within some region in phase space together with its equations of motion to be within some region of phase space at some arbitrary later time. More specifically, the trajectory of a system is predictable if and only if there is a region η constraining the initial conditions at t_0 such that the equations of motion will ensure that the trajectory of the system will pass within some region ε at some time t_1, where the region η is chosen to satisfy ε. For indeterministic systems, the values are determined to the extent determined by the probabilistic factors in the laws. Predictability in this sense applies to all closed Hamiltonian (specifically, conservative, holonomic) systems, including those without exact analytical solutions, such as the three body problem. The systems without exact analytical solutions can be numerically calculated in principle, if we have a large enough computer. The macrostate of a microsystem can be predicted similarly by composing the trajectories of the microcomponents and averaging to get the expected macrovalues.

If we want to undermine predictability, at least one of the assumptions must go. The assumptions are 1) the system is closed, 2) the system is Hamiltonian, and 3) there exist sufficient computational resources. The last condition (3) is a shorthand way of saying that the information in all properties of the system can be computed from some set of boundary conditions and physical laws, where information is understood as an objective measure of asymmetry as in (Muller, 2007, also, but less rigorously in Collier, 1990b, 1996). As I will demonstrate later, all three of these assumptions are violated for some simple physical systems, including some in the solar system. It is worth noting that so-called emergent computation (Forrest, 1991) is really not a case of a violation of 3, nor are many models of 3 body systems that seem to demonstrate chaos or emergence. These are artifacts of the modeling process, and have no ontological significance. On the other hand, there are some systems that violate 3 because no computer could have sufficient power, let alone one connected to the system under study. I will give an example below in terms of Newtonian particle mechanics with gravity and friction that serves as an exemplar for emergence. More complex cases are just more nuanced.

Novelty does not necessarily follow from mathematical unpredictability, since there may be no new properties formed in unpredictable systems, but novelty is impossible without unpredictability, except in the trivial sense that a pile of blocks is novel with respect to the block components. The predictability of the macrostate of a system from its microstate (states of the components of its substrate) is just the condition of reducibility, so unpredictability is also required for and sufficient for irreducibility. The advantage of the mathematical rendition of the characteristics of emergence is that we have reduced three to one, except for possible additional requirements to ensure novel properties. Now the problem is to determine when computability fails in dynamical systems. That is when emergence begins.

2. Dynamical Realism

Dynamical realism is a name that C. A. Hooker and I have given to a metaphysics that holds that what is real is either dynamical or explicable in dynamical terms. Something is dynamical if and only if it can be described completely in terms of forces and flows. We use the term in a book in progress on reduction in complex systems, but some of the basic ideas are in (Collier & Hooker, 1999) and expressed in an analysis of asymptotics and reduction in (Hooker, 2004). Why dynamical realism? Basically, because nothing that is not dynamical can have any effect on anything else, so it is impossible to have meaningful knowledge of it. (This is just a material version of Peirce's pragmatic maxim that any difference in meaning must make a difference to experience.) A similar consideration lies behind (Ladyman & Ross, 2007, p. 29), except in that book structure plays the role of dynamics in Collier and Hooker. Depending on how science works out, the two may coincide, but I prefer dynamical realism because structure can be inert, and do nothing.

Logical characterizations can be useful, but they still need to be hooked up to the world in order to apply to anything. The problem with understanding emergence is to hook up the computational characterization to dynamical conditions. This turns out to be somewhat easier than it might appear, and involves the failure of one or more of the three conditions mentioned in section 1b above.

3. Reduction and supervenience

Before showing how the logical conditions for emergence can be connected to dynamical conditions, it is useful to clear up some confusions about reduction. Most of this has been done already by Ross and Spurrett (2004), Hooker (2004) and myself (2004a), so I will be brief. Kim (1998, 1999, 2005) argues that if supervenience holds (as I have granted above) then a supervenient system has no causal power that its substrate does not, therefore reducibility holds and emergence is false. We can grant the first conclusion that reducibility holds (in a certain way), but it is irrelevant to the conclusion that emergence is false, which I shall challenge.

Reduction is ambiguous in three ways. It might mean intertheoretic reduction, the reduction of fundamental kinds of things (substance, traditionally), or that certain particular entities (objects, processes or properties) can be eliminated without any loss of explanatory power in principle. Intertheoretic reduction is irrelevant here. The reduction of the number of fundamental kinds of things is best called *ontological deflation*. It is a reasonable hypothesis that all that exists is physical. Kim's argument shows that if supervenience, then ontological deflation – all causation is physical causation. I suppose it is obvious that this is not very controversial these days.

However, despite supervenience, if reducibility fails in principle for some entity, then it is emergent. If there is no possible argument (deductive or inductive) from the parts, their intrinsic properties, and (the computational closure of) their binary relations to the full causal powers of the entity itself, then reductive explanation fails in principle. In these cases, even if physicalism is true, they are emergent. This idea of emergence as irreducibility to components fits C. D. Broad's criteria (Collier & Muller, 1998, see also Reuger, 2000a, 2000b, 2004). Basically, Kim has committed a philosophical howler, and has missed the point entirely. He got on the wrong boat.

A slightly different approach to show Kim's mistake is due to Paul Humphrey's (1997a, 1997b) account of emergence, based in the idea of *fusion*. The idea is that dynamically connected components form a fusion, such that the properties of the components are not the same in the fusion as they are in the isolated components. Suppose the Earth and the Sun form a system. The fused system gives the Earth and the Sun properties that they would not have independently. Some of the properties of the independent components (like following rectilinear paths) no longer exist (the two orbit a common centre of gravity). Properties are emergent if they cannot be computed from the properties of the unfused components. In the Earth-Sun case the computation is relatively trivial, so there is no emergence. But this is not always the case, and I will give an example in section 5 below.

Whether we take the component approach or Humphreys' (they are not so different in spirit), Kim's argument is irrelevant. Kim's causation argument, on Humphreys' approach, concerns the component fused system, but does not consider the relation between the separated (unfused) and fused systems. On the component account Kim considers that causal properties of the already combined system, without considering the relation between the properties of the components and those of the system. In either case, Kim is looking at the wrong thing. The only reason his argument gives any appearance of being relevant is that he plays on the ambiguity between ontological reduction and ontological deflation.

4. Hamiltonian systems and holonomic constraints

This is a difficult technical issue, with many complications, especially for specific systems, but it is central to my argument for both the dynamical characterization of, and existence of, emergent entities. I will therefore be painting a picture that ignores many subtleties, and I will be saying some things that seem to violate things that are well established in the literature of physics. Rather than go into details, I will point out right now that these apparent violations apply to specific systems and ignore the complete description of the systems in which they are embedded, or else use a very broad notion of a Hamiltonian system, or both. Thus we have descriptions of Hamiltonian chaos, quantum chaos and nonholonomic constraints on Hamiltonian systems that I will be saying are ruled out by my definition of a Hamiltonian system. The set of Hamiltonian systems in the sense I use here is, I believe, equivalent to the set of trivial machines delimited by von Foerster (2003), and the set of mechanical systems as defined by Robert Rosen (1991). Alas, I do not yet have a proof that satisfies me.

Newtonian mechanics is a very open theory that allows such things as unpredictability, indeterminate but mathematically fully describable systems, nonconservation of energy, and other bizarre phenomena that have been described over the years. Physicists intuitively rule out such cases with implicit or explicit assumptions that restrain the set of models to those we recognize as mechanistic. These restrictions have been formalized first in the Lagrangian formulation, and later in the Hamiltonian formulation of Newton's dynamics. The restrictions are often ignored in physics texts, so it is easy to let them slip past unnoticed.

The Lagrangian formulation for simple systems sets $L = T - V$, where L is the Lagrangian, T is the kinetic energy, and V is the potential energy. The integral of this is stationary on dynamically possible paths (Principle of Least Action). Dynamically, T is the flow part and V is the force part. Variation of the Lagrangian is determined by the force law (connecting forces to flows), generally in terms of generalized coordinates and their first derivative (velocity) – so the resulting equations are second order. The Hamiltonian can be based on the Lagrangian such that $H(q,\dot{q},t) = \sum_i \dot{q}_i p_i - L(q,\dot{q},t)$, where q is a generalized coordinate and p is a generalized momentum. The main difference, obviously, is the dependence on generalized momenta, thus the use of a *2n* dimensional phase space instead of a n dimensional coordinate space. If L is a sum of functions homogeneous (i.e., no products of different degrees) in generalized velocities of degrees 0, 1, and 2 and the equations defining the generalized coordinates are not functions of time, then $H = T + V = E$, where E is a constant (i.e., the system is conservative) and I call such a system a *Hamiltonian system*. If the generalized coordinates do depend on time, then H is not constant, and $H \neq E$, and the system is generally complex. Since all other constraints can be put into the formulation of the generalized coordinates, energy conservation is the only additional constraint on a closed Hamiltonian system. The same is true for quantum systems, which for closed systems are always Hamiltonian in current formulations of quantum mechanics. Quantum systems, therefore, are always simple, and cannot show either true chaos or emergence (Ford, 1986). (Despite this, quantum chaos and emergence have been investigated; if real, these would require violation of the conditions on $H = T + V$.)

Hamiltonian systems have an overall force function (*T*) that is holonomic, i.e., depending only on the position coordinates and time (Holonomic Constraints, 2007), if and only if the force is conservative, an example being particles in a gravitational field. It is possible that component forces are nonconservative, but their combination must be. Being constant, E is also holonomic, as it depends only trivially on position coordinates and time. In general, if a system is holonomic it can do no *virtual work* because all virtual displacements are perpendicular to the forces of the constraints, so there is (would be) no force on them. This is really just another way of saying that the H of Hamiltonian systems depends only on (appropriately chosen) generalized coordinates and E. This is of central importance to the theory of dynamical emergence, as I will argue below.

An alternative way to express holonomic systems is in terms of the Lagrangian: a system is holonomic when the Lagrangian can in principle be expressed in terms of as many coordinates as the system has degrees of freedom. Such systems are integrable, though integration may in practice require numerical approximation. So holonomic systems can be understood as a whole through the integration of their parts and their partwise interactions. A nonintegrable system must be non-holonomic, and must thus not be a Hamiltonian system.[3] An important characteristic of nonholonomic systems is that their equations of motion cannot be separated from their boundary conditions. Conrad and Matsuno make clear the consequences for dynamical systems:

> Differential equations provide the major means of describing the dynamics of physical systems in both quantum and classical mechanics. The indubitable success of this scheme suggests, on the surface, that in principle it could be extended to a universal program covering all of nature. The problem is that the essence of a differential equation description is a separation of itself from the boundary conditions, which are regarded as arbitrary. (Conrad & Matsuno, 1990, pp. 67-68)

Conrad and Matsuno go on to draw conclusions about the application of the method to the whole universe (they claim the system breaks down, but it is actually compatible with the requirement on cosmological theories that they have no boundary conditions). Of more significance here is the breakdown of the separation of differential equations and boundary conditions in nonintegrable systems, exactly the ones that are nonholonomic (in which constraints like boundary conditions cannot be separated from the dynamics). In these systems, computation from partwise interactions fails, and the system is in a sense holistic. In any case, its dynamics cannot be reduced to the dynamics and partwise relations. This is one of the conditions for emergence.

I've shown above that non-Hamiltonian systems are also nonconservative. The next step is to bring the two conditions governing nonholonomicity together and argue for a common basis for emergence in dissipative nonholonomic self-interactive systems.

5. Radically non-Hamiltonian systems

It is generally recognized that Hamiltonian systems are mechanical. This idea of mechanical is summed up by their holonomic character, in an engineer's sense that all their constraints can be expressed algebraically and are basically geometric. Nonholonomic systems, on the other hand, must have a constraint that is expressed as a rate of change, so their form cannot be integrated to an algebraic form, and they cannot be understood geometrically. Some examples of nonholonomic systems are a rolling wheel (friction matters) or a planet experiencing tidal dissipation (recall that holonomic systems are nondissipative).

Some systems are non-Hamiltonian, but are close to Hamiltonian. We can deal with such systems with approximations. This is a common method. Other non-Hamiltonian systems step rapidly from one state to another (rapid is relative here),

---

3. The necessity of nonholonomic constraints was pointed out to me by Howard Pattee, 10 Aug 2000, on my mailing list Organization, Complexity, Autonomy, see also Pattee, 1967.

such as the onset of convection in a Bénard cell. The dynamics of these systems can be analyzed by comparing the micro- and known macromechanics, along with knowledge of the transition. This is how Bénard cells were in fact analyzed. However, there is a large range of systems that are not close to step functions or close to smooth Hamiltonian systems. Such systems typically show sudden changes, for example, a wheel can loose friction suddenly, and a planet can slip from one resonant attractor to another. I conjecture that this sort of radically non-Hamiltonian behaviour underlies all emergence. In particular:

1. The system must be nonholonomic, implying the system is nonintegrable (this ensures nonreducibility)
2. The system is energetically (and/or informationally) open (boundary conditions are dynamic)
3. The system has multiple attractors (see below)
4. The characteristic rate of at least one property of the system is of the same order as the rate of the non-holonomic constraint (radically non-Hamiltonian)
5. If at least one of the properties is an essential property of the system, the system is essentially non-reducible; it is thus an emergent system

I don't claim that these conditions are independent; in fact, I think they are not. I choose them because they are relatively easy to argue for in specific dynamical cases, and from that to emergence. I do claim, however, that the conditions are necessary and sufficient dynamical conditions for emergence. All are required for the emergence of systems, and all but the last for emergence of properties. If any is violated (perhaps implying the violation of others), there is no emergence.

Condition 3 is debatable. Bénard cells are a good case in point. They are set up so that only one possible state can be reached by the transition (there is only one possible attractor). It is possible to predict the convecting state from general knowledge of fluids and knowledge of the specific conditions, unlike systems with multiple attractors, for which it is possible to predict that one of several attractors will be reached, but the ultimate attractor is not predictable. On the other hand, it is impossible in the case of the Bénard cell to predict from the microscopic equations of motion what the macroscopic state will be. So in this sense Bénard cells show both unpredictability and novelty. I don't think we need to make a decision about how to classify such cases as long as we realize that they differ from the more general case.

6. Determinism, nonreducibility, unpredictability

Systems that satisfy the above conditions may be deterministic, but they must be dissipative. If dissipation is irreducibly statistical, then determinism is ruled out to at least this extent. However, since there is good reason to think that, overall, particle systems are deterministic, there is also reason to think that the Second Law of Thermodynamics, in its statistical mechanical form, must be compatible with determinism, and that we need some nonepistemic explanation for the chance or probabilistic character of dissipative systems, for example, some form of relative chance based on relative information in the macrostate to the microstate (see Collier, 1990a). This problem is too difficult to go into here, and is not really relevant. However, systems satisfying conditions 1-5 are irreducible and unpredictable. This is best shown with an example (Collier, 2004a).

Mercury was found in the 1960s to rotate on its axis three times for each two times it revolves around the Sun. This was extremely surprising, since it had been thought that it would be in the same 1:1 harmonic as our Moon-Earth system. There are several more complex harmonic relations in the Solar System. It is well known that the three body gravitational problem is not solvable analytically, but it can be solved numerically, in principle, to any degree of accuracy we might require for any finite time (this is true for any Hamiltonian system – see discussion above). However, this case involves the dissipation of energy through tidal torques, unless the system is in some harmonic ratio. We would like, ideally, a complete explanation (possibly probabilistic) of why Mercury is in a 3:2 harmonic. Due to the high mass of the sun and the proximity of Mercury to the Sun, the high tidal torque dissipates energy reasonably quickly in astronomical time, so Mercury is very likely to end up in some harmonic ratio in a finite amount of time. The central explanatory problem then becomes "why a 3:2 ratio rather than a 1:1 ratio like our Moon, or some other harmonic ratio?"

We cannot apply Hamiltonian methods, since the rate of dissipation is roughly the same as the characteristic rate of the phenomenon to be explained. It is neither a step function nor near Hamiltonian. If the dissipation rate were small, then we could use an approximate Hamiltonian; if it were large, we could use a step function.[4] We are left with the Lagrangian. It is well known that these are not always solvable even by numerical approximation, if and only if the system is nonholonomic (see section 4 above). I will give an intuitive argument that the Mercury's harmonic is such a case. Each of the possible harmonics is an *attractor*. Why one attractor rather than another? If the system were Hamiltonian, then the system would be in one attractor or another. In principle we could take into account the effects of all other bodies on Mercury and the Sun (assuming the universe is finite, or at least that the effects can be localized), and decide with an arbitrarily high degree of accuracy which attractor the system is in. However, given the dissipative nature of the system, it ends up in one attractor or another in finite time. If we examine the boundaries between the attractors, they are fractal, meaning that every two points in one attractor have a point between them in another attractor, at least in the boundary region. This is as if the three body gravitational problem had to be decided in finite time, which is impossible by numerical approximation (the problem is non computable, even by convergent approximation). Therefore there can in principle be no complete explanation of why

---

4. This is what we do in the Bénard cell case, in which the rate of increased dissipation during the transition is high relative to the rates of dissipation in the two stable states.

the Mercury-Sun system is in a 3:2 harmonic. There is approximately a 1/3 chance of 3:2 capture, 1/2 of a 1:1 capture, and the rest of the harmonics take up the rest of the chances. The chances of a 3:2 capture are good, but not that good. The system is obviously physical, but it has a nonreducible property. This property fits Broad's notion of emergence.

Note that condition 1 is satisfied, since the system is nonintegrable: boundary conditions are dynamically involved in the capture in harmonic resonance. Condition 2 is satisfied for this reason as well, plus the system dissipates energy. Condition 3 is obviously satisfied by the existence of multiple attractors. Condition 4 is satisfied because the rate of capture equals the rate of dissipation (also implying radical non-Hamiltonicity). Condition 5 is not satisfied in this case, but it is satisfied for the specific property of the ratio of harmonic resonance. This property is an emergence candidate because it is nonreducible (condition 1) and unpredictable (conditions 3, 4 and 5). Since there is nothing specific about the way the Mercury-Sun system with respect to harmonic resonance satisfies the conditions, all cases fitting conditions 1-5 above will have the same unpredictability and irreducibility.

To show necessity is fairly trivial. If condition 1 is violated the system is at least numerically computable, and hence predictable. If condition 2 is violated, the boundary conditions are fixed rather than dynamic, so they are holonomic. If condition 3 is violated we can predict the single attractor as we can in the Bénard cell case (which is a bit ambiguous in the context of emergence). If condition 4 is violated, then the system can be treated as approximately Hamiltonian, and it is predictable. If condition 5 is violated, there is no emergent property, perhaps just a chaotic system. Since none of these conditions are specific to the example, they apply to all cases. So I have given necessary and sufficient (but probably not independent) dynamical conditions for nonreducibility and unpredictability.

7. Novelty

Novelty is a tricky issue with dynamical emergence, since all of the causes are driven in some sense at the lower level. This is where Humphreys (1997b) idea of fusion is useful. The property of the fusion is not the properties of the fused components. Given that conditions 1-5 are satisfied, the new property is not a sum of the properties of the components either. The fusion is genuinely novel. In my own work I have focused on cases in which the emergent entity is a system, rather than a system property, and I have called the fusion of the dynamical unity property of the system *cohesion* (Collier & Muller, 1998; Collier & Hooker, 1999). This is just Humphreys' fusion applied to the system unity property. One could reverse the approach, and talk of the cohesion of properties wherever there is fusion (Ladyman & Ross, 2007). Thus, novelty, rather than being hard to get, is rather easy to achieve. This might be reflected in Broad's view that water is emergent from its components (whether or not he was right about this).

8. Individuation and Autonomy

Cohesion is also a property of individuation, because it not only binds together the components, but because the binding must be stronger overall than any binding with other objects (Collier & Hooker, 1999). This is reflected in the apt description of cohesion as *the dividing glue* (Collier, 2004b). The basic notion can be used effectively to distinguish levels in dynamic hierarchies (Collier, 2003). One variety of cohesion is autonomy, which is an organizational closure that maintains the closure so that the autonomy survives (Collier, 2006). Autonomy is thus a self sustaining form of cohesion, with its components contributing to the maintenance of the autonomy. Thus autonomy is functional in that it produces survival, and the components are functional inasmuch as they contribute to autonomy. This is the most basic form of function: contribution to survival, from which all other forms of function derive (Collier, 2006). Levels of autonomy are possible, just like levels of cohesion (as in Collier, 2003), and we may have functional conflicts, as between body and cells, mind and body, and society and individual minds. Teleology is not a direct result of emergence, but it is made possible by it. There is nothing mysterious going on. It is all a result of comprehensible dynamics.

Acknowledgements

I am grateful to Cliff Hooker for collaboration that led to this article and for numerous corrections, suggestions and queries on the current version. Any errors that remain are, of course, my responsibility.

References

Broad C. D. (1925). *The mind and its place in nature*. London: Routledge and Kegan.

Campbell, D. T. (1974). "Downward causation" in hierarchically organized biological systems. In F. J. Ayala & T. Dobzhansky (Eds.), *Studies in the philosophy of biology* (pp. 179-186). New York: Macmillan.

Collier, J. (1990a). Two faces of Maxwell's demon reveal the nature of irreversibility. *Studies in the History and Philosophy of Science, 21*, 257-268.

Collier, J. (1990b). Intrinsic information. In Philip Hanson (Ed.), *Vancouver studies in cognitive science, Vol. 1: Information, language and cognition* (pp. 390-409). Oxford: University of Oxford Press.

Collier, J. (1996). Information originates in symmetry breaking. *Symmetry: Culture & Science, 7*, 247-256.

Collier, J. (2003) Hierarchical dynamical information systems with a focus on biology. *Entropy, 5*, 100-124.

Collier, J. (2004a). Reduction, supervenience, and physical emergence. *Behavioral and Brain Sciences, 27*(5), 629-630.

Collier, J. (2004b). Self-organization, individuation and identity. *Revue Internationale de Philosophie, 59*, 151-172.

Collier, J. (2006). Conditions for fully autonomous anticipation. In D. M. Dubois (Ed.), *Computing anticipatory systems: CASY'05 - Sixth International Conference Proceedings, 839*, pp. 282-289. Melville, New York: American Institute of Physics.

Collier, J. & Hooker, C. A.(1999). Complexly organized dynamical systems. *Open Systems and Information Dynamics, 6*, 241-302.

Collier, J., & Muller, S. (1998). The dynamical basis of emergence in natural hierarchies. In G. Farre and T. Oksala (Eds.), *Emergence, complexity, hierarchy and organization: Selected and edited papers from the ECHO III Conference, Acta Polytechnica Scandinavica, MA91*. Espoo: Finnish Academy of Technology.

Conrad, M., & Matsuno, K. (1990). The boundary condition paradox: A limit to the universality of differential equations. *Applied Mathematics and Computation, 37*, 67-74

Ford, J. (1986). Chaos: Solving the unsolvable, predicting the unpredictable! M. F. Barnsley & S. G. Demko (Eds.), *Chaotic dynamics and fractals* (pp. 1-52). New York: Academic Press.

Forrest, S., (Ed.) (1991). *Emergent computation*. Cambridge, MA: The MIT Press.
Wikipedia. (2007). *Holonomic constraints*. Retrieved July 9, 2007 from http://en.wikipedia.org/wiki/Holonomic_constraints
Hooker, C. A. (2004). Asymptotics, reduction and emergence. *British Journal for the Philosophy of Science, 55*, 435-479.
Humphreys, P. (1997a). Emergence, not supervenience. *Philosophy of Science, 64*, S337-S345.
Humphreys, P. (1997b). How properties emerge. *Philosophy of Science, 64*, 1-17.
Kim, J. (1978). Supervenience and nomological incommensurables. *American Philosophical Quarterly, 15*, 149-156.
Kim, J. (1998). *Mind in a physical world*. Cambridge, MA: The MIT Press.
Kim, J. (1999). Making sense of emergence. *Philosophical Studies, 95*, 3-36.
Kim, J. (2005). *Physicalism or something near enough*. Princeton, NJ: Princeton University Press.
Kincaid, H. (1987), Supervenience doesn't entail reducibility. *Southern Journal of Philosophy, 25*, 343-356.
Ladyman, J., & Ross, D. (with D. Spurrett & J. Collier) (2007). *Every thing must go: Metaphysics naturalised*. Oxford: University of Oxford Press.
Muller, S. J. (2007) *Asymmetry: The foundation of information*. Berlin: Springer-Verlag.
Nagel, E. (1961). *The structure of science*. New York: Harcourt, Brace and World.
Pattee, H. H. (1967). Quantum mechanics, heredity and the origin of life. *Journal of Theoretical Biology, 7*, 410-420.
Pattee, H. (2000). Posting on mailing list *Organization, Complexity, Autonomy*, Retrieved August 10, 2000 from http://www.nu.ac.za/undphil/collier/oca2000c.mbx.txt
Rueger, A. (2000a). Physical emergence, diachronic and synchronic. *Synthese 124*, 297 – 322.
Rueger, A. (2000b). Robust supervenience and emergence. *Philosophy of Science, 67*, 466–489.
Rueger, A.(2004). Reduction, autonomy, and causal exclusion among physical properties. *Synthese, 139*, 1-21.
Rosen, R. (1991). *Life itself*. New York: Columbia University Press.
Rosenberg, A. (1978). The supervenience of biological concepts. *Philosophy of Science, 45*, 368-386.
Rosenberg, A. (1985). *The structure of biological science*. New York: Cambridge University Press.
Ross, D., & Spurrett, D. (2004). What to say to a skeptical metaphysician: A defense manual for cognitive and behavioral scientists. *Behavioral and Brain Sciences, 27*(5), 603-627.
Von Foerster, H. (2003). *Understanding understanding: Essays on Cybernetics and Cognition*. New York: Springer.

Forsythe, K. (2008). *Summer Lunch*. 100 cm x 120 cm, tempera on paper.

Cybernetics And Human Knowing. Vol. 15, nos. 3-4, pp. 87-96

From a Dynamical to a Semiotic Account of Emergence
Comments on Collier's Paper "A Dynamical Account of Emergence"

Eugenio Andrade[1]

Summary

Collier offers a physicalist account of emergence that I welcome. Emergence is, thus explained as a property of non-Hamiltonian, non-Holonomic physical systems and can be detected by its non computability. Emergence constitutes a necessary and sufficient condition for the emergence of living systems or agents that process information and generate the corresponding informative records. By distinguishing between analog and digital information processing, I will show that analog information processing corresponds to a physical property of radical non-Hamiltonian, non-Holonomic systems that are responsible for emergence in general terms, but also more specifically to living systems that process digital information. In the way from dynamics to semiosis an intermediary model of physical systems that process both analog and digital information is needed. In consequence a contrast between Collier's Physical Information Systems (PIS) and Zurek's Information Gathering and Using Systems (IGUS) will be advanced in order to show that the latter best accounts for the origin of semiosis for it implicitly assumes that information from the environment can be recorded by means of structural adjustments that create the conditions for the appearance and selection of digital informative records. These systems fulfill the properties of a Peircean sign because they are dynamical systems that serve as a medium for the transmission of form. Thence individuation, autonomy and teleology are best understood as the outcome of information processing, made possible by dynamics.

Comments on Collier's dynamical account of emergence

Against the current prejudice according to which, irreducibility to atomic components is beyond physical account, Collier proposes the understanding of emergence in physical terms by showing that it also applies to physical systems. In this quest Collier follows the path followed by a number of authors like Volkestein (1994), Kauffman (1993), Salthe (1993), and Rosen (2000) just to name a few. My aim will be to examine the applicability of Collier's tenets to the study the emergence of living

---

1. Department of Biology, Universidad Nacional de Colombia. Email: leandradep@unal.edu.co

systems, in particular the origin of life one of the most puzzling emergent phenomena ever occurred. Despite the fact that explanations of emergence in terms of substance are no longer relevant, vitalistic approaches have not been completely dispelled since the appearance of new properties is often conceived as a sudden jump, providing the false impression that the continuity of nature was severed at least on very rare occasions. I hail Collier in taking the challenge of offering a physical account of emergence because it highlights the principle of continuity. The preservation of this principle that Peirce named as *synechism* or "the tendency to regard everything as continuous" (CP 7.565) is the best way to overcome the traditional polarity between reduction and emergence.

In previous papers, Collier asks about the ontological status of the different levels that are organized in a pattern of nested hierarchies (Collier & Muller, 1998), now he proposes a dynamical account of emergence. He starts by examining the conditions for a physical ontological reductionism: R1) The existence of "logical constructs" that are made to correspond to real atomic entities. R2) Closure or independence from external fluctuations. R3) Finitism, or finite computation. Therefore, reductionism and predictability require artificial logical constructions like the assumption of atomic entities (R1) and artificial closure given by the definition of boundary conditions or fixed environmental parameters (R2). If these two conditions are met, it follows that there must be computability (R3). As stated by Collier these are not conditions of a Newtonian systems but the result of the Lagrangian formulation that assumes the complete transformation of potential into kinetic energy in agreement with the principle of energy conservation, ruling out losses by friction and energy exchanges with dissipation. Reductionism according to Collier is a theoretical possibility only for closed Hamiltonian, holonomic systems, acted by conservative forces so that their description depends solely on the position coordinates and time. Consequently a dynamical linear superposition of trajectories that are not mutually affected, would allow an analytic decomposition and reduction applicable even for ideal irreversible processes with temporal asymmetry, as in Boltzmann approach.

It is important to be reminded of Peirce's views about the principle of energy conservation that lies behind reductionist approaches.

> Still, as a scientific generalization, it [the law of the conservation of energy] can only be a probable approximate statement, open to future possible correction. In its application to the ordinary transformation of forces, it has been pretty exactly verified. But as to what takes place within organized bodies, the positive evidence is unsatisfactory, and, in connection with the question of free will, we cannot feel sure the principle holds good without assuming a partisan position which would be unwise and unscientific. (Peirce, 1975-1982, Vol. 2, p. 115)

> The law of conservation of energy is equivalent to the proposition that all operations governed by mechanical laws are reversible; so that an immediate corollary from it is that growth is not explicable by those laws, even if they be not violated in the process of growth. (CP 6.14)

If the principle of energy conservation does not apply for organized bodies, reductionist approaches will not do either. Computation requires ideal conditions given by the assumption that forces act conservatively, thus neglecting the effect of friction and dissipation. If a conservative system requires very large computability like in the case of the "three body problem," still it is computable. Predictability is a direct outcome of condition R1 and R2, however if we lift one of the above conditions, reduction becomes impossible. Moreover reductionism cannot account for the coupling between genotype (lower level informational possibilities), and phenotype (organizing higher level entities) in the context of a specific environment. Nonetheless the claim that life is an irreducible phenomenon does not imply that it cannot be physically explained, all the contrary, it only points out at the insufficiency of mechanical approximations.

By negating one by one the above conditions of reduction, Collier (2008) gets the following conditions of emergence: E1. Non-reducibility to components. E2. Openness to external fluctuations. Likewise, if E1 and E2 are met, thence it follows (E3) non computability and unpredictability. Therefore, one must tackle the problem by focusing on the computational conditions of emergence that is to determine when computation fails. As he says, "the problem with understanding emergence is to hook up the computational characterization to dynamical conditions" (this issue, p. 78). In this point Collier follows the road paved by Rosen (2000) when he stated that the most distinct characteristic of a complex system is its non-computability since the causal entailments on which they depend cannot be encoded into the models we are using to compute it.

In his definition of *dynamical realism*, Collier (2008) is equating emergent systems with complex systems, where everything real is dynamic and therefore can induce an effect on anything else. Such a dynamical world would manifest itself as a complex network of interconnected entities acting on each other, making meaning possible. Therefore, emergent phenomena result from the non-linear interactions of their components that induce new system dynamics.

I will put the emergence problem in the following way: let us have a physical system A that acts as a lower level and let B be the higher level. "A brings forth B," but "B cannot be explained solely in terms of A," or "B is not deducible from A." The reduction of B in terms of A becomes impossible because something new in B has emerged. Where do novelties come from? What is new in B and was absent in A is its *form* or organization pattern that results from the interaction of A with its surroundings (E). Then, $A + E = B$. But, E is currently obliterated in classical approaches that assume the stability and constancy of fixed boundary conditions (environmental parameters). Thence, artificial closure or the isolation from the environment is basically the source of the emergence problem. The emergence problem appears every time that one tries to understand the passage from A to B disregarding E. This fact explains why there cannot be emergence in a closed system (Andrade, 2003). The search for causal explanations of emergence involve the environment, since the interactions among cohesive parts always occurs in the context of a specific environment. Open ended evolutionary physical systems cannot be accounted solely in terms of their basic constitutive components. Consequently the understanding of emergence would permit to deal with the problem of how a hierarchical system is organized, more specifically how genotype phenotype coupling is achieved, for instance between protein sequence and protein structure (Balbin & Andrade, 2004).

Collier (2008) in his search for the limits of computation argues that the conditions of radically, (I would prefer far from equilibrium) non-Hamiltonian behavior that underlie all emergences are: 1) the presence of non-holonomic constraints; 2) Energetic and informational openness; 3) The existence of multiple attractors; 4) The characteristic rate of at least one property of the system is of the same order as the rate of the non-holonomic constraint; and, 5) A system is emergent if at least one of the properties is an essential property of the system, in other words if at least one of the properties is irreducible.

With reference to condition 1, non computable, non integrable system must be non-holonomic, in other words its computation requires an additional non-holonomic constraint expressed as a rate of change dependent on the path it actually follows that is usually a function of environmental parameters, so that the number of coordinates required to represent them completely is more than their degrees of freedom. With regard to condition 2, openness allows the emerging system's capability to probe (measure and interact) the environment. In this manner information processing systems gather information about energy resources that are to be captured and spent in structural organization and maintenance, as well as in keeping the capacity to further probing the environment in search of newly available energy resources. With regard to 3, it is worth to note that whereas for closed systems, multiple microstates correspond one equilibrium macrostate, for open systems, to one specific set of microstates may correspond different macrostates depending on environmental parameters. Therefore, I do not think that the third condition is debatable, even if it seems not to apply to Benard's cells, on the contrary it is an essential condition that implies that for a given lower level informational source, and there can be more than one attractor that characterizes the higher level.

Complex emergent systems are unpredictable not only epistemologically, but also ontologically. According to the former, the slightest uncertainty in the knowledge of the state of a system in a present time leads to an informational lost about its future states, according to the latter there are events highly sensible to initial conditions that make impossible the exact determination of these conditions and the predictability of future states, (Barrow, 1991, p. 167-168). This latter case applies best to far from equilibrium, non-Hamiltonian systems that cannot be computed and are emergent though they are entirely physical. A rolling wheel submitted to friction and a planet that experiences tidal dissipation like the sun-mercury system, exhibit emerging properties that result from rapidly changing parameters. However these cases might not be easily extrapolated to explain the passage from non-living to living systems, since something else not included in dynamics but causally dependent on it, must be included. I will develop this idea below.

Collier (2008) makes also use of Humphrey's approach according to which properties are emergent if they cannot be computed from the properties of the unfused components. A fused system that can be computed from the properties of the unfused components is not emergent. Cohesive objects are dynamical systems. Novelty emerges as a result of fusion of some preexisting components. The emergent entity is a system. Methodologically it is wise to assume that most phenomena are mere manifestation of the underlying level (epiphenomena) until the basis of their cohesion or causal interactions among the parts is fully explained. Cohesion, thus, represents the set of factors that causally link the components through space and time, resulting in coherent behavior and resilience to external and inner fluctuations. When Collier defends that "water, if it is emergent, is emergent because of some facts about water, no about our theories of water" (Collier & Muller, 1998, p. 6), he is assuming a degree of internal cohesion that is responsible for causal interactions among the components of water. For him, a description of H2O requires parameters not needed to describe H and O separately.

Collier correctly concludes that emergence must be defined in terms of causal relations that permit to uncover causal autonomy, novelty, irreducibility and unpredictability of emergent phenomena. Cohesion is the base of dynamical identity that is a key distinctive feature of emergent systems, for they are more cohesive with themselves than with any other subsystem, since they are more stable and resistant to random internal and external noise. Cohesion is dependent on the system's physical context, and is not a subjective matter.

> Cohesive objects have properties that are not merely effects of the properties of their components (though they are too). They differ from epiphenomenal objects in that, far from being merely effects, they can act as causes as well, independent of the particular contingencies of their composite parts. (Collier & Mueller, 1998, p. 8)

Can higher levels be logically reduced to lower ones? From a logical stand point the description of new properties requires new parameters not needed to describe the lower level. Therefore candidates for hierarchical emergence are molecules, dissipative structures, chaotic systems, self-organizing systems, autocatalytic phenomena, biological functions, human communities, etc., but agreeing with Collier (2008), for each level it is, thus, crucial to demonstrate that they are not just logically inferred but a real cohesive dynamical systems. Also, I agree with Collier (2003) that hierarchical levels are not just mere aggregates (scalar hierarchies) or logical categories (specific hierarchies) in the sense of Salthe (1993), but real cohesive entities. Nonetheless Collier (2003) is wrong to criticize Salthe for not considering hierarchies as cohesive systems. In Salthe (1993, p. 152) it is clearly stated that the development of a self organizing system can be explained in terms of changing connectivity patterns going from immature (overconnected with weak communications between almost all the components) to mature (less connected with more definite hubs that make a dominant loop with stronger cohesive links) to end up in senescence (appearance of redundant loops with diminishing strength). Furthermore, Salthe explains how self-organizing systems support the emergence of a hierarchical organization by the action of internal forces. More explicitly emergence is referred to as a sudden increase (or decrease) in system's cohesion (Salthe, 1993).

> When internal forces are strong, as in immature systems, they determine the results; however, as these forces weakens, as a system moves toward equilibrium, idiosyncrasies can come into play that were suppressed by the central tendency of the far from equilibrium situation. (Salthe, 1993, p. 202).

To summarize, the characteristics of emergent phenomena are: E1) Irreducibility to the properties of the lower level. Reductionism invokes the information necessary to specify the identity and macroscopic properties of an object, by identifying what is reduced (higher level) to the reductive components (lower level). Cohesion explains why it is not possible to do that. E2) Individuality, so that the whole becomes a unity as a result of internal binding forces expressed as causal interactions that make it resistant to external and internal fluctuations. Cohesion accounts for individuality or the space temporal continuity of an entity with high specificity and stability that exerts an impact on the environment. E3) Downward causation in the sense that the dynamics of the whole constraints lower components dynamics. E4) Unpredictability and novelty. E5) In order to account for living systems it is needed to add information processing with the ensuing production of informative records of a digital character like DNA, RNA, and proteins.

The emergence of living systems

Collier asserts that individuality is a self-sustained form of cohesion, with its components contributing to the maintenance of the autonomy. If the maintenance of closure is assured autonomy survives. In this vein he states rightly that cohesion accounts for autonomy as an emergent characteristic and with it functionality and teleology can be understood as the result of comprehensive dynamics. *Autopoiesis* commonly considered as an exclusive property of living entities is associated to autonomy and requires an organizational closure. According to Collier dynamics opens the way to semiosis; this seems to be a bold leap that yet has to be bridged with an intermediary model of an information processing agency, in order to avoid the current misinterpretations that consider semiosis as the last trench of vitalism. In the road to semiosis the ideas of Collier's (2003) PIS, Zurek's (1989, 1990) IGUS, and Andrade's (2007) Evolving Developing Agents (EDA), whatever their limitations aim to conceptualize physical systems that are semiotic. Semiosis is here understood as the action of signs. It suffices here to remind that a *sign* is a dynamical system that serves as media for the processing of information needed for the communication of a form (Queiroz & El-Hani, 2006). The mediation between an informative record (DNA) and the corresponding form (phenotype) is made possible by the action of an interpretative agent that played the roll all along development and evolution of a code maker (Barbieri, 2003; Andrade, 2007). In a more general sense semiotic agents (interpretants sensu Peirce) not only encode information, but record, replicate, transfer, translate, interpret, use, preserve, alter, erase, and dispose it.

Collier is right in insisting that emergence is a physical causal process. But considering that living systems collect, record and use environmental information in order to extract free energy, the question turns out to be whether information processing can be considered a form of causation. In order to answer this question one must be clear about what is meant by information processing. If we accept Hoffmeyer and Emmeche's (1991) distinction between analog and digital information, then the term *information processing* has two aspects.

A) Analog information processing. Living beings are communication systems that are integrated as a whole within its own boundaries by signals, but they are also integrated to their environment by interpreting and reacting to external signs (i.e. the state of a cell is modified by the presence of a determinate signal). Analog processing of information refers to what Root-Berstein and Dillon (1997) define as complementarity that embraces all kind of cohesive forces that permits the formation of non random stable aggregates, that is at the molecular level complementarity is best understood as chemical affinity.

The point I want to address is that analog information thus described is the source of cohesion, becoming the crucial step in emergence (Andrade, 2003). This form of information processing by non-random interactions between constitutive components, is the causal agency of the formation of macromolecular aggregates that generate organelles, prokaryotic cells that interact to generate eukaryotic cells, cells that interact to generate tissues, and so forth, so leading to the emergence of a new ontological level with a distinctive qualitative behavior that is characteristic of a new organized functional structure that acts as a coherent whole. Consequently analog information-driven emergence (Andrade, 2003) is the result of the establishment of new cohesive analog-analog interactions between already existing components constrained by environmental conditions. This type of emergence provides the clue to approach the study of evolutionary transitions like the origin of life (Root-Berstein & Dyllon, 1997; Fox, 1984). In agreement with Collier, cohesion results in closure of causal relations among the dynamical parts of a dynamical structure that determines its resistance to external and internal fluctuations. Semiosis accepts the existence of physical agents for whom information is meaningful. Of course that agents may act randomly, but the point is that as information is gathered and encoded their behavior becomes more directed to specific goals. The introduction of self referential agents for whom information is meaningful creates a closed loop that makes computation impossible. This way of interpreting information cannot be formalized in purely syntactic terms because it expresses the self-referential generative process of an agent with its partially describable external environment. Agents' capacities to choose among a random set of components those with which they will interact are the very source of creative and unpredictable interactions with external referents. Emergence exists because new unforeseen semiotic relations can always be established.

B) Digital information processing. Digital information corresponds to what after Shannon and Crick is properly understood as information and suits very well Collier's (2003) concept of lower level information. Digital information refers to encoded information in the form of a record that has the structure of a text composed of basic symbols (DNA) that can be modified by discontinuous variations such as mutations and recombination. But the processing of this information refers to a more abstract operation in which a polymer built out of monomers that are equivalent to symbols, are formed and selected not only for their catalytic functions (chemical affinity) but also for their use as replicating templates that streamline the production of more polymers. This is the starting point of a genetic record that characterizes life as we know it. Once specific sequences are selected for the functionality of their encoded products to the extent that they contribute to cell maintenance and reproduction, the coupling phenotype genotype is produced. Digital encoding of information facilitates the emergence of new functions by permutations of existing strings, only if the new information is expressed in the phenotype and functionally selected.

These two ways of processing information (analog or selection by structural complementarities and digital through the expression of digital codes) causally operate within the restrictions imposed by physical and thermodynamic constraints. There is nothing mysterious about them. In the process of enzyme substrate recognitions new structures are formed and degraded that give rise to a network that is able to stabilize. However the production of polymers that help to specify the structures of enzymes facilitates the maintenance and as a by product their continuous production, making from then onwards the replication of templates a critical step that opened the way to Darwinian evolution.

Analog interactions between organisms and external factors are agent's responses to local and immediate challenging external circumstances in the form of structural adjustments. This form of analog information is the sufficient and necessary condition for selection of a digital record that registers the partial internalization of external referents by the agent. Digital records are created, replicated, mutated, selected, used and eliminated within the context of local interactions established with the surroundings. The random reorganization of previously encoded records provide the possibility to react successfully to unforseen situations. There will always be a number of undefined motifs that can be potentially recorded, and which one is to be incorporated in evolutionary time, into the digital record cannot be predicted beforehand. The origin of a digital description that has all the features of an abstract operation executed by physical systems results from their pragmatic drive to capture free energy and optimize its use conferring evolutionary advantage. Pragmatics is thus, the source of meanings and is always for the sake of someone. Zurek (1989, 1990) pointed out why the shorter the digital record the more efficient the extraction of energy by the agent and later Kauffman (2000) proposed to apply this idea to living systems as I have developed in my book (Andrade, 2003). The origin of semiosis lies in the fact that information processing is meaningful for the agents only as long as it is required for survival through energy capture and use.

Before I make the parallel between Collier's physical information system (PIS) and Zurek's Information Gathering and Using Systems (IGUS), I summarize Collier's

Hierarchical Dynamical Information Systems (HDIS) concept. Collier (2003) defines a HDIS as:

> A system of a number of relatively stable units that can combine more or less freely to form somewhat less stable structures has a capacity to carry information in a more or less arbitrary way. I call such a system a *physical information system* if its properties are dynamically specified. (Collier, 2003, p. 101)

He states that such systems are hierarchical with respect to the expression of lower level information at the higher level. While lower level information is syntactic, the expression at the higher level (dubbed biological information) is functional and has the capacity of development and evolution. Lower level information, he argues, is purely syntactical and can be treated without reference to meaning and is chemical (DNA, RNA, and proteins). I cannot agree with this viewpoint since RNA and proteins exhibit also three dimensional structures, a form that makes them liable of complementary interaction and chemically active as catalysts of chemical reactions. Even more if we consider that life may have originated from a preexisting RNA world or from a protein world then the existence of digital records in the form of DNA may be seen as an outcome of a previous evolutionary process and not a departing point. Higher level or biological information is embodied in the phenotype and also at an even higher level the species. There is also the emergence of new macro level information that is only potential in the lower level, but not specifically determined by it.

My tenet is that Zurek's IGUS are emergent systems because they fulfill the following Collier's requirements for PIS (Collier, 2003): 1) Non-reducibility to atomic components. As explained above this is a direct result of being open systems that are formed by internal structural interactions in the context of causal formative factors that are located in the environment. 2) Dynamical systems that can have effects on others. Information processing systems causally provoke effects on other systems, though they might not be deterministic. 3) Physically based. 4) They do work since they are far from equilibrium systems. In order to be able to act on something an expenditure of energy is required. 5) They are dissipative, a conclusion derived from the fact of being both open and far from equilibrium.

Thence, there is nothing mysterious about PIS. What I aim to point out is that Zurek's requirements for an IGUS are openness, memory, and being far from thermodynamic equilibrium. As mentioned above these three criteria are met in Collier's conditions. With openness to the environment comes unpredictability and novelty in emergence. Memory implies that the systems has an inner structure kept stable by cohesive interactions, though plastic enough that a plurality of microstates and macrostates can be attained, and finally the fact of being far form thermodynamic equilibrium ensures that it can do work and dissipate energy in the form of entropy.

Consequently IGUS also meet the conditions that define a nonholonomic non-Hamiltonian system. As dynamical emergent systems, living entities like IGUS display individuation and autonomy manifested in the process of establishing new interactions and the creation of informative records. They are thus semiotic agents. Autonomy, as Collier asserts means that such PIS use their own information to modify themselves and their environment to enhance their survival, responding to both environmental and internal stimuli to modify their functions to increase viability. The IGUS model not only accounts for what PIS accounts but goes beyond by stating that by means of agents' measurements and interactions, the establishment of structural adjustments provide the conditions for the creation and selection of digital records. In this manner, the path from dynamics to semiosis is really bridged.

References

Andrade, L. E. (2003). *Los demonios de Darwin. Semiótica y termodinámica de la evolución biológica* (2nd ed.). Bogotá:UNIBIBLOS.

Andrade, E. (2003). The processing of information (analog/digital) is the causal factor of the emergence of natural hierarchies. *Ludus Vitalis: Journal of Philosophy of Life Sciences, IX* (20), 85-106.

Balbin, A. & Andrade, E. (2004). Protein folding and evolution are driven by the Maxwell demon activity of proteins. *ActaBiotheoretica, 52* (3), 173-200.

Barbieri, M. (2003). *The organic codes: An introduction to semantic biology.* Cambridge: Cambridge University Press.

Barrow, J. D. (1991). *Theories of everything: The quest for the ultimate explanation.* New York: Fawcett Columbine.

Collier, J. D., & Muller, S. J. (1998). The dynamical basis of emergence in natural hierarchies. In G. Farre & T. Oksala (Eds.), *Emergence, Complexity, Hierarchy and Organization.* Selected and Edited Papers from the ECHO III Conference, Acta Polytecnica Scandinavica, MA91. Espoo, Finland: Finish Academy of Technology.

Collier, J. 2003. *Hierarchical dynamical information systems with a focus on biology. Entropy, 5,* 100-124.

Collier, J. (2008). A dynamical account of emergence. *Cybernetics & Human Knowing, 15* (3-4), 75-86.

Fox, S. W. (1984). *Proteinoid experiments and evolutionary theory.* in M.-W. Ho & P. T. Saunders (Eds.), *Beyond neo-Darwinism* (pp. 15-60). London: Academic Press, Inc.

Hoffmeyer, J., & Emmeche, C. (1991). Code duality and the semiotics of nature. In M. Anderson, & F. Merrell (Eds.), *On semiotic modeling* (pp. 117-166). Berlin: Mouton de Gruyter.

Kauffman, S. (1993). *The origins of order: Self-organization and selection in evolution.* New York: Oxford University Press.

Kauffman, S. (2000). *Investigations.* New York: Oxford University Press.

Peirce, C. S. (1931-35, 1958). *Collected Papers,* Vols. 1-6 (C. Hartshorne & P. Weiss, Eds., 1931-35), Vols. 7-8 (A. W. Burks, Ed., 1958). Cambridge, MA: Harvard University Press. (cited in text as: CP volume.paragraph)

Peirce, C. S. (1975 – 1987) *Charles Sanders Peirce: Contributions to the nation,* Vols. 1-4. (K. L. Ketner & J. Cook , Eds.). Lubbock, TX: Texas Tech University Press.

Queiroz, J. & El-Hani Nino, C. (2006). *Semiosis as an emergent process. Transactions of the Charles Peirce Society, 42* (1), 78-116.

Rosen, R. (2000). *Essays on life itself.* (Complexity in ecological systems series). New York: Columbia University Press.

Root-Berstein, R. S., & Dillon P. F. (1997). Molecular complementarity I: The complementarity theory of the origin and evolution of life. *Journal of Theoretical. Biology, 188,* 447-479.

Salthe, S. N. (1993). *Development and evolution: Complexity and change in biology.* Cambridge, MA: The MIT Press.

Volkestein, M. V. (1994). *Physical approaches to biological evolution.* Berlin: Springer-Verlag.

Zurek, W. H. (1989). Algorithmic randomness and physical entropy. *Physical Review A., 40* (8), 4731 - 4751.

Zurek, W. H. (1990). Algorithmic information content, Church – Turing thesis, physical entropy, and Maxwell's demon. In W. H. Zurek (Ed.), *Complexity, Entropy, and the Physics of Information* (SFI Studies in the Sciences of Complexity, Vol. VIII, pp. 73-89). Reading, MA: Addison-Wesley.

Forsythe, K. (2005). *Network of Networks* (detail). 32.5 cm x 60 cm, acrylic on paper.

Cybernetics And Human Knowing. Vol. 15, nos. 3-4, pp. 97-99

The Dynamics of Emergence:
Response to Eugenio Andrade's Comments, "From a Dynamical to a Semiotic Account of Emergence"

John Collier[1]

Despite wide agreement between us, Andrade makes several claims about what I say in my paper that are not quite correct, or at least not quite what I meant. Perhaps I did not make myself clear, and I will take this opportunity to try to make these points clearer. Andrade says, "Reductionism according to Collier is a theoretical possibility only for closed Hamiltonian, holonomic systems, acted by conservative forces so that their description depends solely on the position coordinates and time" (this issue, p. 88). In fact, I was more concerned with getting necessary and sufficient dynamical conditions for emergence than for the failure of reduction. The two probably form a *complete and disjoint* set over dynamical systems, but although reduction is most readily possible in closed Hamiltonian systems with holonomic constraints, there is a large class of systems that do not satisfy these conditions that I believe to be reducible by way of numerical approximations, if not by analytical solutions. Although such systems may not fit the reductionist paradigm, I do not think they are emergent. These include "near" Hamiltonian systems with minor dissipation, as well as those with step functions (such as used in phase transitions, or indeed the integral of the Dirac delta function used in Quantum mechanics), or "close to" (approximate) step functions. The problems for reduction arise when the systems are radically non-Hamiltonian. This condition is manifest during transitions of state in dissipative systems, but not necessarily in steady state systems, even far from equilibrium. By extension, though, systems that are the result of such transients will be unpredictable from their prior state, and the novel states will be emergent with respect to the prior states, for example, in Bénard cells, to take a simple case. Emergence is relative to a particular set of dynamical resources: Bénard cells are quite well behaved themselves, and are subject to standard analytical treatment. This is generally true of steady-state systems in which transients have died out. There are typically dynamical parts of such systems, like the cells in Bénard cell convection, whose dynamics sum quite nicely in the best form of typical reductionist models. One has to be very careful, then, to specify what a system is supposed to be emergent on, not just that it has dynamical properties that imply that it could have emergent properties, or else one is likely to become confused about what is reducible (to what) and what is not.

The advantage of a dynamical account of emergence that matches the logical/computational accounts that are found more widely in the literature is that dynamical

---

1. School of Philosophy and Ethics, University of KwaZulu-Natal, Durban 4041, South Africa, Email: collierj@ukzn.ac.za, Website: Http://www.ukzn.ac.za/undphil/collier

conditions can be measured, whereas it is difficult to tell whether or not logical conditions like computability hold of a system rather than of specific system models that may or may not be correct. It also helps to distinguish accidental conditions associated with emergence from the necessary ones. I regret that apparently I have not made this clear enough, as Andrade mentions several conditions often associated with emergence that I would not sanction as being involved in emergence per se. For example, he asserts that closed systems cannot be emergent. Indeed, I hinted at this in my condition 2: The system is energetically (and/or informationally) open (boundary conditions are dynamic). It might look like this implies openness of the system in the traditional sense (all subsystems of the universe are energetically open, so this is at best a very weak condition), but I would like to point out that the Universe itself is both closed and isolated (by definition), yet it has emergent properties. Cosmology typically assumes a "no boundary conditions" condition on possible models, but the historical development of the universe constrains its future development such that it becomes self-constraining, and its dynamics cannot be fully separated from its constraints, which is really the condition I intended by condition 2. Universal expansion allows for the increase of both order and disorder (Landsberg, 1984), giving room for complex self-interaction; information appears, but it comes from inside. This is also, perhaps, a better model for Brooks and Wiley's claim (1988; as justified in Collier, 1986) that information systems in biology expand, allowing for self-organization within the biological information system. There must be an underlying far from equilibrium energy system to support the information system, but the dynamics of the information are on top of this, being more or less independent. The reasons for information being best treated as an internal product of the system are different in the two cases, but the results are similar. Perhaps it would have been better if I had used *open-ended* in condition 2, rather than simply *open*, with its established meaning. Andrade alludes to this idea in the early part of his comments. In a somewhat similar vein, although far-from-equilibrium conditions are associated with emergence, and are required for it, they certainly do not imply it, and many far-from-equilibrium systems are reducible in all respects, insofar as we know. Nor is complexity itself a reliable sign of emergence, and I barely mention it in my article. If anything, complex organization is a product of emergence, and not a cause.

On the general issue of cohesion, I think it is important to recognize that it involves not just internal forces (following Andrade's account of Stan Salthe's 1993 work), but the relative difference between internal and external forces (Collier, 1988; Collier & Hooker, 1999), which gives both a principle of individuation and one of differentiation through the same dynamics. This view of the dynamical formation and disruption of cohesion originated in Collier (1986), and is an essential part of the idea. Salthe and I have moved closer over the years, and I think his views are currently much closer to my 1986 view. Be that as it may, the dynamical maintenance of cohesion often involves manipulation of boundary conditions and even loops through the environment. The former almost ensures nonreducibility, and the latter involves a feedback between system and surroundings that can make it impossible to systematically separate the two without doing violence to the system dynamics. Nonreducibility and cohesion lead to a non-localizability of certain important system properties in emergent systems, which is an important but often overlooked aspect of emergence. This non-localizability is a consequence of the inseparability of system laws and system constraints in the system dynamics.

I regard Andrade's remarks on information and semiosis towards the end of his comments largely favorably. The elements of his sketch will I think eventually lead to a dynamical account of semiosis. I tried to produce a similar sort of account in Collier (1999), though I was guided there less by emergence than autonomy, which I now think must be emergent to be of any significance, and by Fred Dretske's (1981) account of analogue and digital information. I think that there is still considerable room for more precision around this whole issue of the connections among information, semiosis and dynamics.

References

Andrade, E. (2008). From a dynamical to a semiotic account of emergence. *Cybernetics & Human Knowing, 15* (3-4), 173-184.

Brooks, D. R., & Wiley, E. O. (1988). *Evolution as entropy: Toward a unified theory of biology* (2nd ed.). Chicago: University of Chicago Press.

Collier, J. (1986). Entropy in evolution. *Biology and Philosophy, 1,* 5-24.

Collier, J. (1988). Supervenience and reduction in biological hierarchies. In M. Matthen & B. Linsky (Eds.), *Philosophy and Biology: Supplementary Volume 14 of the Canadian Journal of Philosophy,* 209-234. Calgary: University of Calgary Press.

Collier, J. (1999). The dynamical basis of information and the origins of semiosis. In E. Taborsky (Ed.), *Semiosis, evolution, energy: Towards a reconceptualization of the sign* (Bochum Publications in Semiotics New Series. Vol. 3, pp. 111-136). Aachen: Shaker Verlag.

Collier, J., & Hooker, C. A. (1999). Complexly organized dynamical systems. *Open Systems and Information Dynamics, 6,* 241-302.

Dretske, F. (1981). *Knowledge and the flow of information.* Cambridge, MA: The MIT Press.

Landsberg, P. T. (1984) Can entropy and 'order' increase together? *Physics Letters, 102A,* 171-173.

Salthe, S. N. (1993). *Development and evolution. Complexity and change in biology.* A Bradford Book. Cambridge, MA: The MIT Press.

Forsythe, K. (2006). *Forest Floor* (detail). 45 cm x 75 cm, collage on paper.

Forsythe, K. (2008). *Bouquet*. 35 cm x 40 cm, acrylic and ink on canvas.

Cybernetics And Human Knowing. Vol. 15, nos. 3-4, pp. 101-134

Emergence and Downward Determination in the Natural Sciences

Fabiano de Souza Vieira [1] *and Charbel Niño El-Hani* [2]

The problem of downward causation – that is, the problem of how a higher-level phenomenon can cause or determine or structure a lower-level phenomenon – is central to emergentism and is also highly debated in the literature on emergence. Downward causation can play, in our view, an important role in the development of our understanding of biological networks and the genotype-phenotype relationship. In order to advance in the discussion of the problem of downward causation, we discuss neo-Aristotelian approaches, which claim that causal modes other than efficient causation are needed to account for this phenomenon, particularly, formal and functional causation. We advocate, rather, that a proper understanding of downward causation demands other kinds of determination, besides causal determination. We develop, thus, an account of downward determination. In particular, we consider two issues: (i) What sorts of "things" are said to be determining and determined in a case of downward determination? (ii) What is the meaning of *determining* in downward determination? By advancing an attempt to answer these questions, we intend to develop a coherent account about how principles of organization constrain and, thus, partially determine the behavior of a system's lower-level constituents. In this account of downward determination, a higher-level organizational pattern, interpreted as a general principle, is the determiner, while lower-level particular processes are determined. The determining influence from a higher-level general organizational principle to particular lower-level processes, in turn, is framed as follows: If lower-level entities $a,b,c,...,n$ are under the influence of a general organizational principle, W, then they will show a tendency, a disposition, to instantiate process p or a set of processes $\{P\}$. The changes in disposition in downward determination can be treated in terms of Popper's propensities, in such a manner that their probability are not just in our minds, but are instantiated in the world.

Keywords: Emergence, Downward determination, Propensities, Downward causation, Reductionism.

1. Introduction

In the end of the 1980s, *emergentism* seemed to be an entirely forgotten philosophical position. Nevertheless, the debate about emergence has re-emerged and the fortune of this philosophical doctrine has changed in the last decade (Kim, 1998, 1999; Stephan, 1999; Cunningham, 2001; Pihlström, 2002; El-Hani, 2002a; Kim, 2006). A great number of works dealing with emergence have been published in the philosophical and scientific literature in the last 20 years,[3] and the concept of emergence has been increasingly used in such diverse fields as artificial life, cognitive sciences,

1. Graduate Studies Program in History, Philosophy, and Science Teaching, Universidade Federal da Bahia/ Universidade Estadual de Feira de Santana. Email: biosv@hotmail.com
2. Professor, Institute of Biology, Universidade Federal da Bahia, Brasil. Graduate Studies Program in History, Philosophy, and Science Teaching, Universidade Federal da Bahia/Universidade Estadual de Feira de Santana. Graduate Studies Program in Ecology and Biomonitoring, Universidade Federal da Bahia. Email: charbel.elhani@pesquisador.cnpq.br

evolutionary biology, theories of self-organization, philosophy of mind, dynamical systems theory, synergetics, and so forth. The role played by the concept in these fields has been directly responsible for revitalizing emergentism as a philosophical trend.

The term *emergence* has both an ordinary use, as when the expression "the emergence of *x*" is employed merely to indicate that *x* has appeared or that *x* has come up, and a technical use. As to the latter, we can refer to a definition of *emergent property* that El-Hani and Queiroz (2005a) modified from a proposal found in Stephan (1998, p. 639): Emergent properties constitute *a certain class* of higher-level properties related *in a certain way* to the microstructure of *a class of systems*. A theory of emergence should, among other things, fill in the open clauses in this definition (shown in italics), providing an account of which systemic properties[4] (of a given class of systems) should be regarded as emergent, and offering an explanation of the relationship between these properties and the microstructure of the systems in which they are instantiated. The reason why such a broad definition, with open clauses, seems at first more adequate than a definition with more content and precision has to do with the fact that the concept of emergence and its derivatives are employed in the most diverse fields, and, consequently, a more detailed definition is likely to apply to some fields but not to others.

Nevertheless, for the sake of both accuracy and clarity, it is important to spell out a number of criteria which should be fulfilled in order to a property or process be treated as emergent. Queiroz and El-Hani (2006) develop a careful treatment of the problems faced when one attempts to build an emergence theory in a particular field, semiotics, addressing both issues related to the open clauses in the above definition and a number of other questions which arise in efforts to interpret a specific phenomenon – in this case, sign processes – within an emergentist framework. Here, we will just introduce some criteria derived from one of the classical works on emergence, *Emergent Evolution* (1923), from Lloyd Morgan.

Morgan characterizes *emergent evolution* as follows:

> Evolution, in the broad sense of the word, is the name we give to the comprehensive plan of sequence in all natural events. But the orderly sequence, historically viewed, appears to present, from time to time, something genuinely new. Under what I here call emergent evolution stress is laid on this incoming of the new. (Morgan, 1923, p. 1)

---

3. Notes: e.g., Klee (1984); Savigny (1985); Blitz (1992); Beckermann et al. (1992); Stephan (1997, 1998, 1999); Kim (1997, 1999); O'Connor (1994); Baas (1996); Newman (1996); Baas & Emmeche (1997); Humphreys (1996, 1997a,b); Emmeche et al. (1997); Emmeche (1997); Bedau (1997, 2002); Azzone (1998); Schröder (1998); El-Hani & Pereira (1999, 2000); Pihlström (1999, 2002); El-Hani & Emmeche (2000); Andersen et al. (2000); El-Hani & Videira (2001); El-Hani & Pihlström (2002a,b); El-Hani (2002a); Symons (2002); Gillett (2002). Emergence has also been the topic of recent special issues of a series of journals, such as Philosophical Studies (1999), International Journal of Systems Science (2000), Grazer Philosophische Studien (2002), Principia (2002) and Synthese (2006).

4. A systemic property is a property found only at the level of a system as a whole, but not at the level of its parts.

He also states that "the emergent step ... is best regarded as a qualitative change of direction, or critical turning point, in the course of events" (Morgan, 1923, p. 5), linking emergent events to the "expression of some new kind of relatedness among pre-existent events" (Morgan, 1923, p. 6). Finally, Morgan observes:

> When some new kind of relatedness is supervenient (say at the level of life), the way in which physical events which are involved run their course is different in virtue of its presence – different from what it would have been if life had been absent. ... I shall say that this new manner in which lower events happen – this touch of novelty in evolutionary *advance* – *depends on* the new kind of relatedness which is expressed in that which Mr. Alexander speaks of as an emergent quality. (Morgan, 1923, p. 16. Emphasis in the original)

These quotations from Morgan's classical work contain some basic criteria for treating properties and processes as emergent. First, they should be (genuinely) new under the sun. This obviously leads to the problems of novelty and unpredictability, which we will not discuss here, since they fall outside the scope of this paper.[5] Second, they should be closely connected with the appearance of a new kind of relatedness (or, for that matter, a new organizational principle) among pre-existent processes and entities, entailing a modification in the way lower-level events run their course (and, consequently, some sort of downward causation). Third, the emergence of properties or processes in a new class of systems (as defined by the above-mentioned new kind of relatedness) should change the mode of systems' evolution. This change, in turn, should be precisely the result of a modification of the behavior of pre-existent entities and processes under the influence of that new kind of relatedness (and this again leads us to the issue of downward causation).[6]

It is also important to take into account that there is no unified emergence theory. In a systematic analysis of emergence theories, Stephan (1998, 1999, 2004, 2006) initially considers three varieties of emergentism – *weak*, *synchronic*, and *diachronic* – and later expands his typology to include six different emergentist positions.[7]

Weak emergentism provides the basis for all physicalist emergence theories, comprising three major tenets: (i) naturalism in the form of physical monism; (ii) the claim that there are systemic properties; and (iii) the thesis of synchronic determination (Stephan, 1998, 1999). The latter thesis, which any physicalist emergentist should assume as a corollary of her commitment to physical monism, will play an important role in our arguments here. It can be explained as follows: Synchronic determination – A system's properties and behavioral dispositions depend nomologically on its microstructure, that is, on its parts' properties and arrangement; there can be no difference in systemic properties without there being some difference

---

5. For discussions of these notions, see, for instance, Emmeche et al. (1997), Stephan (1998, 1999).
6. For an application of these criteria for characterizing events in the origins of life as being 'emergent', see El-Hani (2002b).
7. Stephan's discussion about theories and concepts of emergence performing different roles in distinct fields is in accordance with a pluralist attitude towards a diversity of pragmatically-workable notions of emergence advocated by El-Hani & Pihlström (2002a,b). We will not deal with the six positions described by Stephan in this paper. For more details, see the original works.

in the properties of the system's parts and/or in their arrangement. (Adapted from Stephan 1998, p. 641; see also 1999, pp. 50-51)

Weak emergentism is compatible with reductive physicalism. Therefore, it faces a fundamental problem as regards the usual motivations underlying the proposal of emergence theories. Emergentism is typically thought of as an anti-reductionist or non-reductive physicalist stance, and weak emergentism is, as Stephan (1998, p. 642) writes, "compatible with contemporary reductionist approaches without further ado." It is just natural, then, that many emergentist philosophers and scientists are engaged in attempts to build stronger accounts of emergence, which are arguably incompatible with reductionism. Nevertheless, it is in this move that emergentist philosophies find the most difficult problems.

Both synchronic and diachronic emergentism comprise strong emergence theories. They are closely related, being often interwoven in single emergence theories, but, for the sake of clarity, it is important to distinguish between them. Synchronic emergentism is primarily interested in the mereological relationship between a system's properties and its microstructure. The central notion in synchronic emergentism is that of *irreducibility*. Diachronic emergentism, by its turn, is mainly interested in how emergent properties come to be instantiated in evolution, focusing its arguments on the notion of *unpredictability*. No strong emergence theory can be properly formulated without coming to grips with the problems of irreducibility and/ or unpredictability.

This paper focuses on the concept of irreducibility and, particularly, on the problem of downward causation. Our main goals here are: (i) to explain a distinction between two modes of irreducibility proposed by Stephan (1998; 1999, 2004) and elaborated by Boogerd, Bruggeman, Richardson, Stephan, and Westerhoff (2005), showing how one of these modes entails downward causation; (ii) to discuss the problem of downward causation and some approaches developed to deal with it, particularly focusing on those which appeal to an Aristotelian understanding of causality; (iii) to propose that the idea of *downward determination* is more adequate than that of downward causation to deal with whole-to-part relationships and, most importantly, to develop a clear account of downward determination.

2. Modes of irreducibility

The thesis of the irreducibility of emergent properties makes synchronic emergentism incompatible with reductive physicalism. But what does it precisely mean to say that a property is irreducible? Many discussions about emergence and reduction appeal to a rather generic reference to the term *reduction*, without considering that this term has a variety of meanings in the philosophical (and also scientific) literature (El-Hani & Emmeche, 2000; El-Hani & Queiroz, 2005b). Therefore, there are also different senses in which an emergent property can be treated as irreducible.

Two general modes of irreducibility were distinguished by Stephan (1998, pp. 642-643; 1999, p. 68). The first mode of irreducibility is based on the unanalyzability of systemic properties:

I1. [Irreducibility as unanalyzability] Systemic properties which cannot be analyzed in terms of the behavior of a system's parts are necessarily irreducible (Adapted from Stephan 1998, p. 643).

This notion plays an important role in debates about qualia and is related to a first condition for reducibility, namely, that a property P will be reducible if it follows from the behavior of the system's parts that the system exhibits P. Conversely, a systemic property P of a system S will be irreducible if it does not follow, even in principle, from the behavior of the system's parts that S has property P.

Since Broad (1925), phenomenal qualities of experiences (qualia) have been usually regarded as irreducible because they violate the condition of analyzability. Qualia are often claimed to be adequately characterized neither by the macroscopic nor by the microscopic behavior of the central nervous system's parts, not even in principle, on the grounds of their being allegedly intrinsic, non-relational properties. This idea has been expressed by Levine (1983), for instance, in terms of an explanatory gap between biological/physical processes and phenomenal states of consciousness. For several philosophers, no advances in scientific knowledge can ever be able to close this explanatory gap (Nagel, 1974; Levine, 1983; Kim, 1993, 1996, 1998).

If a phenomenon is emergent by reason of being unanalyzable, it will be an unexplainable, brute fact, or, to use Alexander's (1920/1979) words, something to be accepted with natural piety. We will not be able to predict or explain it, even if we know its basal conditions. In the philosophy of mind, the concept of irreducibility is often used in this sense, as we can observe, for instance, in Kim's (1992, 1993, 1996, 1997, 1998) discussions about irreducibility, in which this notion is typically combined with that of unexplainability, constituting a single thesis. Moreover, qualia are the primary example of emergent property for Kim, precisely because they are, in his view, intrinsic, non-relational properties, and, consequently, are unexplainable from the perspective of our understanding of brains as biological/physical systems.

In our view, if the understanding of the irreducibility of emergent properties is limited to this rather strong sense, we may lose from sight the usefulness of the concept in other domains of investigation. Indeed, claims about emergence turn out to be so strong, if interpreted exclusively in accordance with this mode of irreducibility, that they are likely to be false, at least in the domain of the natural sciences (with are our primary interest in this paper). After all, unanalyzable emergent properties cannot be naturalistically explained and the search for explanations grounded on natural causes plays a central role in the scientific system of values. If an emergent property is taken to be unexplainable, the vast majority of natural scientists will tend to be suspicious about claims concerning it, perceiving them as committed to some sort of mysteriousness, which could not bring significant contributions to the understanding of the systems they investigate. In these terms, the emergence concept would hardly come to play a significant role in the natural sciences.[8]

A second notion of irreducibility is based on the non-deducibility of the behavior of the system's parts:

I2.   [Irreducibility of the behavior of the system's parts] A systemic property will be irreducible if it is synchronically determined by the specific behavior the parts show within a system of a given kind, and this behavior, in turn, does not follow from the parts' behavior in isolation or in other (simpler) kinds of system (Adapted from Stephan 1998, p. 644).

This mode of irreducibility is related to the notion of downward causation, since it is plausible to assume that the influence of the system where a given emergent property *P* is observed on the behavior of its parts is the reason why we are not able to deduce the latter from the behaviors the very same parts show in isolation or as parts of simpler systems.

A second condition for reducibility is violated in this case, which entails that a systemic property *P* of a system *S* will be irreducible if it is realized by parts of *S* whose behaviors do not follow, even in principle, from their behavior in systems simpler than *S*.

Recently, Boogerd and colleagues (2005) grasped the notions of irreducibility as unanalyzability and as non-deducibility in two conditions for emergence they call vertical and horizontal. They took Broad's works (1925) as a starting point to distinguish between these two independent conditions, which Broad himself did not explicitly differentiate (Figure 1).

The vertical condition captures the situation in which a systemic property *P* is emergent because it is not explainable, even in principle, with reference to the properties of the parts, their relationships within the entire system $R(A,B,C)$, the relevant laws of nature, and the required composition principles.

The horizontal condition grasps the situation in which a systemic property *P* is emergent because the properties of the parts within the system $R(A,B,C)$ cannot be deduced from their properties in isolation or in other wholes, even in principle.

Since these two conditions are independent, there are two different possibilities for the occurrence of emergent properties: (i) a systemic property *P* of a system *S* is emergent if it does not follow, even in principle, from the properties of the parts within *S* that *S* has property *P*; and (ii) a systemic property *P* of a system *S* is emergent, if it does not follow, even in principle, from the properties of the parts in systems different from *S* how they will behave in *S*, realizing *P*.

---

8.   One may argue, for sure, that we should not worry so much about what natural scientists think about a philosophical debate as that about emergence. Nevertheless, we are particularly interested in the role the concept of emergence can play in theories and models developed in the natural sciences. Accordingly, it is crucial to our purposes how natural scientists grasp the idea of emergence.

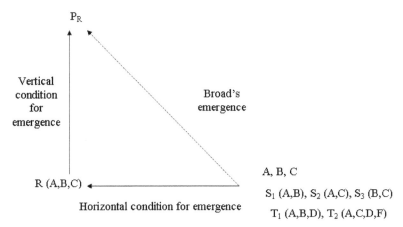

Figure 1: Vertical and horizontal conditions for emergence. A, B, and C are the parts
making up the system R(A,B,C), which shows PR, a systemic property. S1(A,B),
S2(A,C), and S3(B,C) are simpler systems including these parts. T1(A,B,D) is a
system with the same number of parts, and T2(A,C,D,F) is a system with more
parts than R(A,B,C). The diagonal arrow represents Broad's idea of emergence.
The horizontal and vertical arrows capture the two conditions implicit in Broad
that Boogerd and colleagues made explicit. (From Boogerd et al., 2005).

The vertical condition for emergence expresses in a different way the idea of
unanalyzability. Even if we know (i) what properties and relations A, B, and C show
within the system $R(A,B,C)$, (ii) the relevant laws of nature, and (iii) all necessary
composition principles, yet we will not be able to deduce that the system has property
P. This is a case in which the condition of analyzability is violated, since it does not
follow, even in principle, from the behavior of the parts A, B, and C in system
$R(A,B,C)$ that the system has P.

The horizontal condition for emergence expresses in a different way the idea of
irreducibility based on the non-deducibility of the behavior of the system's parts. In
this case, if we know the structure of the system $R(A,B,C)$, we will be able to explain
and predict the behavior of the parts within it, and, also, the instantiation of property P.
Boogerd et al. (2005) discuss the resources available for deducing the behavior of the
parts within $R(A,B,C)$ from their properties and behaviors in other kinds of systems, in
order to establish what would be the proper basis for this inference. We may deduce
the behavior of the parts in $R(A,B,C)$ from their properties and behaviors in systems of
greater, equal or less complexity (see Figure 1).[9] The possible bases for deduction of
the parts' behavior in $R(A,B,C)$ include: (i) more complex systems, such as
$T_2(A,C,D,F)$; (ii) systems with the same degree of complexity, such as $T_1(A,B,D)$; (iii)
simpler systems, such as $S_1(A,B)$, $S_2(A,C)$, and $S_3(B,C)$; and (iv) the parts A, B, and C

---

9. It is important to stress that Boogerd et al. (2005) are obviously aware that complexity does not depend only on
    the number of components of a system, but also on its structure and the nature of the interactions among the
    parts. They indicate differences in complexity through number of parts only for the sake of the argument.

in isolation. Boogerd and colleagues convincingly argue that only (iii) is an interesting basis for deduction, since (iv) trivializes emergence (i.e., in this case, each and every property of a system would seem to be emergent), and (i) and (ii) trivialize non-emergence (i.e., in this case, each and every property of a system would seem to be non-emergent). They conclude, thus, that the key case for understanding the horizontal condition for emergence is (iii), in which we attempt to deduce the behavior of $R(A,B,C)$ or its parts on the basis of less complex systems.

Boogerd et al. (2005) do not address downward causation. Nevertheless, we believe it is clear that the major, if not the only, reason why one cannot deduce the behavior of the parts in a given kind of system from their properties and behaviors in simpler systems lies in the downward influence of the system on their parts, that is, in downward causation. Therefore, the horizontal condition for emergence (or the mode of irreducibility as non-deducibility) can be said to necessarily involve one of the main problems in the emergence debate, namely the problem of downward causation.

3. The problem of downward causation

The problem of downward causation is the problem of how a higher-level phenomenon can cause or determine or structure a lower-level phenomenon (El-Hani & Emmeche, 2000).[10] To be more precise, what is at stake in this problem is what Kim (1999) calls reflexive downward causation, which takes place when some activity or event involving a whole has a causal influence on the events involving its own micro-constituents.

Kim discussed in several works the importance of downward causation to emergentism (e.g., Kim, 1993). More recently, he wrote that "emergentism cannot live without downward causation but it cannot live with it either. Downward causation is the raison d'être of emergence, but it may well turn out to be what in the end undermines it" (Kim, 2006, p. 548). But why is the problem of downward causation so central to emergentism? And why, paradoxically, could downward causation—as Kim suggests—put into question emergentism itself? If we assume, as Kim (1992, 1993, 1996), that, for something to be real, it should have causal powers, it will follow that to ascribe reality to emergent properties—an ascription that seems at first necessary for avoiding the conclusion that they are merely epiphenomenal properties—we will have to show that these properties instantiate new causal powers of their own. As Kim puts it:

> The claim that emergents have causal powers is entirely natural and plausible if you believe that there are such properties. For what purpose would it serve to insist on the existence of emergent properties if they were mere epiphenomena with no causal or explanatory relevance. (Kim, 1999, p. 19)

---

10. The expression *downward causation* was introduced by Campbell (1974) to account for the idea that the higher level is characterized by organizational principles, law-like regularities, that have a downward effect on the dynamics, distribution, and magnitude of lower level events and processes.

The causal powers of emergent properties should, moreover, be irreducible to the causal powers of their basal conditions. Emergent properties are typically supposed to represent novel additions to the ontology of the world. But it seems that this can only be the case if they bring with them genuinely new causal powers, going beyond the causal powers of the lower-level basal conditions from which they emerge.

An argument against Kim's criterion for reality can be derived from C. D. Broad's (1925) distinction between existents and abstracta in connection with the concept of properties. Broad distinguishes between the part of reality which *exists* and the part which is *real* but not *existent* (corresponding to abstracta). Notice that we can plausibly treat emergent properties as immanent universals, and, therefore, include them among abstracta, that is, *real* but not *existent* universals.[11] Kim assumes that emergent properties, to be real, should possess causal powers. He then derives from the claim that emergent properties do not possess causal powers, given that their causal roles are preempted by causal relations between their basal conditions, the conclusion that an eliminative reduction of emergent properties obtains, that is, that they should be eliminated as properties, being retained only as concepts or expressions (Kim, 1999). But we can plausibly claim that the requisite that, to be real, something should possess causal powers applies to the domain of existents within reality, and not to the whole of reality, given the idea that there are abstracta, which are real but not existent. In this sense, causal powers would be necessary to ascribe existence to something, but not reality. Then, Kim's criterion (or, as he calls it, Alexander's dictum) could be turned into the idea that something to be existent should possess causal powers. Then, if we consider emergent properties as immanent universals, and, thus, taken them to be real but not existent universals, there will be no necessity of ascribing causal powers to emergent properties in themselves in order to argue that they are real. Surely, it would be necessary to ascribe such causal powers if we were to say that emergent properties are existent. Nevertheless, since we would be claiming from the start that they are real but not existent parts of reality, Kim's requirement would not bother us anymore.

But, even though we may put aside this first reason to worry about downward causation, a second one is inevitable: Downward causation must provide a way of reconciling the notions of irreducibility and synchronic determination. As we argued above, downward causation is closely related to the notion of irreducibility as the non-deducibility of the behavior of the system's parts. Furthermore, downward causation

---

11. This certainly demands that one takes a position as regards the nature of properties. This is not the space for a more careful and detailed treatment of this issue. Nevertheless, a few clarifying words are indeed necessary. Ontological theories about properties have either postulated universals (realism) or denied their existence (nominalism). Realists about universals, in turn, have favored either Platonic transcendental universals, which are supposed to exist independently of the particulars in which they may be instantiated, or Aristotelian immanent universals, which are always instantiated in concrete particulars. Nominalists advocate, generally speaking, that only particulars are real and properties are nothing more than their classifications in terms of language or concepts. A kind of via media has been proposed by trope theorists, who claim that there are indeed properties, but these properties are particulars' individual modes of being (tropes), and not universals instantiated in several particulars at the same time. As we stated above, as regards these alternative positions, we are assuming, for the sake of our arguments, that emergent properties are immanent universals.

offers a possible explanation of how an emergent property can be irreducible and yet dependent on, and determined by, the micro-structure from which it emerges, as established by the notion of synchronic determination.

Then we have to face the legion of difficulties besetting the notion of downward causation. After all, downward causation has struck a number of thinkers as incoherent and paradoxical. Once more, we can mention Kim, who has repeatedly argued that the combination of upward determination (as in synchronic determination) and reflexive downward causation may threaten the very coherence of emergentism (e.g., Kim 1992, p. 137; 1999, p. 25). But, first, let us take a look at the possible role that downward causation can play in the current development of our understanding of biological networks and the genotype-phenotype relationship.

4. Downward Causation in Biological Networks: The Missing Element in the Understanding of the Genotype-Phenotype Relationship

We are also motivated to tackle the problem of downward causation by recent advances in molecular biology, genomics and proteomics which pushed researchers into adopting a systemic perspective, which has given rise, in turn, to the current wave of systems biology. Systems biology is often presented as a non-reductionistic approach (Chong & Ray, 2002; Kitano, 2002; McCarthy, 2004; Stephanopoulos et al., 2004; Barabási & Oltvai, 2004; Nature, 2005), and many genomic researchers seem quite eager, indeed, to declare that they have overcome *fallacies* such as determinism and reductionism (see, e.g., Venter et al., 2001, p. 1348), even though a sort of embarrassed determinism (cf. Leite, 2006) lives on in their writings. In fact, it is not clear, at present, what systems biology really means in these fields (Keller, 2005), and, furthermore, it can be put into question if it is really such a non-reductionistic approach as many of its advocates claim (Bruni, 2003), much in the same sense that systems ecology was previously charged of being nothing but a large-scale reductionistic approach (e.g., Levins & Lewontin, 1980; Bergandi, 1995). When one reads, for instance, that "a key aim of postgenomic biomedical research is to systematically catalogue all molecules and their interactions within a living cell" (Barabási & Oltvai, 2004, p. 101), one is led to suspect that what is at stake in this approach, after all, is not so much a non-reductionist, but rather a large-scale reductionist approach. And, when we read, in the follow-up of this same argument, that "rapid advances in network biology indicate that cellular networks are governed by universal laws" (Barabási & Oltvai, 2004, p. 101), a sense of bewilderment is inevitable: if cellular networks are indeed governed by universal laws, why would it be necessary to catalogue all molecules and interactions? Might it not be the case that other, more systemic approaches would reveal in a more efficient (and cheaper) way how cellular networks function?

It is clear, however, that the current deluge of systems-biological approaches involves at least a tension between previous, more reductionist approaches in molecular biology, and a current tendency to raise the level of analysis of cell systems back to the level at which cellular phenomena indeed emerge. Even though we should say that it is not clear that the current move in molecular biology and genomics can be really treated as a shift from reductionism to whole-istic biology (Chong & Ray, 2002), it can be said that we may be witnessing a movement towards less reductionist approaches in these fields.

We believe that emergentist philosophies have much to contribute to this movement, particularly as regards the attainment of the goal of a global approach to living systems which does not disdain the role of analytic methods, but argues for a pluralistic research strategy combining analytic and synthetic methods (Bruggeman, Westerhoff & Boogerd, 2002). This research strategy is likely to have a significant impact on the understanding of the relationship between genotype and phenotype, and, consequently, can also contribute to the development of new approaches to the treatment of diseases, particularly of those which are complex in nature. Strohman, for instance, argues for a shift from a genetic deterministic view, in which complex traits are explained as being caused by single genes, to a more systemic view, in which such traits are treated as "complex context-dependent entities to which our genes make a necessary, but only partial, contribution" (Strohman, 2002, p. 701). In this latter view, phenotypes are thought to be controlled by "lawful self-organizing networks that display system-wide dynamics" (Strohman, p. 701). This leads us to emphasize, once again, that if such networks are lawful, a large-scale reductionistic approach does not seem to be the single, or not even the best, alternative to study them.

Strohman also states that "molecular biologists have rediscovered the profound complexity of the genotype-phenotype relationship, but are unable to explain it: Something is missing" (Strohman, 2002, p. 701). And he goes on to claim that the missing element to close the gap between genotype and phenotype is found in Polanyi's notion of boundary conditions, symptomatically a central concept in most treatments of downward causation. In systems biology, boundary conditions are conceptualized as levels of constraints or control constraints, again, a concept much discussed in the literature on downward causation. These control constraints are found at several levels of regulation, many of them above the level of the genome. Thus, the regulation of gene expression—and, in general terms, regulation as a whole—can be treated as a top-down influence of a system over its components, and this influence can be in turn conceptualized in terms of boundary conditions for the operation of lower-level entities and processes (Salthe, 1985; Emmeche et al., 2000; El-Hani & Emmeche, 2000). This is exactly what emergentists mean by downward causation!

The role of regulation in living systems can be illustrated by the context-dependence of gene function. Differences in animal designs and complexity, for instance, are mostly related to changes in the temporal and spatial regulation of patterns of gene expression (Carroll, Grenier & Weatherbee, 2005), and not so much to the evolution of genes themselves, as shown by sequence comparison between several animal genomes. Peltonen and McKusick (2001) argue that a shift from a focus on gene action to an emphasis on gene regulation is one of the features of a possible paradigm change in current molecular biology and genetics. Keller (2000), in turn, sees the seeds of this change emerging a long time ago, when Jacob and Monod's model of gene regulation brought into focus the idea of gene activation rather than gene action. Be that as it may, regulation is a process which entails an influence of higher-level processes on molecular processes, such as transcription, RNA splicing, translation, and so forth, that is, it involves a kind of process which has not been clearly conceptualized yet in biological thought, namely, downward determination. The time and place in which a given set of genes is activated or not crucially depend on downward regulation, and this regulation is something to which genes are submitted, rather than something that genes do, command, control, program, etc.

We would like to reinforce the need of an adequate theoretical/philosophical approach to the nature of networks in biology. To the extent that these networks are lawful, the lawful regularities found in their dynamics naturally become a key research target. These regularities have to do with self-organizing processes in these networks and the influence of the system-wide dynamics on the components, the latter being precisely the central issue in debates about downward causation. In the progression from genotype to phenotype, many levels of control are introduced, and a number of important transitions can be identified: from genome to transcriptome; from transcriptome to proteome; from proteome to dynamic networks or systems; from dynamic systems to phenotype (Strohman, 2002). It is here that the missing element perceived by Strohman enters the scene: "each control level is defined by a dynamic system of self-organizing proteins, the output of which is governed by laws that are still poorly understood" (Strohman, 2002, p. 701). We believe that a proper understanding of biological networks cannot result simply from large-scale extensive data gathering, as it is typically (and inductively)[12] attempted, but crucially demands a clear formulation of the regularities governing the system-wide dynamics of these networks.[13] For this purpose, we need a coherent and heuristically powerful conceptual toolkit. Our goal in this paper can be seen as an attempt to offer some contributions to build such a toolkit, based on the tradition of debates about the downward influence of systems over their components in the emergentist literature.

5. Synchronic and diachronic downward causation

When considering the influence of wholes over parts, it is important to distinguish between synchronic and diachronic downward causation. In synchronic reflexive downward causation, a whole and its parts are involved in an instantaneous causal relationship:

> [Synchronic reflexive downward causation] At a certain time *t,* a whole, *W,* has emergent property *M* where *M* emerges from the following configuration of conditions: *W* has a complete decomposition

---

12. For a defense of the role of inductivist approaches (or discovery science, described as having the objective of defining all of the elements in a system and creating a database containing that information, much in the sense of a large-scale reductionistic approach) as a necessary (but not sufficient) element in systems biology, see Ideker et al. (2001). For a critical appraisal of this inductivist strategy, see Allen (2001).

into parts $a_1...a_n$; each has Property P_i; and relation R holds for the sequence $a_1 ... a_n$. For some a_j, W's having M at t causes a_j to have P_j at t. (Kim, 1999, p. 29)

This kind of downward causation looks like a bizarre metaphysical bootstrapping phenomenon (Symons, 2002). For instance, how could an organism by having a given property M at t really causes one of its constituents to have property P_j at the same time t? By acting on a part of the very micro-structure by which it is synchronically determined, an emergent property would be changing its own basal conditions. But wouldn't this entail, then, that the identity of the emergent property would itself be changing, in such a way that it becomes, after all, impossible to understand what might be happening in such a case? The whole idea of synchronic downward causation seems, at first, to reduce to absurdity.

This circularity comes from the fact that causation, as typically understood, takes place over time and involves property changes that make 'self-causing' paradoxical – for instance, because of their transitivity. Taking into account that this picture is committed to the usual interpretation of causes in terms of efficient causation, a possible way out of the bootstrapping problem would be to understand causation in a way which makes it encompass a wider variety of modes. We shall consider this possibility later. For the moment, let us discuss another way out of the bootstrapping problem.

An emergentist thinker might claim that the problems related to the synchronic case can be overcome through a treatment of a second case, in which the whole-to-part relationship takes place over time:

[Diachronic reflexive downward causation] As before W has emergent property M at t, and a_j has P_j at t. We now consider the causal effect of W's having M at t on a_j at a later time $t + \Delta t$. Suppose, then, that W's having M at t causes a_j to have P_j at $t + \Delta t$. (Kim, 1999, p. 29)

---

13. Strohman quotes an analogy, proposed by Polanyi (1968), between the strategy of a chess player and the moves in this game, and the strategy of systems imposing boundary conditions on their components and the activities of these components. Polanyi argued that the interest in biological research lies rather in the strategies of living systems, and not so much in the several moves of the components (even though,we should add,this knowledge is also necessary). Biology is a science of living organization (El-Hani & Emmeche, 2000), not a sort of applied physics and chemistry. To understand biological systems, we should consider how they orchestrate their physical and chemical components to instantiate a constrained set of properties and processes. Accordingly, we agree with Strohman's (2002) plea for a greater focus on the strategies observed in dynamic biological networks that generate – through development – phenotype from genotype, i.e., on how boundary conditions at several levels of organization are imposed on the components of such networks. This focus would help bringing systems biology to fulfill its promise of being a global, systemic approach, rather than a large-scale reductionistic, inductivist, and cataloguing approach. The efforts to predict gene function from genomic databases have come to failure (Stephens, 1998; Keller, 2000), and, as Strohman (2002) argues, it is also likely that proteomic databases will not be enough to this predictive task, since they "do not contain sufficient information to specify the behavior of a complex system." Something more is required and we believe this is indeed network biology (Barabási & Oltvai, 2004), but we also think that network biology should be pursued not only as an exhaustive cataloguing effort. But, despite this criticism, we should recognize that important insights are already arising from network biology (see, e.g., Gavin et al., 2002; Lee et al., 2002), and, consequently, the conceptual approach proposed in this paper is directed towards complementing this approach, rather than advocating its upheaval.

In the diachronic case, the problematic circularity discussed above is removed, but at the expense of the reflexive aspect of the causal relation at stake. The reason is shown by Kim's argument of causal/explanatory exclusion. Kim (1999, p. 24) derives a general principle, the principle of downward causation, from his arguments about inter- and intra-level causation in the context of a layered model of the world: To cause any property to be instantiated, you must cause the basal conditions from which it arises. When we consider that any higher-level property has, according to the supervenience concept, a supervenience base (or realizer) that is sufficient to bring about its instantiation, the problem of causal/explanatory exclusion enters the scene. Considering that for any single event there can be no more than a single sufficient cause, if both a higher-level property Q and its physical supervenience base P are sufficient causes of another physical property P^* and, hence, of its supervenient property Q^*, one of them must be excluded from this causal picture. It is reasonable to claim that the role of Q in the causation of P^* (an instance of downward causation) should be preempted by P, so that we end in the following picture: P causes P^*, and Q supervenes on P, and Q^* supervenes on P^*. In this picture, causal processes at the micro-level are taken as fundamental and all events of macro-causation (including downward causation) are regarded as supervenient, or dependent, on micro-causation.

In short, cases of diachronic reflexive downward causation seem to easily reduce to supervenient causal relations, in which its aspect of reflexivity is lost. This picture poses a serious problem for the emergentist's interpretation of downward causation as a causal power that could change the behavior of lower-level entities and processes, since the causal powers instantiated at a higher level are taken to be, in the case of both same-level causation and downward causation, utterly derived from causal powers at the micro-level.

Given the problem of causal/explanatory exclusion, if an emergentist thinker wishes to insist on the idea of irreducible downward causation, a violation of the physical causal closure will seem to follow. After all, irreducible downward causation would be, in these terms, a causation of physical processes by nonphysical properties (see Kim, 1996, pp. 232-233; Kim, 1998, p. 44).[14]

If we intend to propose a coherent and plausible physicalist synchronic emergence theory, we must (i) either make sense of downward causation without committing ourselves to a violation of the causal closure of the physical domain, and at the same time avoiding the problem of causal/explanatory exclusion; or (ii) circumvent the incoherence in synchronic reflexive downward causation. Kim (1993, p. 356; 1998, p. 46) claims that the only plausible solution to the problem of downward causation would be some form of reductionism, allowing us to discard, or at least moderate, the claim that mental properties (or any other higher-level properties) are distinct from their underlying physical properties. Then the result is, as shown by Kim's argument

---

14. See El-Hani & Pereira (1999, 2000) and El-Hani & Emmeche (2000) for a criticism of the interpretation of the term *physical* in this claim, to the effect that the idea that downward causation would involve nonphysical causes fails to grasp the thesis that all levels of reality are contained in a global physical level — i.e., the thesis of the inclusivity of levels (Emmeche, Køppe & Stjernfelt, 1997, 2000).

itself, the impossibility of postulating any new and irreducible causal powers at the higher level.

Downward causation is interpreted in Kim's arguments as a sort of efficient causation (for a treatment of this issue, see El-Hani & Pereira, 1999, 2000; El-Hani & Emmeche, 2000), and, furthermore, the causes in downward causation are understood by him, following Sperry, as concrete, particular events (Hulswit, 2006). These two features in Kim's account of downward causation can be put into question. One may explore, for instance, the possibility of interpreting downward causation as a type of causation other than the efficient causal mode. This is the move made by neo-Aristotelian accounts of downward causation. But let us first take a look at an argument for a coherent account of synchronic downward causation put forward by Symons.

6. An argument for synchronic downward causation

The diachronic downward causation model does not fit the descriptions of the kinds of phenomena that elicit the idea of downward causes (Hulswit, 2006). This is one of the reasons why many authors insist on synchronic downward causation. Therefore, we will focus here mainly on the second horn of our description of the downward causation dilemma, addressing ways of circumventing the putative incoherence of synchronic reflexive downward causation.

Symons (2002) developed an argument for a putative case of a non-contradictory synchronic relation between the causal behavior of parts and the emergent properties of the systems (wholes) including those parts. He assumes, first, an interpretation of causality in terms of probability, stressing that probability and structure are related notions. Basically, what he intends in his paper is to show that an interpretation of causes as objective probabilities (see below) allows one to see the structure of the whole as playing a role in shaping the causal powers of the constituents. Or, to put it differently, a probabilistic interpretation of causality would make it possible to imagine the structure as having an effect on the system's parts which is distinct from the causal powers of the latter. That is, Kim's causal inheritance principle, according to which the causal powers of a given property are merely a product of the causal powers of its basal conditions (Kim, 1998, 1999), would not hold in the probabilistic case.

In order to make it clear the influence of an emergent property, more specifically, the property of a system's having a given structure, on a system's components, Symons (2002) asks us to consider the example of a dean at Harvard Law School telling the students to look to their left, and then to their right, and finally saying: "By the end of the year, one of you will not be here." Surely, this would be just a way of expressing the fact that there is a one-third attrition rate during the first year at that school. But Symons asks us to think about the dean's utterance as a graphic way of pointing out that 1 out of 3 people (33%) on average would have abandoned Harvard Law School by the end of the first year. Symons argues that his statement would have the unintended effect that students sitting at the ends of the rows would be more likely to drop the school than their neighbors. Then, he asks us to suppose that the seating arrangement at that occasion would be important to the outcomes of the dean's statement. A change in this arrangement would change the likelihood that specific students leave the school.

Considering, for the sake of the argument, that the dean's utterance played proxy for a law of nature, we can ask: What is the relationship between a student's chances of graduating and his location in the seating arrangement? Symons argues that, if the students are seated in a row, the students at the end of the row are less likely to graduate, but, on average, students have a 66% chance of making it through the school. But suppose the students were seated in a circle. Then, he argues, the average chance of a student graduating would decrease to 50% simply by virtue of the structural or spatial relationship between them.

Symons uses this example in order to show that structural arrangements, treated by him as emergent properties, can have a significant effect on the causal powers of systems and their constituents, causally affecting them in a downward synchronic way. He admits, however, that this example is pretty contrived, since it relies on the specification of a hypothetical law of nature that already includes some consideration of structure (Symons, 2002, p. 198). He characterizes the effects of structural arrangements on the causal power of systems and their components as constraints, interpreting them not as particular events, as Kim does, but as general principles. Finally, he claims that, in the context of a probabilistic interpretation of causality, the behavior of the components can be understood as altered or enslaved by their participation in a given structure. These constraints on the components' behavior amount, in Symons' arguments, to a downward causal effect resulting from an emergent property, the structural arrangement of the system's components.

According to Symons, this is not a case of diachronic downward causation, but rather of an instantaneous, synchronic influence of the structure *qua* emergent property on its constituents. He argues that, in a probabilistic interpretation of causality, one can envision a meaningful sense in which a whole can act on its parts without becoming something other than itself. Thus, the incoherence shown by Kim in synchronic reflexive downward causation would be overcome. The basic argument is that, in the example sketched above, the properties of the parts that are being affected at t are not constitutive of the whole at time t. The change in the constituents' properties that takes place in the downward causal event is interpreted as a change in the probability that the students graduate or not at Harvard Law School. As Symons (2002, p. 200) summarizes: "the structural property exerts a change on the causal power of the parts, but a funny kind of change, namely a change in their potential for behavior in the moment immediately following their entry into the whole."

It is not clear whether and how the alteration or enslavement of the components due to the influence of a structural arrangement can be conceptualized as the effect of an efficient cause. Alternatively, we might understand such an influence in terms of another causal mode. But, then, we should ask which causal mode might be adequate to understand the sort of structural effect at stake in Symons' arguments.

The same is true also of other arguments about downward causation. Stephan (1998, p. 644), for instance, writes that downward causation "would not amount to a violation of some widely held assumptions, such as, for example, the principle of the causal closure of the physical domain. Within the physical domain, we would just have to accept additional types of causal influence besides the already known basal types of mutual interactions". Similarly, in his discussion of Sperry's emergentist-interactionist account of human consciousness, O'Connor claims that Sperry may be assuming, in his explanation of downward macrodetermination, "that the emergent *structurally* determines ... the systems' relational structure" (O'Connor, 1994, p. 102, emphasis in the original), being *structural determination* conceived as "a species of causation distinct from ordinary efficient causation through time" (O'Connor, 1994, p. 103, n. 18). But what do Stephan and O'Connor exactly mean by appealing to other types of causality in their arguments? In our view, this is precisely the sort of clarification that neo-Aristotelian approaches to downward causation intend to offer.

7. Neo-Aristotelian approaches to downward causation

What does it mean to claim that the structure of a system, as an emergent property, changes the causal powers of the components by enslaving them? Emmeche, Køppe, and Stjernfelt's (2000) systematic analysis of different notions of downward causation offers a good starting point to answer this question. They advance an Aristotelian understanding of causality as a way of grasping the nature of the influence of wholes over their parts.[15] They identify three versions of downward causation, each making use of a particular way of interpreting the causal mode (or modes) involved in this sort of causation: strong, medium, and weak downward causation.

Strong downward causation interprets the causal influence of a whole over its parts as a case of ordinary, efficient causation. Nevertheless, to claim that a higher level exerts an efficient causal influence over a lower one, we need to postulate a sharp distinction between these two levels, regarding them ultimately as being constituted by different kinds of substances (Emmeche, Køppe & Stjernfelt, 2000; El-Hani & Videira 2001; Hulswit, 2006). In other words, strong downward causation demands an acceptance of substance dualism, and, thus, it is blatantly incompatible with a scientific understanding of emergence. Moreover, this notion faces other important difficulties, such as the bootstrapping problem discussed above. Therefore, Emmeche and colleagues (2000) rightly emphasize that there are only two viable candidates for a scientifically acceptable account of downward causation, both committed to an

---

15. Other authors also take Aristotelian causal notions as an inspiration to think about causal processes in biological and other complex systems, such as, for instance, Salthe (1985, 1993), Rosen (1991), Riedl (1997), Van de Vijver, Salthe, & Delpos (1998), Ulanowicz (1999), El-Hani & Pereira (1999, 2000), El-Hani & Emmeche (2000), El-Hani & Videira (2001). In this connection, we can also refer to Putnam's (1994, 2000) claim that a return to Aristotle can be a fruitful approach in the philosophy of mind.

interpretation of downward causation as a case of synchronic formal causation: medium and weak downward causation.

We can summarize the key points of Emmeche and colleagues' arguments for medium downward causation as follows: (i) a higher-level entity comes into being through the realization of one amongst several possible lower-level states. (ii) In this process, the previous states of the higher level operate as factors of selection for the lower-level states. (iii) The idea of a factor of selection can be made more precise by employing the concept of boundary conditions, introduced by Polanyi (1968) in the context of biology, particularly in the sense that higher-level entities are boundary conditions for the activity of lower levels, constraining which higher-level phenomenon will result from a given lower-level state. (iv) Constraints can be interpreted in terms of the characterization of a higher level by organizational principles – law-like regularities – that have a downward effect on the distribution of lower-level events and substances. (v) Medium downward causation is committed to the thesis of constitutive irreductionism, namely, the idea that even though higher-level systems are ontologically constituted by lower-level entities, the higher level cannot be reduced to the form or organization of the constituents. (vi) Rather, the higher level must be said to constitute its own substance and not merely to consist of its lower-level constituents, or, else, a higher-level entity should be regarded as a real substantial phenomenon in its own right. (vii) This interpretation of downward causation may assume either a thesis Emmeche and colleagues call formal realism of levels, stating that the structure, organization or form of an entity is an objectively existent feature of it, which is irreducible to lower-level forms or substances, or a thesis they designate as substantial realism of levels, claiming that a higher-level entity is defined by a substantial difference from lower-level entities. The difference from strong downward causation is said to lie in the necessary commitment, in this position, to the thesis of a substantial realism of levels.

In turn, Emmeche and colleagues' treatment of weak downward causation can be summarized in terms of the following arguments: (i) in the weak version, downward causation is interpreted in terms of a formal realism of levels, as explained above, and constitutive reductionism, that is, the idea that a higher-level entity ontologically consists of lower-level entities organized in a certain way. (ii) Higher-level forms or organization are irreducible to the lower level, but the higher-level is not a real substantial phenomenon, that is, it does not add any substance to the entities at the lower level. (iii) In contrast to the medium version, weak downward causation does not admit the interpretation of boundary conditions as constraints. (iv) By employing phase-space terminology, Emmeche and colleagues explain weak downward causation as the conception of higher-level entities as attractors for the dynamics of lower levels. Accordingly, the higher level is thought of as being characterized by formal causes of the self-organization of constituents at a lower level. (v) The relative stability of an attractor is taken to be identical to the downward governing of lower-level entities, that is, the attractor functions as a whole at a higher level affecting the processes that constitute it. (vi) The attractor also functions as a whole in another sense of the word, given that it is a general type, of which the single phase-space points in its basin are tokens.

Emmeche and colleagues' contribution to the debates about downward causation has a lot of merit, particularly because it stressed a diversity of downward causation accounts that has been often neglected, and, moreover, tried to make some advance in organizing the variety of such accounts. As Hulswit (2006) sums up, Emmeche and colleagues made "a valiant attempt at creating some order in the conceptual chaos that characterizes the discussion regarding downward causation" (Hulswit, p. 276).[16] Nevertheless, their typology faces a number of problems, something which is not really surprising. After all, many attempts to explain downward causation available in the literature are confronted with important difficulties. In the case of Emmeche and colleagues' arguments, in particular, the distinctions between strong, medium, and weak downward causation should be further clarified. For instance, it seems necessary to describe in more detail in what sense strong and medium downward causation differ as regards the idea that a higher-level entity is a substantial phenomenon, or, else, how one would differentiate medium versions committed to the thesis of a substantial realism of levels from strong downward causation.

We do not intend, however, to pursue these lines of reasoning in this work. For the sake of our arguments, we will simply work below with an interpretation which comes close to medium downward causation by interpreting boundary conditions as constraints, but, at the same time, departs from it, by resolutely rejecting constitutive irreductionism. It also comes close, thus, to weak downward causation. But we will not try here to classify our account in terms of Emmeche and colleagues' typology. We will rather concentrate on explaining how we conceive the relationship between downward causation and constraints.

To go on with our attempt to answer our initial question – what does it mean to say that the structure of a system, as an emergent property, changes the causal powers of the components by enslaving them? – we will appeal to Juarrero's (2000) approach to complex adaptive systems, which also employs an Aristotelian understanding of causality in order to account for part-whole relationships in complex systems. She stresses that modern science conceives that, to explain anything, it is necessary to identify the role that each cause plays in bringing about the phenomenon to be explained. Even though this idea itself has Aristotelian roots, it is also implicit in Aristotle's account of causes another appeal, concerning the idea that nothing, strictly speaking, can move, cause, or act on itself in the same respect, or, to put it differently: "Contemporary causal theories of action have consistently adhered to Aristotle's principle that nothing moves or changes itself; intentions, volitions, and other alleged causes of action are supposed to be other than the behavior they cause" (Juarrero, p. 25).

---

16. One of the authors of the present paper (C. N. El-Hani) was greatly influenced by Emmeche and colleagues' treatment of downward causation, discussing it in several papers (El-Hani & Pereira 1999, 2000; El-Hani & Emmeche 2000; El-Hani & Videira 2001; El-Hani, 2002a).

In order to support the thesis that hierarchical systems are self-referential and exhibit inter-level effects, she claims that the notion of causality should be recontextualized so as to include more than efficient causes. Then, she advances the conceptual framework of the theory of complex adaptive systems as

> a 'theory-constitutive metaphor' that permits a reconceptualization of cause, and in consequence a rethinking of action. A different logic of explanation — one more suitable to all historical, contextually embedded processes, including action — arises from this radical revision. (Juarrero, 2000, p. 25)

The framework put forward by Juarrero can be summarized as follows: (i) complex adaptive systems are typically characterized by positive feedback processes, in which the product is necessary for the process itself to take place in an appropriate manner. This leads to a kind of circular causality, or self-cause, which contradicts the Aristotelian proposal. (ii) Interactions between certain dynamic processes can create a system-level organization with new properties that cannot be reduced to the simple sum of their lower-level components. (iii) The global dynamics of the emergent system not only determines which parts are to be allowed within the system, but also regulates and constrains the behavior of the lower-level components. In contrast to the usual scientific understanding, Juarrero claims that the whole is not an inert epiphenomenon, but a complex dynamical whole that exerts — in a distributed manner — active power on their parts, in such a manner that the overall system is maintained and enhanced. Thus, to understand the dynamics of such a system, she claims that we should revive the Aristotelian concepts of formal and final causes, in a similar vein to Emmeche and colleagues' proposal. Another similarity between these proposals lies in the appeal to the notion of constraints in order to account for these other kinds of causality:

"Since the active power that wholes exert on their components is clearly not the go cart-like collisions of a mechanical universe, the causal mechanism at work between levels of hierarchical organization can better be understood as the operations of constraint." (Juarrero, 2000, p. 30)

Juarrero also introduces a distinction between two kinds of constraints exerted by wholes over their parts: "context-free constraints, which take a system's components far from equiprobability, and context-sensitive constraints, which synchronize and correlate previously independent parts into a systemic whole" (Juarrero, 2000, p. 26).

We believe that we can effectively explore the relationship between downward causation and constraints based on Juarrero's complex adaptive systems framework. We can begin by considering that, when lower-level entities are composing a higher-level system, the set of possible relations among them is constrained, since the system causes its components to have a much more ordered distribution in spacetime than they would have in its absence. This is true in the case of both entities and processes, since processes also make the elements involved in them assume a particular distribution in spacetime. We can take a first step, then, towards explaining why the same lower-level entity can show different behaviors depending on the higher-level system it is part of—the basis for a concept of irreducibility based on the non-deducibility of the components' behavior. As we saw above, while discussing Symons' arguments, we can plausibly argue that lower-level entities are enslaved by a particular pattern of constraints established by the higher-level structure in which they are embedded, so that their relations to each other are modified, and, consequently, their causal powers. We are dealing, then, with higher-level constraints on the components' relations which results from the fact that the components are part of the space-time form, or pattern, of the system's structures and processes. We can conceptualize, then, the modification suffered by the system's parts as a constraint resulting from being part of a (spatio-temporal) pattern. This modification is not the same as an effect in an efficient causal event. It should be rather thought of as the consequence of a multi-nested series of constraints on the possible interactions of the components (Emmeche et al., 2000).

Then, we can arguably interpret downward causation as a formal cause by basically recasting the notion of higher-level constraints (or constraining conditions) in terms of Aristotle's set of causal concepts (see Emmeche et al., 2000; El-Hani & Pereira, 2000; El-Hani & Emmeche, 2000; El-Hani & Videira, 2001).[17] A given set of constraining conditions acting on the parts of a given whole can be interpreted, in a neo-Aristotelian approach to causality, as an instance of formal causality.[18] Moreover, we can interpret the specific functions that many components come to perform as their relations are constrained within a given higher-level structure (contributing to the dynamical stability of the system itself), in terms of a functional causality.[19]

The notion of boundary conditions, introduced by Polanyi (1968), is useful for characterizing these higher-level constraints (see also van Gulick, 1993). Polanyi

17. Notice that a case can be made for sticking to the vocabulary of constraints without introducing a potential source of contention, such as the Aristotelian formal causal mode. We will come back to this possibility later. For the moment, consider that it is quite natural that, as the problem we are dealing with concerns causation, it seemed worth exploring, for a number of authors, the consequences of recasting the treatment of constraining conditions in terms of formal causal influences of wholes over parts. Nevertheless, we should not lose from sight that the very difficulties faced by the concept of downward causation, which are indeed the main motivation for emergentist thinkers to seek new ways of understanding causality, can be seen as evidence that causality is the wrong issue when it comes to emergence (at least in some domains. See Pihlström (2002) and, generally speaking, complex systems see Van de Vijver, Van Speybroeck & Vandevyvere (2003).

18. Emmeche et al. (2000, p. 7) characterize formal causality as corresponding to the form or pattern into which the component parts of a given entity or process are arranged. This is entirely compatible with Aristotle's definition of the formal causal mode: "A second way in which the word [cause] is used is for the form or pattern (i.e. the formula for what a thing is, both specifically and generically, and the terms which play a part in the formula" (Physics II.3, 194b26-28. Aristotle 1996, p. 39).

19. Emmeche et al. (2000, p. 17) substitute a new notion of causality, functional causality, for the original meaning of the Aristotelian final causality, describing it as amounting to the role played by a part in an integrated processual whole, or the purpose of a behavior as seen from the perspective of a system's chance of remaining stable over time. Aristotle characterized the final causal mode as a way of specifying the cause "in the sense of end or that for the sake of which a thing is done ... The same is true also of all the intermediate steps which are brought about through the action of something else as means towards the end" (Physics II.3, 194b32-35; Aristotle, 1995, pp. 332-333). Given the ongoing debates concerning the relationships between the concepts of function, teleology, and finality, and their explicit intention of reinterpreting Aristotle's causal modes under the light of contemporary theoretical frameworks, it is understandable that Emmeche and colleagues preferred to avoid either identifying function with the Aristotelian final cause or using the notion of finality at all.

argued that a living system, as a naturally designed entity, works under the control of two principles: The higher one is the principle of design or organization of the system, and this harnesses the lower one, which consists in the physical-chemical processes on which the system relies. As the physical-chemical processes at the lower level are harnessed, the components come to perform functions contributing to the maintenance of the dynamical stability of the system as a whole.

To explain further the ideas of constraint and boundary conditions, we can argue that, as the parts of a system are enslaved by a particular pattern of constraints which is characteristic of that kind of system, they partly lose, so as to say, their freedom to behave, while the system, conversely, acquire more freedom to behave, precisely by coordinating the behaviors of its components. Consider, first, a set W of all possible behaviors the constituents of a system may show. The boundary conditions established by the system's organization select, among all the possible behaviors the constituents might show, a more limited set $(W - x)$ of behaviors they will effectively show, as parts of that kind of system.[20] In turn, by constraining the behaviors of its parts, the system shows enhanced capacities, in the sense that it becomes capable of displaying behaviors we would not observe if the system did not constrain, and, thus, coordinate, orchestrate the processes which take place within it. Constraints increase the likelihood that the parts of a system be engaged in relations which, in turn, are embedded in a certain set of particular processes, which is smaller than the set of processes they could be part of in the absence of the system. And, in turn, the instantiation of these processes in a coordinated manner allows the system to show novel higher-level behaviors, increasing its freedom to behave.

The interpretation of downward causation as a formal cause, in terms of higher-level constraining conditions influencing the behavior of a system's components, has an additional bearing on current debates about emergence. A downward causal influence is usually ascribed to emergent properties in a rather general way, that is, each and every emergent property is supposed to exert such an influence on the microstructure. Emergentist thinkers usually claim that emergent properties, in such a general sense, bring to the world new causal powers of their own and that those properties have powers to influence and control the direction of the lower-level processes from which they emerge (cf. Kim, 1998, p. 100, 1999, pp. 6 & 22). But, according to the interpretation of downward causation presented above, a specific kind of emergent property is supposed to exert a formal influence over a system's parts, namely, the property of a class of systems $\{Z\}$ having a given kind of structure S. This

---

20. In fact, a model for explaining emergence needs to consider not only boundary conditions established by a higher level – in relation to the level in which a given emergent property or process is instantiated (we can call it, following Salthe, the focal level) – but also initiating conditions described at a lower level. As Salthe (1985, p. 101) argues, the phenomena observed at the focal level should be "among the possibilities engendered by permutations of possible initiating conditions established at the next lower level," but "what actually will emerge will be guided by combinations of boundary conditions imposed by the next higher level." This entails the necessity of explaining emergence in the context of a model comprising three, and not only two levels. The reason why our arguments throughout this paper will consider only two levels lies in the fact that our problem here is that of explaining downward causation. A development of a model in three levels to explain the emergence of a particular kind of process – namely, sign processes – can be found in Queiroz & El-Hani (2006).

is an important outcome of our treatment of downward causation: downward macrodetermination should be thought of as stemming from the structure of systems, as a particularly important emergent property.[21] It is worth stressing the primary role of structures in downward causation for several reasons, among them, most importantly, because the downward influence of systems' structures on their components plays a crucial role in the explanation of other emergent systemic properties.

This explanation of downward causation can arguably provide appropriate grounds for understanding in what sense parts and wholes can be involved in mutually determinative relations. Synchronic determination, as a determinative upward relation, is combined in this account with a determinative downward relation. In these terms, the codetermination of parts and wholes is grounded on the conjunction of two distinct asymmetric determinative relations, synchronic determination and downward causation. The putative incoherence of combining upward and downward determinative relations, rightly pointed out by Kim in a causal structure admitting only efficient causal relations, would be avoided, in the present case, by the use of a richer array of causal concepts.[22]

8. A critique of neo-Aristotelian approaches to downward causation

Nevertheless, we can put into question whether neo-Aristotelian accounts of downward causation satisfy basic requirements for a theory of causation. Hulswit (2006), for instance, criticizes these accounts on the grounds of two fundamental questions: (i) What sort of things are said to be causing and caused in the case of downward causation? (ii) What is the meaning of *causing* in downward causation?

Hulswit concludes that the concept of downward causation is fuzzy with respect to the nature of causes and effects and muddled as regards the meaning of causation. Concerning the first problem, we should take into account a distinction found in the literature about downward causation between two types of downward causes: general principles and particular events or substances. In his original formulation, Donald T.

---

21. It is possible that the characterization of the structure of a system as an emergent property gives room for confusion, since we mentioned above the relationship between emergent properties and the microstructure of systems. It is important to avoid losing from sight, however, that the structure (even though referred to as 'microstructure', to stress its role as a realizer of a given emergent property) is itself a systemic property (see Kim 1998). Maybe a good way of avoiding this confusion is to dispense with the term 'microstructure', notwithstanding its currency in contemporary philosophy of mind. We can think of the situation as follows: the structure of a system is a macroproperty, which is realized by a set of relations among the components of the system, at the lower level. This macroproperty, in turn, has a downward formal influence over these components, creating a condition in which they can produce other emergent properties, at the systemic level.

22. A fully developed argument about the prospects of assuming both synchronic and downward determination in a coherent emergentist account also demands a claim about the mode of irreducibility one should ascribe to emergent properties. We will not develop this argument here, but refer the reader to another paper in which we argue that synchronic determination creates problems for a specific mode of irreducibility, particularly popular in the philosophy of mind, namely, irreducibility as unanalyzability, but not for the mode of irreducibility indeed related to downward causation and more relevant to the natural sciences, irreducibility as non-deducibility of the behavior of a system's parts (see El-Hani & Queiroz, 2005b).

Campbell (1974) interpreted downward causes as general principles, in the sense that, say, the behavior of a molecule inside a cell is not only determined by physical-chemical laws, but it is also constrained by the laws (in the very broad sense of general disposition) of the higher levels. Thus, in Campbell's account, the causal relata in downward causation are concrete *processes* (effects) at the lower level and *laws* or *law-like general principles* (causes) at the higher level.

It was in this sense that we explained above the relationship between higher-level organizational principles and lower-level processes that are constrained by the former. This is consistent with Polanyi's (1968) interpretation of boundary conditions as higher-level general principles that control lower-level processes. As Hulswit (2006) summarizes, Campbell, Polanyi, and also Van Gulick understand downward causation as "a selective activation of lower-level causal processes by higher-level boundary conditions, which basically are general principles" (Van Gulick, 1993, p. 268). Moreover, Hulswit takes this position to mean that "'downward causes' are not *causes in the strict sense* but general principles" (Hulswit, p. 269). This has important bearings on a claim we will advance below, namely that the influence of a system over its components is better understood in terms of other kinds of determination, rather than in terms of causal determination.

It is particularly important to avoid – as we explicitly do in this paper – an interpretation of downward causes as particular events, as we find, for instance, in Roger Sperry's (1969, 1980, 1983, 1986, 1991) and Kim's accounts.[23] Even though the bootstrapping problem does not disappear if downward causes are interpreted as general principles, we can say that it certainly becomes worse when the causal *relata* in downward causation are taken to be particulars at different levels of organization.

Hulswit (2006) also argues that the meaning ascribed to the term *causation* in debates about downward causation usually refers to ideas closer to explanation and determination than to causation, provided we understand causation in the intuitive sense of bringing about, that is, in the current sense of efficient causation. Not surprisingly, he considers the expression *downward causation* badly chosen. Even though one of the authors of the present paper has argued in previous works for a neo-Aristotelian interpretation of downward causation, we should stress we basically agree now with Hulswit's conclusions. In fact, his work reinforced our feeling that the idea of downward determination was better than that of downward causation and added to our motivation to make the move presented in this paper.

Although verbs usually related to the causing activity of a higher level in downward causation, such as *to restrain, to select, to organize, to structure, to determine,* and so forth may be understood as being related to causing (in the sense of bringing about), they are certainly not equivalent to causing (Hulswit, 2006). This can be seen as a result of an impoverishment of the meaning of the term *cause* in modern

---

23. We should not neglect the fact that Sperry provides most of the standard examples of downward causation in Kim's works. Thus, Kim's understanding of downward causation as involving concrete events as causes is certainly strongly influenced by Sperry's view. Thus, we can even say that at least some of the flaws Kim finds in the concept of downward causation can be traced back to problems which are specific of Sperry's position.

science, due to the fact that classical physics critically appraised, and, ultimately, denied a number of theses related to Aristotelian philosophy, many of them concerned with the principle of causality (El-Hani & Videira, 2001). Ultimately, only two of the four Aristotelian causal modes, efficient and final causes, came to be included in the meaning ascribed to the term *cause* in most modern languages. Symptomatically, the Greek word translated as cause (*archai*) in Aristotle's works does not mean cause in the modern sense (Ross, 1923/1995, p. 75; Lear, 1988, p. 15).[24] For Aristotle, a cause was not only an antecedent event sufficient to produce an effect or the goal of a given action, but the basis or ground of something. In other terms, to refer to Aristotle's archai as causes is very misleading; they should be rather treated as principles. It is in this sense that Aristotle can conceive matter and form as also having the nature of causal modes – in terms of his material and formal causal modes. It is not surprising, then, that, if we stick to our currently intuitive ideas about causation, Aristotle's causal modes are more similar to modes of explanation than to modes of causation. Aristotle seemed to be thinking mainly about the grounds for our understanding, while pondering about causal modes.

Another relevant critique of the neo-Aristotelian appeal can be derived from Mario Bunge's (1979a) work. In his view, causation is not the only single source of change and novelty in nature. He treats determination as a broader category than causation, and claims that the lawfulness of the world lies in the processes of determination operating in it. Causation is, he argues, but one kind of determination, and contemporary science should thus understand that determination is not limited to simple cause-and-effect relationships. As an example of how inadequate it is to appeal to causation as the single principle of determination, Bunge considers the well-known Einstein's equation, $E = mc^2$. This equation shows, for instance, that a loss of radiant energy by an atom leads to an associated mass loss. In this case, Bunge argues, there is determination, but no causation, since we are not dealing with an event bringing about another event, or even with a relation between events. Instead, what we see in this case is a relationship between two properties of a system, mass and energy.

On the grounds of his idea that determination is not limited to causation, Bunge distinguishes between some categories of determination: quantitative self-determination, causal determination, interaction (treated as reciprocal causation or functional interaction determination), mechanical determination, statistical determination, structural (or wholistic) determination, teleological determination, and dialectical determination. Even though no well-defined category of determination might be reduced to one another, Bunge thinks of these categories as constituting hierarchies of types of determination, in such a manner that no type of determination can be found alone, in some pure form, except in ideal cases. There are certainly problems with this scheme, since many of the kinds of determination he discriminates are so deeply interwoven that it becomes difficult to separate them into distinct

---

24. Translated into Latin, archai turned into causae, which in turn was translated into English as 'cause' (and, equivalently, in the case of other languages).

categories. Consider, for instance, mechanical determination, taken to be a "peculiar combination of purely quantitative self-determination ... and reciprocal action, which can often be polarized into cause and effect" (Bunge, 1979a, p. 20).

It would be possible to use the above claims about the impoverishment of cause in modern science as a ground for counteracting Hulswit's and Bunge's arguments. But we do think important limitations in recent accounts of downward causation can be discerned from these perspectives, particularly Hulswit's. Indeed, downward causation, as explained by neo-Aristotelian approaches, seems closer to determination than to causation. But how should we understand the relationship between the higher-level activities usually related to downward causation and the meaning of *causing*? It seems to us that the important relation between the ideas usually connected to downward causation in neo-Aristotelian accounts and the basic ideas about causation concerns the fact that, in both cases, we are dealing with some kind of determination.

As Hulswit (2006) stresses, the main difference between determining and causing is that the former primarily involves necessitation (in the sense of "it could not be otherwise" or, to put it in terms more consistent with probabilistic events, "it would not tend to be otherwise") while the latter primarily involves the idea of bringing about. We would like to invite our readers, then, to consider three issues: first, that most of the debates about downward causation are really about determination or explanation rather than causation; second, that efficient causes are typically regarded as individuals (usually events, facts, or substances), and downward causes are more properly interpreted (in our view) as general, law-like organizational principles;[25] and, third, that a similar move has been made in the case of another determinative but mereological relation, namely physical realization (and, consequently, supervenience), which cannot be properly accounted for as causal (see Kim, 1993, 1996).

We will be able to see, then, how proper it may be to advance the claim that it would be better to refer to downward (formal) determination, rather than downward causation. Instead of proposing that an understanding of the influence of wholes over parts demands causal categories other than efficient causation, we can rather claim that such understanding requires other kinds of determination than just causation. Indeed, causes are not the only sort of determining factors in the world and it is largely accepted in other current philosophical debates, such as those about supervenience, the introduction of non-causal determinative relations.

9. From downward causation to downward determination

The Aristotelian formal cause intended to explain the stability of the world in terms of the structure of things. It is, thus, a concept strongly committed to an ontology of substances. It is likely, however, that a theoretical framework to be employed to understand complex systems and phenomena, involving ideas such as self-

---

25. For this reason, Campbell (1974) himself remarked that the expression *downward causation*, which he first explicitly used, was awkward.

organization, emergence, complex networks, fractal patterns, and so forth, can be more fruitfully built if the stability of the world is explained in terms of dynamic relationships between events (e.g., Hulswit, 2006). This explanation should be embedded into a process philosophy, that is, a philosophical tendency of treating processes as being more fundamental than entities as ontological categories. A process was defined by Rescher (1996, p. 38) as "a coordinated group of changes in the complexion of reality, an organized family of occurrences that are systematically linked to one another either causally or functionally." To give ontological primacy to coordinated, organized family of occurrences clearly contradicts the priority historically given to entities in most of the Western thinking, substantially influenced by Aristotelian philosophy. This tension, in turn, can be seen as part of a criticism of the substance paradigm or the myth of the substance (Seibt, 1996), associated with thinkers such as Alfred North Whitehead, Charles Sanders Peirce, Charles Hartshorne, Paul Weiss, Samuel Alexander, Conway Lloyd Morgan, and Andrew Paul Ushenko (see Rescher, 1996, 2002).

It is not that process philosophy should necessarily claim that the idea of entities has to be abandoned. It is only that, when considering entities, we should always bear in mind that processes should be treated, in a dynamical world, as more fundamental than entities, since "substantial things emerge in and from the world's course of changes" (Rescher 1996, p. 28). Or, to put it differently, entities are just relatively stable bunches of processes, which emerge from processes and subsequently vanish into processes.

In a recent paper, El-Hani and Queiroz (2005a) appealed to Peirce's theory of signs in order to advance an account of downward determination, following Hulswit's (2001) thesis that a Peircean process and semiotic treatment of causation can play an important role in the construction of a process philosophical approach aiming at explaining the stability of the world in terms of dynamic relationships between events. Another helpful idea in Peirce's theory is that forms are treated as having a relational nature, and not as something embodied in a substance. In the present paper, we try to advance beyond this initial attempt to tackle the problem of downward determination based on Peirce's philosophy. But before we discuss how contributions from other philosophical positions can help in this endeavor, let us state here the basic ideas in our approach.

When we consider a system *A* and a set of *B*-elements that constitute *A*, we will say that the behavior of the *B*-elements is partly determined by *A*. This is a stronger claim than the assertion that the behavior of the *B*-elements cannot be adequately explained without reference to *A*. After all, the latter is an epistemological statement, and the former is an ontological one. At the same time, the former claim is weaker than the assertion that the behavior of the *B*-elements is partly brought about by *A*, since this latter statement is related to the idea of efficient cause.

It is clear that these ideas about determination have consequences for our explanatory endeavors, but it is necessary to formulate in consistent terms the idea of determination itself, and then subsequently derive epistemic consequences, such as those regarding efforts to explain part-whole relationships in complex systems. If we intend to develop a theory about downward determination, we should answer the following two questions: (i) What sorts of things are said to be determining and determined in a case of downward determination? (ii) What is the meaning of *determining* in downward determination? We intend to develop a coherent account about how principles of organization constrain and, thus, partially determine the behavior of a system's lower-level constituents. In this account of downward determination, a higher-level organizational pattern, interpreted as a general principle, is the determiner, while lower-level particular processes are determined.

To ascribe a clear meaning to the notion of determination, we should distinguish between causal and other kinds of determination, particularly, the kind involved in downward determination. Peirce himself may have been the first to suggest that downward causation may be regarded as a sort of formal causation (see EP 2, pp. 115-132. See also Hulswit, 2006). In the context of his philosophy, one finds a distinction between kinds of determination, namely the idea that determination has a logical and a causal sense (Ransdell, 1983). In dynamical terms, determination is associated by Peirce to the idea of production of an effect. We are thus dealing with causal determination in the intuitive sense of bringing about, elaborated in the modern theory of causality in terms of efficient causation. If we consider the logical sense of determination, in turn, it will be related to material implication: if p, then q. El-Hani and Queiroz (2005a) argued that, in this sense, determination should be understood as a constraining rather than a causally deterministic process, and used this sense of determination to conceptualize downward determination.

But there seems to be a problem with this appeal to Peirce, since, at first, the idea of logical determination seems to lead us from ontological to logical and/or epistemological discourse. Thus, the determinative relations would seem to have just an epistemological, not ontological (and, therefore, in a certain reading of the term, real) value, as Bunge (1979b, pp. 13-14) claims: "the higher levels cannot command or even obey the lower ones. All talk of interlevel action is elliptical or metaphorical, not literal." Maybe this is not a fatal problem, since, under the light of Peircean pragmatism, the logical structure of thought, rules, and generals is the same (Hulswit, 2001). Moreover, for Peirce, generals were not abstractions of the thinking mind, but real features of the world. Peirce was a realist about generals. He would probably agree with Emmeche and colleagues' (2000) formal realism of levels, which states that the structure, organization or form of an entity is objectively existent and is irreducible to lower-level forms or substances.

Juarrero explicitly opposes Bunge's assertion in the following terms:

> Complex adaptive systems have proven Bunge wrong; their interlevel relationships, however tangled, are real, not just epistemological. The emergence of relatively autonomous levels of organization carries with it the emergence of relatively autonomous qualities; quantitative changes produce qualitative changes. (Juarrero, 2000, p. 32)

As we will see below, it is possible that Juarrero's account, combined with Peirce's idea of logical determination, can offer us a clearer view about how downward determination can be said to take place in the world, not only in our logical abstractions.

Downward determination does not have a causal nature in the sense that it does not concern productive events, which bring about an effect. To expand on this issue, we can take as a point of departure the idea that the relations between the components at the lower level of a given system, which instantiates a token of a given type of structure, are constrained by the organizational, regulatory influence of this structure. From this idea, we argue that a logical determinative relation holds between higher-level organizational principles and particular processes at the lower level. Nevertheless, in order to allow for statistical relationships between organizational principles and particular processes, we treat this determinative influence as a propensity relation: If some lower-level entities $a,b,c,...,n$ are under the influence of a general organizational principle, W, they will show a tendency to behave in certain specific ways, and, thus, to instantiate a set of specific processes. The determining influence in this case is from a higher-level general organizational principle on particular lower-level processes, and can be framed as follows: if $a,b,c,...,n$ are under the influence of W, then they will show a tendency, a disposition, to instantiate process p or a set of processes $\{P\}$. In other terms, we treat downward determination here as a would-be tendency, a relation leading to a higher likelihood that a given process or set of processes will happen.

When we deal with propensities in probabilistic terms, we can appeal to Popper's propensities theory of probability, first put forward in 1957 and developed in a series of papers and books (Popper, 1959, 1983, 1990). Popper's propensity theory puts probability in the world,[26] instead of leaving it to our minds or logical abstractions:

> probabilities must be 'physically real' – they must be physical propensities, abstract relational properties of physical situation, like Newtonian forces, and 'real', not only in the sense that they could influence the experimental results, but also in the sense that they could, under certain circumstances (coherence), interfere, i.e. interact, with one another. (Popper, 1959, p. 28)

In these terms, probability comes to be seen as a physical propensity, or disposition, or, else, a tendency that a given type of physical situation produces a certain kind of result or a limit of relative frequency of such a result. As it is the case with all dispositional properties, propensities show some similarities with Aristotelian potentialities. Nevertheless, while disposition is conceived in the Aristotelian system as an inherent property of things, in the propensity theory nothing is inherent in the

---

26. Popper needed a theory of objective probability to account for probability as applied to single events. In his book *The Logic of Scientific Discovery* (Popper, 1959/2002), he defended a version of the frequentist theory to lead with the problem, but afterwards perceived that that theory was inadequate and a new theory of objective probability had to be introduced. The frequentist theory could say nothing about single events, and only a subjectivist theory of probability was available to account for those events. But an objectivist like Popper could not be satisfied with a subjectivist theory of probability (Gillies, 2000).

object, and propensities are rather taken to be relational properties (Popper, 1959). Propensities are not inherent properties of an object, but are inherent just in a situation, of which the object is obviously a part. Just as a newly synthesized chemical compound generates new possibilities of forming new compounds, new propensities always create new possibilities, and these new possibilities tend to be realized so as to create, once again, new possibilities (Popper, 1990). Ulanowicz (1999) argues that one of the conclusions we can drawn from these ideas is that, since propensities occur juxtaposed, interfering with one another, in such a manner that new possibilities tend to arise, "conversely, one must add constraints in order to 'organize' the more indeterminate configuration." (Ulanowicz, p. 133).

In these terms, we can speak of a downward determinative influence of a higher-level organizing principle, W, so that there is a greater physical propensity that a given process, p, or set of processes $\{P\}$, occurs than in a situation in which the components of this process are not under the influence of W. Or, to put it differently, a general organizational principle, W, operates as a physical constraint over the occurrence of a given process, p, or set of processes $\{P\}$, if, given the instantiation of W, the physical propensity that p occurs is higher than the propensity of its occurrence in the absence of W. Therefore, Popper's propensity theory can give us the tools for putting in the world, and not in our minds, downward determination interpreted as a change in the propensity of the occurrence of a given process resulting from its being under the influence of a general, higher-level organizational principle.

It is heuristically fruitful, in our view, to formulate the idea of downward determination in terms of such a propensity account. Such a formulation is reinforced by its connections with Juarrero's thesis of top-down constraints (discussed above), which claims that the influence of wholes over parts consists in altering the prior probabilities of the components' behaviors:

> The higher-level's organization is the change in probability of the lower-level events. Top-down causes cause by changing the prior probability of the components' behavior... (Juarrero, 1999, p. 146)

The difference between causal and downward determination is striking: While causal determination is a *productive* event, which brings about effects, structural determination is rather a *subtractive* event, which, as explained above, constrains the possibilities of behaviors of a system's components. The top-down constraints imposed by the organizing principle W are limiting in the sense that they constrain the possible behaviors of the parts, and, thus, eliminates possible effects rather than produces new effects, and, by doing so, makes it possible that the system as a whole show an enhanced set of capabilities, due to the coordination of the behavior of its parts. Thus, these constraints are also creative, in a functional sense, since they enable the components to efficiently take part in a set of processes, by channeling their behavior, so as to say, towards a particular collection of activities. As components of a larger system, the parts come to play new functional roles. Certainly, if we framed this account, as we did above, in terms of downward determination, it will become relatively close to the neo-Aristotelian perspective on downward causation, with the caveat that we shall rather refer to downward determination and embed this notion within a process-oriented approach—which is at odds with an Aristotelian view, which shows a clear bias in favor of entities and substances.

10. Concluding remarks

It is quite clear to us—as it certainly is for our readers—that the idea of downward determination sketched above demands further work in order to be formulated in a clearer and more fruitful way. We should clarify, however, that it is not the case that the arguments put forward here merely means that we are naming differently the same basic idea expressed in several accounts of downward causation. Notice, first of all, that even though the issue at stake in this paper is partly a terminological one, this does not mean it is unimportant. From a pragmatist standpoint, which we assume here as a metaphilosophical position, terminological issues are rather fundamental since philosophical problems and views are constituted by how we speak about them in different philosophical traditions (see El-Hani & Pihlström, 2002a, 2002b, for a similar discussion with regard to the concept of emergent properties). Secondly, it is not a just a terminological issue we are addressing here, because it is in fact embedded within an effort to make the central ideas in downward determination clearer, by confronting important difficulties in the previous literature on the theme. Thirdly, from a strategic point of view—which we do think it is consequential to consider—to speak about downward determination instead of causation can help increasing the acceptance of the idea that a whole can indeed alter the behavior of its parts, since it is basically the same move made when it was perceived that it was incoherent to speak of supervenience (and, for that matter, also physical realization) as a causal determinative relation. Finally, as commented above, by avoiding the Aristotelian framework, we move away from a substance-oriented—which can hamper, in our view, a proper understanding of part-whole relationships—to a process-oriented approach.

Acknowledgements

We are indebted to CAPES, CNPq, and FAPESB for grants and funding that supported the research project with which this paper is associated. We are also thankful to João Queiroz and Claus Emmeche for important discussions about topics related to emergence and downward determination.

References

Alexander, S. (1979). *Space, time, and deity.* Gloucester: Peter Smith. (Originally published in 1920).
Allen, J. F. (2001). Bioinformatics and discovery: Induction beckons again. *Bioessays, 23,*104-107.
Andersen, P. B., Emmeche, C., Finnemann, N. O., & Christiansen, P. V. (Eds.). (2000). *Downward causation: Minds, bodies and matter.* Aarhus: Aarhus University Press.

Aristotle. (1995). *The complete works of Aristotle*. (The Revised Oxford Translation, 2 Vols., J. Barnes, Ed.). Princeton: Princeton University Press.

Aristotle. (1996). *Physics*. Oxford: Oxford University Press.

Azzone, G. F. (1998). The cement of medical thought: Evolutionary emergence and downward causation. *History and Philosophy of the Life Sciences, 20* (2), 163-187.

Baas, N. A. (1996). A framework for higher-order cognition and consciousness. In S. R. Hameroff, A. W. Kaszniak, & A. C. Scott (Eds.), *Toward a science of consciousness* (pp. 633-648). Cambridge, MA: The MIT Press.

Baas, N. A., & Emmeche, C. (1997). On emergence and explanation, *Intellectica, 25,* 67-83.

Barabasi, A. L., & Oltvai, Z. N. (2004). Network biology: Understanding the cell's functional organization. *Nature Reviews Genetics, 5,* 101-113.

Beckermann, A., Flohr, H., & Kim, J. (Eds). (1992). *Emergence or reduction?: Essays on the prospects of nonreductive physicalism*. Berlin: Walter de Gruyter.

Bedau, M. (1997). Weak emergence. *Nous* (Suppl. S), 375-399.

Bedau, M. (2002). Downward causation and autonomy of weak emergence. *Principia, 6*(1), 5-50. (Special Issue on Emergence and Downward Causation, C. N. El-Hani, Ed.)

Bergandi, D. (1995). "Reductionist holism": An oxymoron or a philosophical chimera of EP Odum's systems ecology? *Ludus Vitalis, 5,* 145-180.

Blitz, D. (1992). *Emergent evolution: Qualitative novelty and the levels of reality*. Dordrecht: Kluwer.

Boogerd, F. C., Bruggeman, F. J., Richardson, R. C., Stephan, A., & Westerhoff, H. (2005). Emergence and its place in nature: A case study of biochemical networks, *Synthese, 145*(1), 131-164.

Broad, C. D. (1925). *The mind and its place in nature*. London: Routledge and Kegan Paul. Retrieved April 6th 2008 from http://www.ditext.com/broad/mpn/mpn.html.

Bruggeman, F. J., Westerhoff, H. V., & Boogerd, F. C. (2002), BioComplexity: A pluralist research strategy is necessary for a mechanistic explanation of the "live" state. *Philosophical Psychology, 15* (4), 411-440.

Bruni, L. E. (2003). *A sign-theoretic approach to biotechnology*. Unpublished dissertation. Copenhagen: Institute of Molecular Biology – Department of Biological Chemistry – The Biosemiotic Group, University of Copenhagen

Bunge, M. (1979a). *Causality and modern science* (3rd ed.). New York: Dover Publications.

Bunge, M. (1979b). *Ontology II: A world of systems*. Dordrecht: D. Reidel.

Campbell, D. T. (1974). 'Downward causation' in hierarchically organised biological systems. In F. Ayala, & T. Dobzhansky (Eds.), *Studies in the philosophy of biology: Reduction and related problems* (pp. 179-186). Berkeley: University of California Press.

Carroll, S. B., Grenier, J. K., & Weatherbee, S. D. (2005). *From DNA to diversity: Molecular genetics and the evolution of animal design*. Oxford: Blackwell.

Chong, L., & Ray, L. B. (2002). Whole-istic biology. *Science, 295* (5560), 1661-1661.

Cunningham, B. (2001). The re-emergence of 'emergence'. *Philosophy of Science, 68* (PSA 2000 Proceedings), S62-S75.

El-Hani, C. N. (2002a). On the reality of emergents. *Principia, 6* (1),51-87. (Special Issue on Emergence and Downward Causation, C. N. El-Hani, Ed.)

El-Hani, C. N. (2002b). Uma ciência da organização viva: Organicismo, emergentismo e ensino de biologia. In W. J. Silva Filho (Ed.), *Epistemologia e Ensino de Ciências* (pp. 199-244). Salvador-Bahia, Brazil: Arcadia/UCSal.

El-Hani, C. N. & Emmeche, C. (2000). On some theoretical grounds for an organism-centered biology: Property emergence, supervenience, and downward causation, *Theory in Biosciences, 119,* 234-275.

El-Hani, C. N. & Pereira, A. M. (1999). Understanding biological causation. In V. G. Hardcastle (Ed.), *Where biology meets psychology: Philosophical essays* (pp. 333-356). Cambridge, MA: The MIT Press.

El-Hani, C. N., & Pereira, A. M. (2000). Higher-level descriptions: Why should we preserve them? In P. B. Andersen, C. Emmeche, N. O. Finnemann, & P. V. Christiansen (Eds.), *Downward causation: Minds, bodies and matter* (pp. 118-142). Aarhus: Aarhus University Press.

El-Hani, C. N., & Pihlström, S. (2002a). Emergence theories and pragmatic realism. *Essays in Philosophy, 3*(2). Electronic journal: http://www.humboldt.edu/~essays/ pihlstrom.html

El-Hani, C. N., & Pihlström, S. (2002b). A pragmatic realist view of emergence. *Manuscrito, XXV* (Sp. number), 105-154.

El-Hani, C. N. & Queiroz, J. (2005a). Downward determination. *Abstracta, 1*(2), 162-192.

El-Hani, C. N., & Queiroz, J. (2005b). Modos de irredutibilidade das propriedades emergentes. *Scientiae Studia, 3* (1), 9-41.

El-Hani, C. N., & Videira, A. A. P. (2001). Causação Descendente, Emergência de Propriedades e Modos Causais Aristotélicos. *Theoria, 16* (2), 301-329.

Emmeche, C. (1997). *Defining life, explaining emergence*. On-line paper retrieved November 28th, 2008 from http:// www.nbi.dk/~emmeche/. Also published in two parts as: Emmeche, C. (1997). Autopoietic systems, replicators, and the search for a meaningful biologic definition of life, *Ultimate Reality and Meaning, 20*(4), 244-264; and, Emmeche, C. (1998). Defining life as a semiotic phenomenon, *Cybernetics & Human Knowing, 5*(1), 3-17.

Emmeche, C., Køppe, S., & Stjernfelt, F. (1997). Explaining emergence: Towards an ontology of levels. *Journal for General Philosophy of Science, 28,* 83-119.

Emmeche, C., Køppe, S. & Stjernfelt, F. (2000). Levels, emergence and three versions of downward causation. In P. B. Andersen, C. Emmeche, N. O. Finnemann, & P. V. Christiansen (Eds.), *Downward causation: Minds, bodies and matter* (pp. 13-34). Aarhus: Aarhus University Press.

Gavin, A.-C., Bösche, M., Krause, R., Grandi, P., Marzioch, M., Bauer, A., et al. (2002). Functional organization of the yeast proteome by systematic analysis of protein complexes. *Nature, 415*, 141-147.

Gillett, C. (2002). Strong emergence as a defense of non-reductive physicalism: A physicalist metaphysics for 'downward' determination. *Principia, 6* (1), 89-120. (Special Issue on Emergence and Downward Causation. C. N. El-Hani, Ed.)

Hulswit, M. (2001). Semeiotic and the cement of the universe: A Peircean process approach to causation. *Transactions of the Charles S. Peirce Society: A Quarterly Journal in American Philosophy, XXXVII* (3), 339-363.

Hulswit, M. (2006). How causal is downward causation? *Journal for General Philosophy of Science, 36* (2), 261-287.

Humphreys, P. (1996). Aspects of emergence. *Philosophical Topics 24* (1), 53-70.

Humphreys, P. (1997a). Emergence, not supervenience. *Philosophy of Science, 64* (proceedings, Philosophy of Science Association) S337-S345.

Humphreys, P. (1997b). How properties emerge. *Philosophy of Science, 64* (1), 1-17.

Ideker, T., Galitski, T. & Hood, L. (2001). A new approach to decoding life: Systems biology. *Annual Review of Genomics and Human Genetics, 2*, 343-372.

Juarrero, A. (1999). *Dynamics in action: Intentional behavior as a complex system.* Cambridge: The MIT Press.

Juarrero, A. (2000). Dynamics in action: Intentional behavior as a complex system. *Emergence, 2* (2), 24-57.

Keller, E. F. (2000). *The century of the gene.* Cambridge: Harvard University Press.

Keller, E. F. (2005). The century beyond the gene. *Journal of Biosciences, 30*, 3-10.

Kim, J. (1992). 'Downward Causation' in Emergentism and Nonreductive Materialism. In A. Beckermann, H. Flohr, & J. Kim (Eds.), *Emergence or reduction? Essays on the prospects of nonreductive physicalism* (pp. 119-138). Berlin: Walter de Gruyter.

Kim, J. (1993). *Supervenience and mind.* New York: Cambridge University Press.

Kim, J. (1996). *Philosophy of mind.* Boulder, CO: Westview Press.

Kim, J. (1997). Supervenience, emergence, and realization in the philosophy of mind. In M. Carrier, P. K. Machamer (Eds.), *Mindscape: Philosophy, science, and the mind* (pp. 271-293). Pittsburgh: University of Pittsburgh Press.

Kim, J. (1998). *Mind in a physical world: An essay on the mind-body problem and mental causation.* Cambridge, MA: The MIT Press.

Kim, J. (1999). Making sense of emergence. *Philosophical Studies, 95*, 3-36.

Kim, J. (2006). Emergence: Core ideas and issues. *Synthese, 151* (3), 547-559.

Kitano, H. (2002). Systems biology: A brief overview. *Science, 295* (5560), 1662-1664.

Klee, R. L. (1984) Micro-determinism and concepts of emergence. *Philosophy of Science, 51*(1), 44-63.

Lear, J. (1988). *Aristotle: The desire to understand.* New York: Cambridge University Press.

Lee, T. I., Rinaldi, N. J., Robert, R., Odom, D. T., Bar-Joseph, Z. Gerber, G. K., et al. (2002). Transcriptional regulatory networks in Saccharomyces cerevisiae. *Science 298*, 799-804.

Leite, M. (2006). Retórica determinista no genoma humano. *Scientiae Studia, 4*, 421-452.

Levine, J. (1983). Materialism and qualia: The explanatory gap. *Pacific Philosophical Quarterly, 64* (4), 354-361.

Levins, R., & Lewontin, R. (1980). Dialectics and reductionism in ecology. *Synthese, 43* (1), 47-78.

Lloyd Morgan, C. (1923). *Emergent Evolution.* London: Williams and Norgate. Retrieved September 19th 2008 from http://www.brocku.ca/MeadProject/Morgan/Morgan_1923/Morgan02_00.html

McCarthy, J. (2004). Tackling the challenges of interdisciplinary bioscience. *Nature Reviews Molecular Cell Biology, 5*, 933-937.

Nagel, T. (1974). What is it like to be a bat? *Philosophical Review, 4*, 435-50.

Nature. (2005). Editorial: In pursuit of systems. *Nature, 435*, 1.

Newman, D. V. (1996). Emergence and strange attractors. *Philosophy of Science, 63*(2), 245-261.

O'Connor, T. (1994). Emergent properties. *American Philosophical Quarterly, 31*(2), 91-104.

Peirce, C. S. (1998). *The essential Peirce: Selected philosophical writings* (Vol. 2, Ed. by the Peirce Edition Project). Bloomington: Indiana University Press. (cited as EP, followed by volume and paragraph).

Peltonen, L. & McKusick, V. A. (2001). Dissecting human disease in the postgenomic era. *Science, 291*, 1224-1229.

Pihlström, S. (1999). What shall we do with emergence? A survey of a fundamental issue in the metaphysics and epistemology of science. *South African Journal of Philosophy, 18*, 192-210.

Pihlström, S. (2002). The re-emergence of the emergence debate. *Principia, 6*(1), 133-181. (Special Issue on Emergence and Downward Causation, C. N. El-Hani, Ed.)

Polanyi, M. (1968). Life's irreducible structure. *Science.* 160, 1308-1312.

Popper, K. R. (1959). The propensity interpretation of probability. *British Journal for the Philosophy of Science, 10* (37), 25-42.

Popper, K. R. (1983). Realism and the aim of science: From the postscript to the logic of scientific discovery. Totowa, NJ: Rowman & Littlefield.

Popper, K. R. (1990). *A world of propensities.* Bristol: Thoemmes Antiquarian Books.

Popper, K. R. (2002). *The logic of scientific discovery.* London: Routledge. (Orignally published in 1959)

Putnam, H. (1994). *Words and life* (J. Conant, Ed.). Cambridge, MA: Harvard University Press.

Putnam, H. (2000). Aristotle's mind and the contemporary mind. In D. Sfendoni-Mentzou (Ed.), *Aristotle and contemporary science* (pp. 7-28). New York: Peter Lang.

Queiroz, J. & El-Hani, C. N. (2006). Semiosis as an emergent process. *Transactions of the Charles S. Peirce Society: A Quarterly Journal in American Philosophy, 42*(1), 78-116.

Ransdell, J. (1983). Peircean semiotic. Manuscript.

Rescher, N. (1996). *Process metaphysics: An introduction to process philosophy.* New York: SUNY Press.

Rescher, N. (2002). Process philosophy. In E. N. Zalta (Ed.), *The Stanford Encyclopedia of Philosophy* (Spring 2008 Edition). Retrieved July 11th 2008 from http://plato.stanford.edu/archives/spr2008/entries/process-philosophy/

Riedl, R. (1997) From four forces back to four causes. *Evolution and Cognition, 3*, 148-158.

Rosen, R. (1991). *Life itself.* New York: Columbia University Press.

Ross, D. (1995). *Aristotle.* London: Routledge. (Originally published in 1923)

Salthe, S. N. (1985). *Evolving hierarchical systems: Their structure and representation.* New York: Columbia University Press.

Salthe, S. N. (1993). *Development and evolution: Complexity and change in biology.* Cambridge, MA: The MIT Press.

Savigny, E. V. (1985). An emergence view of linguistic meaning. *American Philosophical Quarterly, 22*(3), 211-220.

Schröder, J. (1998). Emergence: Non-deducibility or downwards causation? *Philosophical Quarterly, 48* (193), 433-452.

Seibt, J. (1996). The myth of the substance and the fallacy of misplaced concreteness. *Acta Analytica, 15*.

Sperry, R. W. (1969). A modified concept of consciousness. *Psychological Review, 76,* 532-536.

Sperry, R. W. (1980). Mind-brain interaction: mentalism, yes; dualism, no, *Neuroscience, 5,* 195-206.

Sperry, R. W. (1983). *Science and moral priority: Merging mind, brain, and human values.* New York: Columbia University Press.

Sperry, R. W. (1986). Macro- versus micro-determination. *Philosophy of Science, 53,* 265-275.

Sperry, R. W. (1991). In defense of mentalism and emergent interaction. *Journal of Mind and Behavior, 12,* 221-245.

Stephan, A. (1997). Armchair Arguments against Emergentism. *Erkenntnis, 46,* 305-314.

Stephan, A. (1998). Varieties of Emergence in Artificial and Natural Systems. *Zeitschrift für Naturforschung, 53c,* 639-656.

Stephan, A. (1999). Varieties of emergentism, *Evolution and Cognition, 5*(1), 49-59.

Stephan, A. (2004). Phenomenal emergence. *Networks, 3*(4), 91-102.

Stephan, A. (2006). *The dual role of 'emergence' in the philosophy of mind and in cognitive science. Synthese, 151* (3), 485-498.

Stephanopoulos, G., Alper, H., & Moxley, J. (2004). Exploiting biological complexity for strain improvement through systems biology. *Nature Biotechnology, 22* (10), 1261-1267.

Stephens, C. (1998). Bacterial sporulation: A question of commitment? *Current Biology, 8,* R45-R48.

Strohman, R. (2002). Maneuvering in the Complex Path from Genotype to Phenotype. *Science, 296,* 701-703.

Symons, J. (2002). Emergence and reflexive downward causation. *Principia, 6* (1), 183-202. (Special Issue on Emergence and Downward Causation, C. N. El-Hani, Ed.)

Ulanowicz, R. E. (1999). Life after Newton: an ecological metaphysic. *BioSystems, 50,* 127-142.

Van de Vijver, G., Salthe, S. N., & Delpos, M. (Eds.). (1998). *Evolutionary systems.* Dordrecht: Kluwer.

Van de Vijver, G., Van Speybroeck, L., & Vandevyvere, W. (2003). Reflecting on complexity of biological systems: Kant and beyond? *Acta Biotheoretica, 51,* 101-140.

Van Gulick, R. (1993). Who is in charge here? And who's doing all the work? In J. Heil & A. Mele (Eds.). *Mental causation* (pp. 233-256). Oxford: Oxford University Press.

Venter, J. C. et al. (2001). The sequence of the human genome. *Science, 291* (5507), 1304 - 1351.

Forsythe, K. (2006). *Ying Cat.* 45 cm x 60 cm, acrylic on canvas.

Cybernetics And Human Knowing. Vol. 15, nos. 3-4, pp. 135-144

Downward Causation Requires Naturalized Constraints:
A Comment on Vieira & El-Hani

Alvaro Moreno[1]

I have no essential objections against the central assumption of Vieira and El-Hani's paper, namely, that downward causation plays an important role in our current understanding of biological phenomena. To tell the truth, I am not even quite sure that my disagreement concerning their proposal of substituting the concept of causation (in downward causation) with that of determination would play a very important role in the issue at stake. However, I have had certain doubts concerning the authors' position throughout the reading of the paper, since they often seem to endorse key arguments against downward causation, and then, several pages later, seem to reject them. And the section of conclusions is not very helpful for clarifying their position. At the end, even though they reject anti-downward causation positions, I have the impression that the authors seem to be more worried about the criticism against the concept of downward causation than about the consequences of dispensing with it. As they say, "we have to face the legion of difficulties besetting the notion of downward causation" (this issue, p. 110). One can ask, however, if the rejection of downward causation would not imply even worse problems for our current understanding of complex systems (Just think about the role played by concepts like selective constraint or regulatory control in biology, and try to restate current biological knowledge without these kinds of concepts).

As I understand the authors' position, developed in the second part of the paper, their central line of argument is articulated around the concept of constraint, interpreted as embodied boundary conditions harnessing lower level dynamics (or laws). In particular, they develop this idea in section 7, where they seem to agree with Juarrero's (1999) explanation of complex systems (and, in our case, biological systems) in these terms. As they say,

> the boundary conditions established by the system's organization select, among all the possible behaviors the constituents might show, a more limited set ($W - x$) of behaviors they will effectively show, as parts of that kind of system. In turn, by constraining the behaviors of its parts, the system shows enhanced capacities, in the sense that it becomes capable of displaying behaviors we would not observe if the system did not constrain, and, thus, coordinate, orchestrate the processes which take place within it. Constraints increase the likelihood that the parts of a system be engaged in relations which, in turn, are embedded in a certain set of particular processes, which is smaller than the set of processes they could be part of in the absence of the system. And, in turn, the instantiation

---

1. Departamento de Logica y Filosofia de la Ciencia, Universidad del Pais Vasco UPV/EHU, Apartado 1249, 20080 Donostia, San Sebastian, Spain. Email: alvaro.moreno@ehu.es

of these processes in a coordinated manner allows the system to show novel higher-level behaviors, increasing its freedom to behave. (this issue, p. 122)

I essentially concur with this perspective. However, the validity of any justification of downward causation on the concept of constraint lies, in my opinion, in the possibility of naturalizing this latter concept. As I have explained elsewhere (Moreno & Umerez, 2000), in physics constraints are embedded boundary conditions, which human observers selectively impose in order to simplify the description of the action of laws. In this sense, constraints are not reducible to laws. But, if constraints are taken only in an epistemological sense, they cannot help us in understanding the very causal structure of complex systems. Whether we conclude either that they have no ontological status (which would undermine seriously the thesis of downward causation) or the contrary; the assessment about the ontological status of constraints seems a crucial issue. Therefore, as long as the origin of constraints remains unanswered, we face serious problems. How to defend at the same time the non-reduction of constraints to laws and avoid dualism? How to pretend that constraints have an ontological status derived from, but not reducible to, laws? If we do not arrive at an explanation of the origins of constraints (i.e., the origins of natural systems endowed with constraints), we will face either an infinite regress or a radical dualism.

Now, since constraints are associated with complex systems, it seems sensible to address the question by looking for the appearance of (a minimal form of) constraints. How is it possible to explain the origin of constraints in an abiotic universe? We can assume that the laws and the initial conditions of the universe have led to a progressively diversified world, in which a great variety of (more or less) stable aggregates of matter is generated. Now, once these stable aggregates appear, things become a little bit different. Let us see in more detail how things change by an example, which I take from H. Pattee:

> Suppose you begin with a glass of water with common salt in solution. The sodium and chloride ions are free to move about in three dimensions. We say "free" only in the sense that they each follow the laws of motion of non-interacting particles with only occasional collisions with other molecules or ions. More precisely, we say that most of the time each particle has three translational degrees of freedom. Now suppose that after some time a collection of ions has formed a substantial crystal. This structure can now act as a constraint for some of the ions that land on one of its surfaces. These ions now have fewer degrees of freedom … [The structure] is a collective constraint on individual elements that make up the collection. … A more realistic variation of this example is the screw-dislocation crystal growth … Instead of each ion binding only at the points of a perfect lattice, there are imperfections in crystal growth which produce a new kind of constraint …[that] has two properties: 1) It speeds up the binding of ions by an enormous factor, and 2) it preserves its screw structure as the crystal grows. (Pattee, 1973, pp. 82-83)

One could say, from this example, that in certain circumstances, many microscopic parts, freezing up their degrees of freedom, constitute stable aggregates. Once a certain threshold of size is attained, these aggregates become macroscopic entities that harness the dynamics of many other microscopic elements in their proximity. Thus we may call them constraints, as Pattee does. But, since there is not any observer for whom this description is more practical than the detailed, microscopic one (i.e., the basal description, as Kim calls it), the question at stake is whether the consideration of the crystal structure as a constraint makes some difference in how things evolve. Anti-emergentists may convincingly argue that in this example (and in many other similar ones) the difference exists only in the eye of the beholder.

However, there is a problem with this view, since the more complex a system, the less probable become a) its appearance, and b) its persistence. Let me explain why: simple building blocks generate spontaneously composite stable structures (atoms, molecules, macromolecules…) due to different levels of forces[2] (Simon, 1969). As a result of this low-level interactions, increasingly complex stable structures appear (in many cases stable structures showing new interactive properties, which are not present in their separate parts, such as superconductivity, chemical affinity, etc.). So far, so good. However, as far as the complexity of the structures increases, its maintenance becomes a problem, because thermal noise increases fragility. In addition, in abiotic conditions the formation of increasingly complex structures becomes also increasingly unlikely, because they require the coincidence or coordination of many highly specific processes (as we will see later, this is the case of enzymes). Even worse is the case of thermodynamically dissipative aggregates, given that no force ensures their cohesion. And yet, we obviously live in a world with plenty of highly complex systems (we, ourselves, are an eloquent example!). Therefore, something else than initial conditions and basic laws is required to explain a world of complex systems. Actually, the problem is even worse, since most of the complex systems we live with are thermodynamically dissipative systems, namely, composite aggregates whose parts are tied together without intrinsic forces ensuring their cohesion. As I will explain, this is where an ontological concept of constraint is going to enter.

How can a dissipative aggregate first appear and, then, persist? Suppose that chance produces from time to time unlikely aggregates made of non-cohesive parts. These aggregates should be ephemeral, since no force keeps together their parts (moreover, they are submitted to permanent fluctuations). But now, suppose that, given certain boundary conditions in far-from-equilibrium conditions, certain ephemeral collective aggregates affect the neighboring microscopic trajectories in such a way that a causal loop is formed, and, therefore, the (macroscopic) aggregate is forced to persist. Actually, we can find in the physical world different examples of this type of process, like hurricanes. They are called *dissipative structures* (Nicolis & Prigogine, 1977). Interestingly, in these dissipative systems the maintenance of the global structure depends not only on a specific set of boundary conditions, but also on the effect they produce on the microscopic dynamics. Once it has appeared, the pattern constrains the dynamics of the system's components so that the produced pattern in turn produces itself. For instance, in the case of Bénard convection cells,

---

2. The strongest force (around 140 mev) holds together the nuclei of the atoms, and the weakest (around 0.5 mev), the tertiary structure of large macromolecules. As defined by Murray Gell-Mann, the (structural) complexity of a given entity is the (outcome of) the sequence of accidental events (from the Big Bang to the constitution of such entity) frozen in the different levels of stability that such entity embodies.

beyond a certain temperature gradient, the fluctuations are reinforced rather than suppressed; then, a new macroscopic order emerges, caused by a macroscopic fluctuation and stabilized by an exchange of energy with the environment. Realize that since heat will be dissipated more rapidly through the formation of a coherent pattern of hexagonally arrayed convection cells than through turbulent boiling (these structures increase the rate of heat transfer and gradient destruction in the system), this pattern is what allows the system to dissipate the available thermal energy most rapidly. That is why—though in a minimal sense—the emergent pattern (the creation of hexagonal cells) contributes to its own maintenance. In other words, they are, at least to a certain degree, self-maintaining structures. We are now talking about a certain type of constraint whose condition of possibility (i.e., maintenance) is the creation of a causal loop. As Van Gulick (1993, pp. 251-252) has pointed out, these patterns exist because they are self-sustaining.[3] Also Juarrero (1999) has tried to naturalize constraints in terms of closure of feedback loops.

More recently, S. Kauffman (2000; see also Kauffman et al., 2008) has proposed a similar way to naturalize the concept of constraint. According to this author, constraints appear (and are propagated) whenever some material configuration in a part of the universe generates a loop he calls a constraint-work cycle. The fundamental idea is that a constraint is any material aggregate that, by its structure, harnesses the flow of matter and energy in such a way that some useful result is created.[4] For example, in a steam machine, disordered molecules of hot water (steam) are harnessed by a set of metallic devices (constraints) in such a way that ordered energy is obtained. When used for several purposes, this ordered energy is called work. Now, how can we, in a prebiotic context, talk about useful energy (work)? Useful for what? Kauffman proposes a very elegant solution to this question: work and constraints co-define each other: Ordered release of energy becomes useful when it is used for the construction of the constraints harnessing the flows of energy that produce them. In other words, a naturalized concept of constraints has to consider them as material structures embedded in a closed organization that (at least partially) they contribute to maintain.

Actually, any attempt of a scientific account for understanding biogenesis should explain not only how constraints arise, but also how they propagate, become

---

3. Of course, in these minimal examples we cannot say that self-maintenance is due to a selective action on the lower-level entities.

4. Kauffman and co-workers (2008) have recently explained the origin of constraints in the following terms: "We consider a single, but complex case in cosmic evolution. It is well known that molecular grains are found in interstellar space. These grains aggregate up to the scale of planetessimals. Now it is also well known that the grains have surfaces with complex molecular features on which complex chemistry appears to be occurring. The grains themselves act as constraints, or boundary conditions, that confine reacting substrates, hence may catalyze reactions … In some cases, the product molecules presumably are bound to the growing grain, thereby modifying the boundary conditions afforded by the grain, which in turn modifies the chemical reactions that can occur. Furthermore, the product molecules can be novel substrates … which again allow novel chemical reactions to occur. In short, the grains appear to behave as constraints that can … create new constraints enabling such processes and linked processes, and can create novel sources of free energy in the form of novel substrates able to enter into new chemical reactions … Then the growing grains appear to be cases in which matter, energy, and continuously evolving boundary conditions and novel sources of free energy emerge, and condition the future evolution of the grains" (Kauffman et al. 2008. p. 43).

progressively more complex and form entangled webs. How, in certain conditions, chemical processes will generate self-maintaining systems, that is, more or less stable configurations of matter (and flows of energy), and how the possibility of reaching further steps will be based (at least in part) on the causal role played by these former configurations (a mechanism allowing a cumulative increase of complexity is fundamental)? In part, Simon's (1969) theory of hierarchical systems is helpful, but since it is assumed that biogenesis implies increasingly complex far-from equilibrium systems, something has to explain the persistent continuity of local situations of lower entropy. Of course, locally low entropy situations are possible without violation of the second law by increasing entropy in the environment, but this is not an explanation of why and how this happens *persistently*. For the scientific community, an explanation of this fact requires a plausible mechanism, which in this case means three things:

1. that the starting point should be a configuration of matter and energy, taken as (a set of) boundary conditions, whose appearance and (relative) stability should be explainable in terms of the known laws of physics and chemistry, which in turn were harnessed by the former history of the universe, that is, laws harnessed by embodied sets of successive accidental events (from the Big Bang to the constitution of this local domain of the universe) frozen at the different levels of stability

2. that each new step will consist not only in the generation of new structural, thermodynamically conservative structures, but also of macroscopic dissipative configurations of matter and energy such that 1) the underlying dynamics of microscopic components becomes affected and 2) the new microscopic dynamics of the system's components contributes, in turn, to the maintenance of this constraint. In other words, dynamically speaking, the appearance of constraints in this context leads the system to a fixed point, which therefore stabilizes both the constraint(s) and what Kim calls its/their *basal conditions*. (Notice that the apparent synchronicity between constraints and their basal conditions is only a consequence of the stabilization. Later, this is what really matters.

3. that from here it becomes more likely the appearance of new, more complex, conservative and dissipative constraints, which in turn would be stabilized if they satisfy recursive interaction with their basal conditions. Therefore, the process can be described as a temporal causal sequence of constraints, harnessing low level conditions, generating stability (by finding recurrent causal loops), thus allowing the exploration of a new level of complexity (a new, more complex constraint), and so on. This process has been called the exploration of the adjacent possible by S. Kauffman (2000).

This exploration of the adjacent possible will depend on the appearance of increasingly complex constraints. An example of this is the origin of a new and interesting form of constraint: enzymes. In current living cells chemical reactions are channeled by enzymes. The action of enzymes is similar in principle to other types of chemical catalysis: By providing an alternative reaction route and by stabilizing intermediates, enzymes reduce the energy required to reach the highest energy transition state of the reaction. The reduction of activation energy (ΔG) increases the number of reactant molecules with enough energy to reach the activation energy and form the product. Thus, enzymes modify the probability of reaching the reaction's transition state by lowering associated activation energy, and, then, reaction speed can be increased in several orders of magnitude without temperature being altered.

The typical way in which enzymes constrain chemical processes is by momentarily adhering to the relevant substrate, providing it with a local surface to interact, creating conditions where its transformation into product is facilitated. Effective catalysis takes place when the *active site* (i.e., the three-dimensional surface that the enzyme provides to the substrate, thus destabilizing it and activating the reaction) *fits* in a more adjusted way into the substrate. The active site is continually reshaped by interactions with the substrate as the substrate interacts with the enzyme.[5] The advantages of the induced fit mechanism arise due to the stabilizing effect of strong enzyme binding. (Obviously, this requires that the size of the enzyme reach a point capable of providing a rich enough variety of 3D specific forms). As a consequence of the fit mechanism, the enzyme lower the activation energy, either by distorting the substrate, by creating an environment with the opposite charge distribution to that of the transition state, or by other means. Since in the absence of the enzyme other possible reactions might lead to different products (because in those conditions these different products are formed faster), enzymes selectively alter the microscopic interactions of the substrates. This causal action takes place by changing the rates of reactions, and there is no way to describe this form of action but as an irreversible and statistical process.

Thus, the first lesson is that, instead of the former types of constraints, which were either solid rigid structures or highly unstable dynamic patterns (fluids), enzymes constitute a flexible and specific, relatively stable form of constraint. Here the constraint harnesses both the rate and the specificity of the low level processes. Accordingly, by producing the suitable enzyme, practically any desirable reaction is feasible (provided it is not forbidden by physico-chemical laws). Second, enzymes can couple two or more reactions, so that a thermodynamically favorable reaction can be used to "drive" a thermodynamically unfavorable one; thus, by linking together many different reactions, a whole constructive system can be feasible, including the synthesis of other enzymes.

Why all that matters? As such, enzymes are highly complex molecular structures, which tend to become degraded into simpler ones very soon.[6] Actually, enzymes persist because they are embedded in chemical networks, which renew them. To be

---

5. The initial interactions between enzyme and substrate are relatively weak, but these weak interactions rapidly induce conformational changes in the enzyme that strengthen binding. These conformational changes also bring catalytic residues in the active site close to the chemical bonds in the substrate that will be altered in the reaction. After binding takes place, one or more mechanisms of catalysis lower the energy of the reaction's transition state by providing an alternative chemical pathway for the reaction.
6. Though enzymes are conservative structures, they are highly fragile.

more precise, enzymes make possible highly specific and unlikely recursive webs of chemical reactions: They produce and maintain a globally far-from-equilibrium self-sustaining network, which in turn produces these very enzymes. It is now widely accepted that metabolic networks appeared when primitive self-maintaining systems driven by rather unspecific catalysts were taken over by modular,[7] much more specific catalysts (probably, ribozymes).

As it is well known, the last step in the origin of life was the take over of primitive metabolisms by a genetic machinery, namely, a set of chemically almost *inert* components – DNA – whose role was (and still is) just to provide a template specifying the sequential order of the building blocks (amino acids) that make up the enzymes. Thus, genetic components are a kind of second-order constraint, since they, almost literally, *in-form* the processes leading to the synthesis of enzymes, processes that already are constrained by enzymes themselves. In other words, only enzymes (or active components) can be *sensu stricto* control constraints, because DNA does not control other events by themselves, but only through the construction of proper control constraints, that is, enzymes. As a result, it seems that nucleic acids only should be considered to be control constraints in an indirect way (Etxeberria & Moreno, 2001).

If so, how to understand this new "formal determination" (as the authors call it) operating upon another level[8] of formal determination? If interpreted in this strongly disembodied way, things appear rather strange. Why not simply saying that the action of constraints is a kind of *meta* efficient causation? As we have seen in the detailed description of the enzymatic action, harnessing the lower-level dynamics is in itself a complex dynamical process involving matter, energy, and time. This fact is often ignored because, from the perspective of the controlled domain, the amounts of matter, time, and energy implicated in the high-level processes are almost negligible. However, the in-formational action of the controlling domain upon the controlled one is always a physical event: we have to remind that in physics any form of control implies entropy generation and, therefore, at least a minimal amount energy dissipation, which is estimated to be larger than $1kT$. Why then not seeing this harnessing as if it were an efficient causation operating on the parameters (the boundary conditions) of another system, such that the operations in the former system are causal but dynamically decoupled (in the sense of belonging to two different dynamical domains)? For example, processes occurring in the nervous domain of an animal may cause metabolic changes, however, the connection between both domains

---

7. A modular catalyst is a kind of (relatively complex) oligomer, which adopts a 3D structure as a consequence of the sequential order, namely, the specific order (and number) of the building blocks (modules) of this oligomer. Whereas the 1D structure - the sequence - is maintained by means of strong bonds, the 3D structure (i.e., the mapping from the linear sequence of building blocks to the 3D structure) is mainly dependent on the weak bonds. Since the capacity for acting as a highly specific and efficient catalyst depends on the 3D structure, in particular, on the binding site, it is possible, in principle, that any desirable 3D structure be produced by a given specific sequence of the building blocks. Accordingly, if natural selection allows a wide enough exploration of the sequential domain, sooner or later evolution will find sets of modular catalysts fitting together in globally viable networks.

8. And in complex multicellular living systems, there are many meta-levels of this kind.

is dynamically arbitrary: the amount of energy of a given neural pattern has no intrinsic relation with the amount of energy in the metabolic domain that it has triggered.

If so, the authors' claim that the action of constraints should be characterized rather as a form of determination than as a form of causation seems less justified. For determination, as opposed to causation, means purely formal entailment, while here we are dealing with connections involving matter, energy, and time. My own argument in support of considering higher-level constraints as materially operating causes is that, when we analyze in detail the operations, what we call constraints appear as rate-dependent, material processes. However, this fact is hidden because in biological systems the causal structure is dynamically decoupled. By this I mean the resulting organization of an integrated system in which the constitutive processes generate and sustain a relatively independent dynamic subsystem, which in turn acts selectively regulating those constitutive processes. This definition implies that in complex systems (for example, biological systems) there are two organizational levels (although in highly complex biological systems there are many more): the *constitutive subsystem*, which is the basic or lower level, and the *regulatory subsystem* (namely, a set of emergent constraints), which is the higher one. Significantly, the higher-level regulatory subsystem cannot exist without the regulated constitutive system, and this later in turn would be disintegrated without regulation: both levels causally depend on each other. Thus, the system is dynamically decoupled but hierarchically coupled. In other words, there are within the system two causal domains,[9] operating at different time scales. Since these subsystems work at different rates and with different operational rules, the system has an increased potential to explore new or alternative forms of global self-maintenance (that are not accessible to *flat* systems without any hierarchy or modularity in their organization). In this way, the higher-level subsystem creates a set of functional constraints on the lower-level dynamics. At the same time, the controlled level plays a fundamental role in the constitution and maintenance of the controller level (and, therefore, of the whole system). For example, the genetic (sub)system in the cell acts harnessing the dynamics of the metabolic reactions (actually, in an indirect way, by specifying the primary structure of the enzymes), but, in turn, metabolic processes contribute to the maintenance, reparation, replication, and translation of genetic components.

One can say that in this picture the higher-level subsystem constrains or harnesses the dynamics of the lower-level subsystem; according to this perspective, constraints may be described as a different type of causes (say, formal causes) than those operating at the lower level (say efficient causes). But these two types of causation appear different only because they operate at different time and space scales. In conclusion, I think that a careful analysis of the underlying mechanisms of what are

---

9. But in many cases there are further levels of regulatory constraints. For example, in the brain the behavior of neurons are in turn constrained by higher levels of organization. From this perspective, it is irrelevant whether the underlying dynamics is in turn constrained or not. What matters is the partial decoupling of the different causal domains, which are globally coordinated.

considered as constraints in biological systems permits an interpretation of the causal structure of these systems both in terms of plurality and, at the same time, in terms of a common material process (I do not enter in the discussion of whether this corresponds to the Aristotelian concept of efficient causation).

The idea I have argued for is that increasingly complex forms of material organization produce (and are maintained by) forms of dynamically decoupled causation – we call them constraints – that materially and temporally over-determine former organizational levels. Detractors of downward causation can say that what we call a constraint is not different from its basal conditions, and, therefore, this term does not add anything, for it is the basal conditions of the structure that harness the microscopic elements. The problem with this argument, however, lies precisely in what is meant by *basal conditions*, namely, the properties and relations characterizing the parts (Kim, 2006, p. 549).

Now, in many cases the causal powers of a complex system are not determined solely by the physical properties of its constituents and the laws of physics, but also by the organization of those constituents within the composite. We cannot say at the same time that a given configuration of matter (in far-from-equilibrium conditions) is extremely unlikely, and that it is likely (i.e., stabilized). For, in this later case, we should add the action of organization, as something that occurs because an emergent, unlikely macroscopic pattern triggers a recursive process, namely, contributes to its own stabilization.

The problem is whether the relations characterizing the parts can be (or not) instantaneously stated. Biogenesis shows that certain relations are progressively unfolded. But even at the ontogenetic scale, the relations characterizing parts in biological systems show different time scales. Biological systems are entities whose existence is rather a *becoming*, a process in which certain relations are brought into existence at much larger temporal scale than others; if so, the set of relations cannot be stated *ab initio*. And therefore, as new larger scale relations come on, former, short-time relations get modified. A whole hierarchy of constraints, most of them in need of renewal (also at different time-scales), maintain living beings alive. That is way living systems are precarious entities, which depend on their own action (as well as on the actions of other living systems) just to stay alive.

Acknowledgements

Funding for this work was provided by grant IT-250-07 from the Basque Government, grants HUM2005-02449 and BFU2006-01951/BMC from the Spanish Ministry of Science and Education (MEC) and Feder funds from the European Union.

References

Etxeberria, A. & Moreno, A. (2001). From complexity to simplicity: Nature and symbols. *BioSystems, 60* (1-3), 149-157.
Juarrero, A. (1999). *Dynamics in action: Intentional behavior as a complex system.* Cambridge, MA: The MIT Press.

Kauffman, S. (2000). *Investigations*. New York: Oxford University Press.

Kauffman, S., Logan, R., Este, R., Goebel, R., Hobill, D. & Shmulevich, I. (2008): Propagating organization: An enquiry. *Biology and Philosophy, 23* (1), 27-45.

Kim, J. (2006). Emergence: Core ideas and issues. *Synthese, 151*, 547-559.

Moreno, A. & Umerez, J. (2000). Downward causation at the core of living organization. In P. B. Andersen, C. Emmeche, N. O. Finnemann, & P. V. Christiansen (Eds.), *Downward causation: Minds, bodies and matter* (pp. 13-34). Aarhus: Aarhus University Press.

Nicolis, G., & Prigogine, Y. (1977). *Self-organization in non-equilibrium systems*. New York: Wiley.

Pattee, H. H. (1973). The physical basis and origin of hierarchical control. In H.H. Pattee (Ed.), *Hierarchy theory* (pp. 73-108). New York: George Braziller.

Simon, H.A. (1969). *The sciences of the artificial*. Cambridge, MA: The MIT Press

Van Gulick, R. (1993). Who is in charge here? And who's doing all the work? In J. Heil & A. Mele. (Eds.). *Mental causation* (pp. 233-256). Oxford: Oxford University Press.

Forsythe, K. (2006). *Yuce Dream*. 50 cm x 50 cm, mixed media collage on board.

Cybernetics And Human Knowing. Vol. 15, nos. 3-4, pp. 145-147

Downward Determination:
A Philosophical Step in the Way to a Dynamic Account of Emergence

Fabiano de Souza Vieira[1] and Charbel Niño El-Hani[2]

Initially, we would like to thank Alvaro Moreno for his comments, which will certainly play the role of inspiring us to go on with our research project about downward determination. We would like to offer some remarks, however, about his commentary.

In the first part of the commentary, Moreno writes that he is not sure that our proposal of replacing the concept of causation by that of determination might play an important role in the understanding of whole-to-parts relationships. He is also doubtful about our position: He argues that we seemed to endorse at some points key arguments against downward causation, while, some pages later, we seemed to reject those very arguments. We will take the opportunity of this reply to clarify our position.

Moreno is right in arguing that we gave a great deal of attention to problems concerning downward causation in the first part of our paper. We were particularly worried about the problems faced by synchronic and diachronic downward causation, as stated by Kim (1999, 2006). However, it is not a correct appraisal of the structure of our arguments that we would have both rejected and accepted downward causation throughout our paper. We agree that this notion has a central role to play in both emergentism, and, generally speaking, our current attempts to understand complex systems, such as living organisms. Nevertheless, we do think it is necessary to address both logical-philosophical conditions, as we discuss in our paper, and dynamic conditions for emergence, which were the main focus of other authors in this special issue, such as Moreno and Collier. While discussing philosophical issues related to emergence, we should be careful enough to both present the cases of the critics of downward causation and emergence in a proper manner, and develop answers to those cases. The perplexing nature of our paper seems to result from the fact that we gave full attention to both features. To the end of our paper, however, we focused on attempts to overcome the challenges of the critics and, consequently, elaborate on the notion of downward causation, which we regard to be fruitful, despite occasional problems. This is the case of the systematic analysis of different renderings of downward causation by Emmeche, Køppe and Stjernfelt (2000) or Juarrero's (1999)

1. Graduate Studies Program in History, Philosophy, and Science Teaching, Universidade Federal da Bahia/Universidade Estadual de Feira de Santana. E-mail: biosv@hotmail.com
2. Professor, Institute of Biology, Universidade Federal da Bahia, Brasil. Graduate Studies Program in History, Philosophy, and Science Teaching, Universidade Federal da Bahia/Universidade Estadual de Feira de Santana. Graduate Studies Program in Ecology and Biomonitoring, Universidade Federal da Bahia. E-mail: charbel.elhani@pesquisador.cnpq.br

account of downward causation in the context of a theory of complex adaptive systems.

Even though we agree that these attempts led to important advances in our understanding of downward causation, making it possible to overcome some problems related to synchronic downward causation (which, we think, is the most fruitful notion to pursue), we think there are other steps to be taken in a way to a dynamic account of emergence, and these steps still have to do with philosophical problems that cannot be ignored.

One of these problems concern the appeal to neo-Aristotelian accounts of causality, which, no matter how enticing they are, still bring problems to treatments of downward causation. In this scenario, Hulswit's (2006) criticism is particularly relevant, since he points out—and we basically agree—that the concept of downward causation is still vague with regard to the nature of causes and effects, and muddled on the subject of the meaning of causation. It was on the basis of such criticisms, which we regard to be sound, that we appealed to the idea that causation is not the only source of change and novelty in nature, and, thus, that it may be the case of considering other kinds of (non-causal) determination in order to account for the relationships between wholes and their parts.

We have, then, four basic steps in our arguments: first, we showed how the notion of downward causation is surrounded by philosophical problems that cannot be simply ignored and were clearly exposed, among others, by Kim, no matter how much we disagree with him; secondly, we discussed neo-Aristotelian approaches to downward causation as a way of circumventing those problems; thirdly, we criticized how the very notion of causation and the causal relata are accounted for in these neo-Aristotelian perspectives; and, finally, we concluded by explaining our own account of downward determination, trying to be clear about two central issues: What sorts of things are said to be determining and determined in a case of downward determination? What is the meaning of determining in downward determination? By answering in a clear manner to these two issues, we hope to have paved the way to our next work, which will focus on the dynamic aspects of emergence and downward causation.

We would like to conclude this reply by making a central issue clear, even if at the cost of looking repetitive. We did not intend to put into question the role that the notion of downward causation plays either in emergentist philosophies or in the natural sciences. But notice that, even if it is true that a rejection of downward causation would result in problems for our current understanding of complex systems, this does not mean that we should take this concept at face value, without trying to come to grips with the philosophical problems that it raises. We gave so much attention to the philosophical strategy of carefully running through arguments against downward causation in order to clarify some central issues related to this notion. Moreno indeed hints at certain grounds on which we can put those arguments into question, such as, for instance, Kim's arguments against downward causation. We do not think, however, that we can overcome the problems surrounding the idea of downward causation by appealing to a concept such as meta-efficient causation, as Moreno suggests. Despite the recourse to this concept, the philosophical problems are still there and should be dealt with. True, we cannot argue for downward determination as a way of treating those problems in a disembodied way. This is why we appealed to Popper's propensities theory of probability (see, e.g., Popper, 1959). Our intension was to put probability in the world when accounting for downward determination as a change in the disposition of a system to instantiate a set of processes due to the downward influence of a higher-level, general organizational principle on its components. Notice the important feature that, in this account, while particulars are determined at the lower level, generals are determiners at the higher level. This is, in our view, a central element in the attempt to go beyond efficient causation and avoid the bootstrapping problem that threatens synchronic downward causation. It is also clear that we are not dealing with purely formal entailments, to be found in our minds or logical abstractions, but, rather, with material processes.

In sum, we insist in our claim that there are advantages in talking about downward determination, rather than causation, when addressing the many philosophical problems related to the synchronic influence of wholes over parts. This is a move often made in attempts to understand another mereological relation, the physical realization or constitution of wholes by their parts. Physical realization has been conceived as a synchronic, non-causal determinative relationship even by strong critics of downward causation and emergence, including Kim himself. Moving towards determination can give room not only to strategic advantages, but also to conceptual clarifications. For instance, the formulation of downward determination in terms of Popperian propensities arguably makes it clearer what is at stake when a higher-level subsystem constrains or harnesses the dynamics of lower-level subsystems.

In our research project about emergence and downward causation, we are now moving to a discussion about the contributions of these notions to the understanding of complex biological systems, and both Moreno's case for naturalized constraints and Collier's defense of a shift from logical to dynamic conditions for emergence will be instrumental to our future work.

References

Collier, J. (2008). A dynamical account of emergence. *Cybernetics & Human Knowing, 15* (3-4), 75-86.

Emmeche, C., Køppe, S. & Stjernfelt, F. (2000). Levels, emergence and three versions of downward causation. In P. B. Andersen, C. Emmeche, N. O. Finnemann, & P. V. Christiansen (Eds.), *Downward causation: Minds, bodies and matter* (pp. 13-34). Aarhus: Aarhus University Press.

Hulswit, M. (2006). How causal is downward causation? *Journal for General Philosophy of Science, 36* (2), 261-287.

Juarrero, A. (1999). *Dynamics in action: Intentional behavior as a complex system.* Cambridge: The MIT Press.

Kim, J. (1999). Making sense of emergence. *Philosophical Studies, 95,* 3-36.

Kim, J. (2006). Emergence: Core ideas and issues. *Synthese, 151* (3), 547-559.

Popper, K. R. (1959). The Propensity interpretation of probability. *British Journal for the Philosophy of Science, 10* (37), 25-42.

Forsythe, K. (2008). *Cave*. 15 cm x 22 cm, acrylic on canvas.

Cybernetics And Human Knowing. Vol. 15, nos. 3-4, pp. 149-161

Social Organizations as Reconstitutable Networks of Conversations

Klaus Krippendorff[1]

This essay intends to recover human agency from holistic, abstract, even oppressive conceptions of social organization, common in the social sciences, social systems theory in particular. To do so, I am taking the use of language as simultaneously accompanying the performance of and constructing reality (my version of social constructivism). The essay starts with a definition of human agency in terms of its linguistic manifestation. It then sketches several leading conceptions of social organization, their metaphorical origin and entailments. Finally, it contextualizes the use of these metaphors in conversation, which leads to the main thesis of this essay that the reconstitutability of networks of conversation precedes all other criteria of the viability of organizational forms. The paper transcends the traditional second-order cybernetic preoccupation with individual cognition – observation and description – into the social domain of participation.

> *Imagine, they gave a war and nobody showed up*
> Carl Sandburg[2]

Human Agency

It is common to associate human agency with the capacity to make choices that cause changes in the world. As such, human agency is closely associated with free will, the philosophical doctrine that distinguishes choices from unthinking causal determinisms. This doctrine also posits that the capacity of humans to act is individual. *Freedom* is another largely individualist if not mentalist and certainly politically loaded idea. Heinz von Foerster (1992, p. 14) touched upon human agency by connecting it with formal indeterminacy when he proposed "Only those questions that are in principle undecidable, we can decide." I agree. Where the answer to a question is not obtainable by applying a logical procedure or algorithm, human agency can be exercised to propose one. I deviate from these conceptions, however, and consider human agency a social phenomenon that reveals itself in the practice of accountability.

The idea of accountability can be traced to C. Wright Mills's (1959) study of *The Power Elite* in the U.S. To obtain data on his topic, Mills inquired into what happened inside that elite by visiting boardrooms, observing meetings and social events where decisions were made and implemented; and where power was exerted, yielded, and

---

1. Gregory Bateson Professor for Cybernetics, Language, and Culture, The Annenberg School for Communication, University of Pennsylvania. Email: kkrippendorff@asc.upenn.edu
2. This phrase, often attributed to Bertolt Brecht was multiply translated from Carl Sandburg (1936). *The People, Yes*. New York: Harcourt, Brace. Page 43: "Sometime they'll give a war and nobody will come."

contested. He soon realized that the traditional macro-theoretical conception of power was too simplistic, and discovered the richness of language used there: language not as a medium of influence, as envisioned by rhetoric; not as a medium of representation, as conceived in the abstract objectivist notion of language of the enlightenment; but as interactions during which the meanings of decisions are created, accepted or dismissed. In a landmark paper, Mills (1940) described the vocabulary of motives that decision makers use to justify their proposals and actions. His approach developed further (Scott & Lyman, 1968; Shotter, 1984; Buttny, 1993) and is now discussed in terms of accountability.

To me, accountability manifests human agency, not in terms of individual/ psychological conceptions, for example, in terms of intentions, awareness of alternatives, or rational criteria for decision making or choices, but in terms of the accounts that human actors give to each other in response to requests or in anticipation of being held accountable for what they say or do. The two kinds of accounts in which agency becomes socially manifest are excuses and justifications.[3] Both are conversational moves.

- *Excuses deny that an actor had agency.* They acknowledge that something untoward has happened but attribute it to causes not under the actor's control, for example, accidents, lack of information, or being under the influence of or command by someone else.
- *Justifications, by contrast, acknowledge an actors' agency.* They are offered by actors who assume responsibility for a given situation, are convinced of the virtue of their actions, and expect others to see their virtue as well.

Accounts may be accepted or not. Rejecting an account may lead to further requests for accounts until the participants in the conversation are satisfied and willing to go on to other issues. The acts of offering, accepting, and rejecting accounts manifest human agency regarding the use of language, even if agency is denied regarding particular occurrences.

The adequacy of accounts does not depend on whether they are true or false in any objective sense, but on whether they are accepted as adequate *within* the conversations in which they are offered. Validity could become an issue, but only if knowledge of what an account claims is deemed relevant and available to those considering it. Typically, accounts appeal to prevailing values or ethical considerations. Whether they prevail indeed, depends not on anyone's unasserted convictions but on being accepted as adequate.

According to John Shotter (1984), people do not speak and act in the presence of others without having appropriate accounts ready if requested. Moreover, people do

---

3. A third account, incidentally occurring most frequently in conversations, is explanation. Explanations have to do with understanding. They indicate conversational competence and cognitive autonomy and have the effect of coordinating understanding, without the assumption of sharing. This ability and its consequence is only marginally related to human agency and not central to this essay.

not offer accounts without anticipation that they have a chance of being understood and accepted by those who matter to them. Thus, explicit human communication always takes place against the background of an implicit operating consensus regarding held values, plausible reasons, and coherent constructions of reality. Where this background is at odds with the articulated foreground, accounting practices bring that operating consensus to the surface and renegotiate it as needed.

Cognitive correlates of conversation, even intents to deceive, are irrelevant unless someone suspects such motivations to be disingenuous, challenges them by requesting appropriate accounts that either expose them or puts the suspicion to rest. The absence of accounts signals acceptance of what was said and done for no apparent reasons.[4]

Accepting excuses certifies a participant's lack of agency in the instance in question, and accepting justifications credits if not expresses appreciation of a participant's exercise of agency in that instance. Thus, human agency, surfaces in accounting practices, and as such is an entirely social and interactive phenomenon, not divorceable from the conversational use of language.

The Metaphorical Grounding of Social Organization

Social organizations exist only virtually. One cannot point to them. One cannot observe them. One cannot talk to them. Yet, people can practice them as members and receive something in return for their participation or are affected in interactions with people who act in the name of an organization. This virtuality invites the use of metaphors to understand and live with their objectifications. It is not surprising, therefore, that most theories of organization rely on metaphors to characterize their objects. What theorists rarely realize, however, is that all metaphors have entailments that unwittingly direct their users' attention to particular features worthy of investigation (Lakoff & Johnson, 1980). Acting on these entailments has ontogenetic implications, here, constructing what organizations "really are." Let me sketch the metaphorical origin of five key conceptions of organization.

- *Family metaphors* are of ancient origin. It is easy to see how the basic idea of family, consisting of individuals and including responsible adults, is metaphorically extendable to larger social forms: tribes, feudal forms, monarchies, even the Catholic Church. One entailment of the use of family metaphors is that members have no choice regarding where they belong, are child-like, and in need of having to be taken care of by those privileged or more knowledgeable. So, rulers have to take care of their subjects, and priests see themselves as shepherds of their followers.

---

4. The unproblematic acceptance of what is said or done includes the acceptance of authority/dependency relations. However, denying accountability or punishing those who are asking for it, which ends up in the fear of holding authorities accountable for what they say and do manifests the exertion of power—I would say "illegitimate power" inasmuch as accountability is a universal of language use.

- *Machine metaphors* of social forms emerged in the industrial era. Factory owners did not own their workers but hired them to perform specific functions which they designed in the service of their factory's purpose. This metaphor made factory workers replaceable when they turned out to be inefficient or defective, like the parts of a machine. Machine metaphors also introduced logical hierarchies with the functions of ordinary workers below and various levels of supervisory functions above them, always leading to factory owners who had no responsibilities to anyone but to that factory yielding a profit as a whole. Max Weber described prototypical bureaucracies (incidentally during the same era) in terms of rational differentiations and assignment of functions to impersonal offices. Their structure logically followed from the overall purpose, (form follows function) and office workers had to perform according to specifications, satisfying the overall design.

- *Biological metaphors* are responsible for the very word *organization*, literally the shaping of something into an organism. Much like machines, organisms tend to be analyzed in terms of hierarchies of functions.[5] However, biological metaphors do not insist on the replaceability of the members of social organizations (see the concept of autopoiesis, Maturana & Varela, 1988) but on harmonious collaboration among them, but always with the larger whole in mind. Collaboration demands that members adjust their functions relative to each other and subordinate their collaboration to an organization's well-being. Conflicts that could arise within organizations, the analogue of diseases, are considered dysfunctional and in need of resolution to restore normality. Parsons (1951) *Social System* and Bertalanffy's (1968) *General System Theory* exemplify metaphorical generalizations of biological organisms.

- *Person metaphors* are at home largely in legal discourse and politics. Legal discourse considers corporations as entities that allow groups of individuals to act as if they were a single composite individual for certain purposes, for example, lawsuits, property ownership, and contracts. By extending laws, originally regulating individual conduct, to corporate entities, legal scholars encountered difficulties and aptly consider corporate personhood a "legal fiction." In politics, states are often personalized as friendly, hostile, authoritarian or democratic, or trustworthy. The attribution of individual characteristics to countries typically directs international relations. Person metaphors of social organization entail little about the nature of individual membership, except that they enable designated individuals, spokes persons, presidents, CEOs, or hired lawyers to represent and speak for them in particular proceedings.

---

5. It is not entirely clear whether the etymology of "function" is routed in technology or in biology. In any case, it is now a defining concept of biological discourse, enabling explanations of how the parts that biologists distinguish within an organism interact in the service of that organism as the a whole entity. Engineers consider functions in their analysis of technological artifacts with the difference that technical functions are intended by design, whereas biological functions offer useful part-whole explanations.

- *Network metaphors*, communication nets in particular, focus attention on the relations among component parts of social organizations. Connections may be close or far apart, direct or indirect, or used heavily or lightly. Calling networks heterarchical suggests them to be antithetical to hierarchies. Hierarchies, however, are mere special cases of networks. Network metaphors of organizations say little about who occupies the nodes of a network – individuals, offices, or whole organizations. There is no implication of functions, suggesting that wholes do not determine the nodes. Networks may cross the boundaries of particular organizations.

Etymologically, family metaphors gave way to machine metaphors. U.S. slavery occurred in that transition. Slaves were traded but still had to be cared for. Machine metaphors were vastly enriched by the introduction of biological metaphors, still dominant in the current literature on organizations. Network metaphors liberalize the biological ones but have not replaced them as is evident in suggestions that organizations *have* networks, for example of communication (Monge & Contractor, 2003). I shall make use of the network metaphor below, suggesting that organizations *are realized* in networks of conversations.

All metaphors have entailments (Lakoff & Johnson, 1980). Except for network metaphors, the above metaphors share three quite unfortunate ones.

(1) *Organizations are whole entities.* At least legal discourse acknowledges that corporations are legal fictions; not in the awareness of their metaphorical construction, but in the experience that corporations—unlike individual human beings—do not speak and thus complicate issues of legal accountability. Organizational theorists rarely recognize the metaphorical ground of their concepts of organization and look for evidence of what are their entailments outside of language. Indeed, such evidence can be found in the enduring manifestations of organizational identities: the consistent use of their names, logos, and uniforms for employees; the buildings, equipment, products, and other assets in their name; and various published records, addresses, advertisements, the trading value of their stocks, and various statistics. Consistent with the idea of organizations as entities is the idea that their manifestations persist for some time. When they exceed the life span of their individual members, these metaphors encourage the belief that organizations are more real and more important than their human constituents.

But it is in language that such manifestations are identified with particular organizations and it is in language that they could vanish by disuse.

(2) *Organizational members continue in their organization.* This is obviously misleading. Unlike machines and biological organisms whose parts or organs cannot rearrange themselves and are permanently in place and coupled to each other, people cannot be so tied up. Most social organizations cease activity after working hours, on weekends and holidays, in the absence of appropriate members, but may reconstitute themselves under certain conditions. People have choices to participate in various

social organizations, typically sequentially. Theories of the internal working of social organizations, which account for almost all organizational research, cannot reveal how organizations are constituted or what creates their reality and for whom.

(3) *The viability of the whole determines the practices of its parts.* This whole→part determinism leads to theories of organizational hierarchies, how power is exercised, and how members of an organization, as a condition of being its member, perform the functions necessary to sustain it. Yet, wholes cannot exist without their constituent parts. Wholes are abstractions that reside in language, including in conversations among the constituents of organizations. Theories that make use of these metaphors effectively reverse the actual determinism involved and are unable to explain how organizations could arise. Such theories of organization are theories of how human agency can be suppressed and directed to abstract ends.[6]

Reconstitutability

To recover human agency in conceptions of social organization I am suggesting that the central feature of all social organizations is not their persistence and overall well being but their *reconstitutability* at different times, with same or different people, and perhaps at different locations.

As already suggested, social organizations do not require continuous existence. A parliament is sometimes in session and mostly not. Taking a seminar at a university, means showing up for agreed upon periods of time, actively participating as a student, but thereafter being free to participate in other organizational forms: eating with co-students at a dining hall, taking part in a political discussion, competing in a sports event, working at a job, populating traffic on the way home, and partying with friends. When the right number and kind of people meet at the right time, such as when employees show up for work at 9 am or when the members of a family sit down for a dinner conversation after everyone worked at various places, appropriate organizational forms can arise.

Individuals who repeatedly reconstitute the same social organizations know each other well and when they meet after a period of practicing other organizations, they may continue where they had left off. In periods of inactivity, a social organization is reduced to a mere possibility.

Not all organizations are reconstituted by a bodily same set of individuals. For example, a court of law comes into being when a case is to be adjudicated, all required constituents are present, and constituents conduct themselves as expected. That court may, however, involve a different cast of individuals each time. The reconstitutability of a court of law is *institutionalized* in the sense that its organizational practices are well known by potential participants who may signify their qualifications to each other. The signification of qualifications is evident in doctors wearing white coats while patients do not; in police officers using flashing lights on their cars while

---

6. Incidentally, this picture of organization is of prime interest to managers of organizations or their CEOs who tend to assume the ability to control their members by defining the purposes of the whole.

ordinary drivers would be prosecuted if they do; in shop keepers standing behind a counter and customers in front of it; and in car mechanics wearing typical working clothes and disallowing clients from entering their workshop. When such signifiers are reliably recognized, and complement one's potential role in a desired organization, it is easy for the potential constituents of an organization to fall into their roles.

Institutionalization may involve impersonal signifiers, place holders that enable individuals to move into institutionally defined spaces: an empty seat on a bus, the public space in a bank, a job application form, or a theatre ticket. Such signifiers invite or license an actor to become a particular constituent of a social organization – a rider on a bus, a bank customer, a job applicant, or a member of a theatre audience – temporarily, by choice, and in the knowledge of what is expected by occupying these places.

Most importantly, reconstitutability presupposes human agency. If individuals would not initiate interactions that reconstitute a social organization, that organization could not come into being. The process of reconstitution distinguishes social organizations from machines, whose parts do not know each other and are assembled by a designer or user, and from organisms that have evolved and must maintain uninterrupted autopoiesis (Maturana & Varela, 1988) as a condition of their living. Even families cannot exist without the bodily participation of their members, whatever their relationships may be. All social organizations are either active, dissolved and waiting to be reconstituted when potential constituents so desire, or have ceased forever. Examples of no longer reconstitutable organizations are lost crafts, dead languages, and dictatorships after a true revolution.

The ability of individual actors to reconstitute a social organization supersedes all other conditions of a social organization's viability. For example, there are viable organizations that make no profit. There are viable organizations that shrink in size. There are viable organizations whose members do not get paid but have to pay their way into it. There are viable organizations that have no apparent utility, like birthday parties or soccer games. There are viable organizations whose members dread what they are asked to do but do it anyway. But there are no social organizations whose members refuse or are unable to reconstitute them for whatever reasons.

Social organizations in which some constituents hold other constituents captive in continuous membership, like in prisons or slavery, offer the latter no alternatives to realize themselves in diverse social organizations, prevent them from developing their own identities, robbing them of their inalienable human agency. Theories of social organization that attend only to how individuals function within organizations flirt with totalitarianism by failing to recognize or deliberately ignoring that individual members of an organization voluntarily, contractually, and temporarily trade some of their human agency for the benefits of participating in that organization, regardless of their motivation. Since reconstitutability is a prerequisite for social organizations to come into being, human-centered research needs to turn its attention to why individuals are willing to give up some of their human agency for benefits they might be receiving while participating in social organizations, and how they manage to reconstitute organizations and negotiate their participation.

Networks of Conversations

I am suggesting that all social organizations are realized, come to life, as networks of conversations (Ford, 1999; Fonseca, 2002, p. 47ff; Krippendorff, 2004, pp. 66-68; Kimberley & Fernbach, 2006). *Conversations* are self-organizing, more or less free flowing verbal interactions among mutually identifiable human actors (Gadamer, 1982, pp. 330-341; Holquist, 1990, pp. 40-66; Nofsinger, 1999; Todorov, 1988; Buber, 1958). Conversations are cooperative practices and what they leave behind are joint accomplishments (Shotter, 1993). Networks of conversations network these practices. Accordingly, organizations are not entities but conversational practices. People practice organization as participants. This is the gestalt switch needed to escape the determinism entailed by the above mentioned metaphors of social organization. In conversations one can distinguish utterances between turns of talk (Volosinov, 1986, pp. 45-98), performatives (Austin, 1962), including the above-mentioned accounts, recursive con-sensual coordinations of actions (Maturana, 1988), speech acts like assertives, expressives, directives, declaratives, and commissives to engage in certain activities (Searle, 1969), language games (Wittgenstein, 1958), stories (Fisher, 1987), and artifacts (Krippendorff, 2006). Conversations are prototypically face-to-face, but may take place also by telephone and electronic communications. The number of participants in a conversation is usually limited to the amount of attention individuals can devote to each other. While it is possible for people to meet in numbers that make individual identifiably difficult – public performances, religious gatherings, or political demonstrations, which include spectators – these meetings almost always are the outgrowth of preceding conversations, temporally make some participants featured performers and others silent but necessary observers, but are likely to fuel subsequent conversations. All conversations coordinate the activities and reality constructions of their participants.

Minimally, conversations leave behind their own histories of what happened, available to all who contributed to them, which serve as the expanding ground for future conversations. Most conversations accompany, define and direct ongoing activity, whether consuming food during a dinner conversation, negotiating a document to satisfy all those present, or committing participants to a policy or course of action and monitoring its results. The realities that may emerge in conversations are not entirely cognitive as Glasersfeld (1995, 2008) insists but social in the sense that they are being coordinated across individual constructions, usually in mutual respect for their differences (Krippendorff, 1996).

Conversations may become networked in at least four ways.

(i)   Most often, conversations are networked *sequentially*, with participants moving from one conversation to another, taking what had transpired in preceding conversations into a current one. Supervisors may so move, introducing coherences that coordinate conversations in effect. So does the complement of supervision: delegation to conversations among representatives of previous conversations. But more typical is that members or organizations rotate through various conversations concerned with different topics of organizational significance.

(ii)   Conversation may become networked *operationally,* such as when the products of one part of an organization serve as the prerequisite for another part to proceed. Operational networks tend to be more horizontal with participants engaged in negotiating the interfaces between their respective conversations.

(iii)   Conversations may also be networked *emotionally* and *informally,* like among friends, people who share extra-organizational interests, or acquaintances willing to do each other favors.

(iv)   Conversations may be networked by *sharing documents* generated in one conversation and made available to others. The reading of documents – reports, rules, and resolutions – can network conversations without direct human contact. Texts circulating in a network of conversations may preserve histories of organizational practices beyond the capacity of individual memories and regulate that network.

Coordinating a network of conversations takes place entirely within that network and consists of conversations about conversations that recursively construct their own conversational realities (Shotter, 1993). As individuals move through various conversations, that network may become more coherent and navigable for its participants. A crucial ingredient of this coordination is the development of vocabularies about conversational practices, including motivational mission statements, working schedules, network ethics, operational practices, success stories, logos, and products – all of which are conversational accomplishments that can give the participants in conversations a sense of making a difference and feeling to belong.

One cannot prevent the above metaphors of organization from entering networks of conversations and causing their entailments to be realized therein, as is common. I am suggesting that the vocabularies of current theories of organization, which may well be regarded as expert accounts, have the effect of concealing their conversational nature, reifying the holistic, abstract, and functional conceptions of organization they describe, and denying places for human agency. This does not need to be so and this essay hopes to discourage the unreflective use of such metaphors in networks of conversation.

In other words, the vocabularies, which are saturated with the above-mentioned metaphors of organization, should be replaced (Rorty, 1989) by vocabularies of the conversational moves that individuals may or may not want to make in reconstituting networks of conversations and *practicing organization.* Practicing organization may well involve suspending some human agency otherwise available, but now reflectively, for limited times, not unconditionally.

Infrastructures of Organization

The reconstitutability of organizations is enhanced when the *histories of conversations* are not merely remembered by their participants, but also encoded in reusable infrastructures: human bodies, texts, and technological artifacts.

Human bodies are not merely biological phenomena. The body we know as ours has passed through a complex history of socializations, causing successful habits, memories, and abilities to develop that, without access to that history, may well appear natural and common. Literacy is just one example. Language is a human artifact with reading and writing being a later invention that has transformed society as it has trained the human body to be part of it. As Bakhtin reminds us, the words we read and write are learned, but their origins are mostly forgotten (Holquist, 1990), together with the alternatives they replaced. We read nearly automatically without knowing how we do it. The word *nearly* is important because human agency, as I defined it, is the exception to bodily automatisms.

   Texts may be read

(i)   As protocols of what transpired in prior conversations. Such protocols may avoid repetition and may serve as an efficient way to induct newcomers into to a conversation. This essay could be regarded as a protocol that acknowledges voices from previous conversations I had, for example with James Taylor from Montreal, Pille Bunnell from Vancouver, and others who commented on its first draft, as well as the works of other authors mentioned

(ii)   As exemplars to be reconsidered or rules of conduct that have proven useful in the past of some conversations, to be generalized to other conversations

(iii)   As contracts to temporarily suspend one's agency in collaboration with present and future practitioners of organization, fixing individual commitments to perform organizational practices inside and across the boundaries of an organization.

Identifying something as text presumes its readability, nothing more. As such, texts contain nothing, mean nothing, possess no symbolic or sign qualities, and convey no information on their own. The meaning of text arises in the process of reading it. Literate bodies make it difficult to read a text idiosyncratically. Conversations coordinate the reading of texts. When reading jointly, starting with parents reading to their children and continuing to discussing a text at a graduate seminar, reading becomes coordinated among participants who can always ask "what do you mean by that," including "I do not understand, please explain" (Krippendorff, 2008). This does not mean that readers read a text the same way, only that answering questions about the meaning of texts amounts to a con-sensual coordination of their interpretations. The reader of documents retrieved from the internet assumes that its author is similarly coordinated. Hence reading assumes belonging to the same or a similar community.

In organizations, all texts have memory and regulative functions, *memory functions* in as much as texts extend the accessible history of recurrent conversations beyond the lifespan of individual participants, and *regulative functions* as they encourage desirable conduct or commit members to perform certain tasks. For example, when an organization is considered a legal entity, members are required to conformity to certain practices, regarding fellow employees, the public, the court, and the state. These requirements certainly direct their conversations.

Networks of conversations are likely to institutionalize their recurrent conversational practices, using *technological artifacts* that improve these networks' efficiency: telephone lines, archives, and computational devices for transmission, storage, retrieval of documents. Such artifacts trade two consequences. On the one hand, they extend desirable human dimensions such as communicating across distances not reachable by the human voice or browsing the internet for documents that would take an individual's life time to find. On the other hand, they impose constraints perhaps considered less important such as using text instead of voice, smell, and touch. Technological infrastructure also includes buildings to house face-to-face conversations, workplaces whose proximity facilitates informal conversations, and access to communicational artifacts.

Revisiting Human Agency

I oppose trivializing the concept of human agency by attributing agency to texts and technological artifacts as in actor-network theory (ANT) (Latour, 1998, 2005). As already suggested, texts are created within a community and acquire meanings by its literate members reading them. Texts may be read for pleasure, information, providing instructions, as declarations, promises or threats. Although speech act theory claims illocutionary forces at work (Searle, 1969), the consequences of reading and acting on what is read or listened to is not causally determined — notwithstanding that literate bodies can be trained to give this appearance. The literary conventions of a community merely favor some readings more than others and thus limit the range of acceptable interpretations. It is not far fetched to extend the notion of literacy to the human use of technological artifacts. Computer literacy is an obvious example. It needs to be acquired. And so is driving a car which is subject to numerous laws and requires one's coordination with other drivers. While technological artifacts exhibit physical constraints on their usability, which are almost completely absent in texts, the use of both is subject to conventions, not inherent to them.

ANT attributes agency to texts and artifacts inasmuch as they impose constraints on their readers or users—just as Niklas Luhmann (1995) attributes agency to communication by suggesting that it produces further communication, regardless of what people do with them. True, in everyday life we might blame a car for breaking down on us and say that a computer guides us through the steps to purchase an airline ticket, but these are artifacts of grammar. Standard European languages happen to provide the option to connect active subjects and passive objects by predicates. But language has other constructions as well. It is also true that the instructions from a boss weigh more than a marginal newspaper story. But this unequal weight does not stem from exposure to a text but from how one's relationship to its author is conceived. The Bible is important to Christians but means little to those who do not believe it to be the word of God. For Latour, an *actant* is anything that behaves, affects something else, or is seen as the source of activity. He conceives human actors as a subspecies of actants and takes from semiotics "the crucial practice to grant texts and discourses the ability to define also their context, their authors –in the text–, their readers –in fabula– and even their own demarcation and metalanguage. All the problems of the analyst are shifted to the 'text itself'" (1998, p. 6).

In response to Latour I wish to point out that one cannot hold texts accountable for how readers read them. Texts contain nothing. Their meanings arise in the process of reading and coordinating one's reading in conversations with other readers. In this sense, meanings are dialogical accomplishments (Krippendorff, 2003). The illocutionary forces that speech acts supposedly possess cannot compel readers to act, They are generated in the process of reading. Texts cannot speak for anyone unless readers imagine their authors from previous conversations. They cannot provide information unless readers read them in the context of what interests them. Texts cannot object to their interpretations. If texts constrain then only because readers construct their meanings as limiting their choices. If texts open opportunities then only because readers come to see opportunities not realized before. Texts do not talk, readers do, including about how they read them. Theorizing the agency of text effectively trivializes human agency.

Attributing agency to technological artifacts amounts to a similar trivialization. All artifacts are created and put in place by human agents. Some artifacts, once set in motion may proceed without further human attention – thermostatically controlled home heating systems, traffic signals, automatic pilots and algorithms for buying and selling stocks. Mechanisms like these are computationally, structurally, or causally determined, but their use is not. Some artifacts survive their creators, cities for example. Settling on cars as a preferred means of transportation, may preempt options available to future citizens. However, options and possibilities are concepts associated with human agents, not with physics. Matter matters but does not determine what human agents do with it. Technological artifacts, like texts, do not speak, cannot account for how they are being used, and what they end up doing.

Attributing agency to non-human entities is way of absolving one's agency. In accounting terms, such attributions are excuses. When accepted, they results in a loss of autonomy and deny future accountability. Thus, trivializing human agency needs to be discouraged.

For the implications of this essay to cybernetics see Klaus Krippendorff (2008, pp. 173-184 in this issue of C&HK)

References

Austin, J. (1962). *How to do things with words*. London: Oxford University Press.
Bertalanffy, L. von (1968). *General system theory: Foundations, development, applications*. New York: George Braziller.
Buber, M. (1958). *I and thou* (2nd ed.). New York: Charles Scribner's Sons.
Buttny, R. (1993). *Social accountability in communication*. London: Sage.

Fisher, W. (1987). *Human communication as narrative: Toward a philosophy of reason, value, and action*. Columbia, SC: University of South Carolina Press.

Foerster, H. von (1992), Ethics and second-order cybernetics. *Cybernetics & Human Knowing, 1* (1), 9-19.

Fonseca, J. (2002). *Complexity and innovation in organizations*. New York: Routledge.

Ford, J. D. (1999). Organizational change as shifting conversations. *Journal of Organizational Change Management, 12* (6), 480-500.

Gadamer, H.-G. (1982). *Truth and method*. New York: Crossroad.

Glasersfeld, E. von (1995). *Radical constructivism: A way of knowing and learning*. Washington, DC: Falmer Press.

Glasersfeld, E. von (2008). Who conceives society. *Constructivist Foundations, 3* (2), 59-64.

Holquist, M. (1990). *Dialogism; Bakhtin and his world*. London: Routledge.

Kimberley, H. & Fernbach, M. (2006). *Research in the middle*. AVETRA Conference, University of Wollongong. Collingwood, Australia: Equity Research Center. Retrieved August 21, 2008 from http://www.avetra.org.au/ABSTRACTS2006/PA%200057.pdf

Krippendorff, K.(1996). A second-order cybernetics of otherness. *Systems Research, 13* (3), 311-328.

Krippendorff, K. (2003). The dialogical reality of meaning.*The American Journal of Semiotics, 19* (1-4), 19-36. (2003 volume was actually published in 2006)

Krippendorff, K. (2004). *Content analysis; An Introduction to its methodology* (2nd ed.). Thousand Oaks, CA: Sage.

Krippendorff, K. (2006). *The semantic turn: A new foundation for design*. Boca Raton, FL: Taylor and Francis, CRC Press.

Krippendorff, K. (2008). Towards a radically social constructivism. *Constructivist Foundations, 3* (2), 91-94.

Krippendorff, K. (2008). Cybernetics's reflexive turn. *Cybernetics & Human Knowing, 15* (3-4), 173-184.

Lakoff, G. & Johnson, M. (1980). *Metaphors we live by*. Chicago, IL: University of Chicago Press.

Latour, B. (1997). *On actor-network theory; A few clarifications*. Staffordshire UK: Keele University, Centre for Social Theory and Technology (CSTT). Retrieved August 18, 2008 from http://www.nettime.org/Lists-Archives/nettime-l-9801/msg00019.html

Latour, B. (2005). *Reassembling the social: An introduction to actor-network-theory*. New York: Oxford University Press.

Luhmann, N. (1995). *Social systems* (J. Bednarz, Jr. & D. Baecker, Trans.). Stanford, CA: Stanford University Press.

Maturana, H. R. (1988). Ontology of observing. In *Texts in cybernetics*. Felton, CA: American Society for Cybernetics Conference Workbook. Retrieved August 8, 2008 from http://www.inteco.cl/biology/ontology/

Maturana, H. R. & Varela, F. J. (1988). *The tree of knowledge; The biological roots of human understanding*. Boston, MA: Shambhala.

Mills, C. W. (1959). *The power elite*. London: Oxford University Press.

Mills, C. W. (1940). Situated actions and vocabularies of motive. *American Sociological Review, 5* (1), 904-913.

Monge, P. R. & Contractor, N. S. (2003). *Theories of communication networks*. New York: Oxford University Press.

Nofsinger, R. E. (1999). *Everyday conversation*. Prospect Heights, IL: Waveland Press.

Parsons, T. (1951). *The social system*. Glencoe, Il: Free Press.

Rorty, R. (1989). *Contingency, irony, and solidarity*. New York: Cambridge University Press.

Scott, M. B. & Stanford M. L. (1968). Accounts. *American Sociological Review, 33*, 46-62.

Searle, J. R. (1969). *Speech acts; An essay in the philosophy of language*. New York: Cambridge University Press.

Shotter, J. (1984). *Social accountability and selfhood*. Oxford: Basil Blackwell.

Shotter, J. (1993). *Conversational realities: Constructing life through language*. Thousand Oaks, CA: Sage.

Todorov, T. (1985). *Mikhail Bakhtin; The dialogical principle* (W. Godzich, Trans.). Minneapolis, MN: University of Minnesota Press.

Volosinov, V. N. (1986). *Marxism and the philosophy of language*. Cambridge, MA: Harvard University Press.

Wittgenstein, L. (1958). *Philosophical investigations*. (G. E. M. Anscombe, Trans.). Englewood Cliffs, NJ: Prentice Hall.

Forsythe, K. (2006). *Sailing*. 25 cm x 60 cm, acrylic on paper.

Forsythe, K. (2005). *In the Garden 2*. 30 cm x 35 cm, mixed media collage on paper.

Cybernetics And Human Knowing. Vol. 15, nos. 3-4, pp. 163-172

A Cybernetic Musing: Five Friends

Ranulph Glanville[1]

Preamble

This column is based on a paper presented at the last "Problems of..." conference organised by Gerard de Zeeuw and myself in the week after Easter, 2001, which formed part of de Zeeuw's University of Amsterdam Professorial retirement celebrations.[2]

Introduction

There are many devices, concepts and such-like that help us think. In my enjoyment of thinking about thinking, I have become particularly aware of the existence of five of these, for I have found I like to go on thinking expeditions with them: they are my "friends." I have mentioned all five in previous columns – but some only in passing. Here, I shall introduce each, and then use them in exploring the idea of intelligence, chosen as an archetypical concept for thinking.

These five are not the only concepts I value in such a way, but they are amongst those I value most.

First Friend: *A description of a thing is not that thing (the description is not the thing described).*

This is the basic premise of representation (as stated so clearly by de Saussure, 1966[3]). Its origin is in the practice of thinking and of communicating, and I suppose it is as old as they are: for (apart from some sort of direct ephemeral union that may or

---

1. CybernEthics Research, Southsea, UK
2. The conferences, initiated by de Zeeuw in 1979, formed a particularly delightful series and ran over 22 years and 12 meetings. They attracted a loyal following because of how they were organised and the style of de Zeeuw's direction, leading to an academic exchange of the highest quality, and a lot of enjoyment, too. Some distinguishing elements were: a full and generous social programme; no parallel sessions; presentation at the conference as refereeing process (final papers were written after the conference); and a theme set by de Zeeuw using a particularly challenging and open form of articulation. The theme for this conference was "Problems of Individual Emergence." For various reasons, publication of the proceedings was much delayed. My paper "A t'Tribute" was omitted due to some misunderstanding (but has since been published in an annex (Glanville, 2007b)). The delay allowed me to develop my thinking, but I still consider the original to contain several important concepts, especially when gathered together. So, after the original delayed publication, I have reworked it, modifying it to take into account some more recent thinking (in particular, the connected notions of sharing and betweenness). I am grateful to the editors Gerard de Zeeuw, Martha Vahl, and Ed Mennuti of the conference proceedings for their permission to republish this renamed, much amended, but still recognisable paper.
3. Ferdinand de Saussure (1857 to 1913) published little. The reference is to an assembly from notes taken during a series of lectures in the 1890's (Saussure, 1966).

may not exist) we know of no thinking or communicating without some form of representation—where the term is used in the most general, liberal sense.[4]

For representation, Saussure required a structure of two elements. One is the represented, the other the representing. These are not inherently connected, being brought together for a moment by the agent making the representation. There is no inherent, logical, symbolic, semiological or other a priori relationship between the two. The agent receiving the representation understands the concurrence and the "two in the one" – the two separate elements brought together in the act of representation (one is normally explicit, the other implicit). Sophisticated accounts of representation and description, depending on complex social constructions, must be founded on this Saussurian act. I can conceive no simpler way representation could be, unless an ephemeral, direct union – which may be communication but probably isn't representation and is certainly beyond this discussion.

In this account, meaning is not transferred. An arbitrary bringing together of two unrelated elements is treated as a representation, allowing both *speaker* and *listener* to create and again represent their own meanings, which they have (individually) constructed. The mechanism that allows this to function as a means of communication was elaborated in Gordon Pask's conversation theory (e.g., Pask, 1975). Conversation (a form, an iterative, circular interaction) is the archetypically cybernetic act.

At the centre of my interest are these two Saussurian requirements: the separation of the represented from the representing; and the lack of inherent connection between them. For Saussure, they are arbitrarily brought together in the instant. Thus, while in the act of representation the two may appear as one, they must always remain different (Glanville, 1980). Bateson (who talked of *explanatory principles*) reminds us (1972) of Korzybski's proclamation "the map is not the territory," which pithily makes the point. Since, in Saussure's account the representing is not the represented, something found in the one may not be assumed to be in the other. Thus, the describing (i.e., the representing) is not the described (i.e., the represented). These two aspects establish my first friend: A description of the thing is not that thing.

Representation is a muddied field. Much of it concerns interpretations, "official" meanings and so forth. Often it ventures into the highly symbolic, and personal opinion seems asserted, all too frequently, as universal truth. Absolute value is claimed for the manipulative and the personal. This aspect of representation neither interests nor communicates to me. My interest is how representation might occur, the structures and conditions that would allow and sustain it. Such an interest is typical of a cybernetician.

---

4. At least three notable cyberneticians, Lars Loefgren, Humberto Maturana and Klaus Krippendorff, have taken the position that we exist in language, and hold that consideration of language is crucial to understanding and developing cybernetics. I find this difficult to accept as such an absolute view. In my experience there are moments that are completely extra-linguistic. Of course, these cannot be told: Our insistence on telling leads to us considering only that about which we can tell. These extra-linguistic moments can be shared and are thus communicable—but not in a "linguistic" manner.

Second Friend: *Circularity*

Circularity (of form) – leading by iterative recursion to a spiral progression in which we circle, ending above where we started – is cybernetics' central theme (Glanville 2002b). Cybernetics is concerned with "circular causal and feedback mechanisms" (see the Macy Conferences[5]). Wiener's (1948) formulation in his eponymous book, writes of communication and control, giving the essential example of the feedback loop (the prototype for control in a world where error is inescapable—but we can act to alleviate its effect). Conversation is circular.

The argument that circularity is more fundamental in cybernetics than the more conventionally fundamental linearity, depends on Occam's Razor (*Pluralitas non est ponenda sine necessitate* – entities should not be multiplied unnecessarily). Occam's Razor is an efficiency decision maker, telling us we should chose the description giving more for less. It is a device that makes intuitive sense, but is very difficult to implement without ambiguity: what exactly do we mean by the intuitively clear terms *more* and *less*?

Under Occam's Razor, we assert circularity is more general than linearity, because linearity can be understood as a special instance of circularity, with feedback so weak it may be ignored. This argument can be related to early cybernetic arguments about the absolute roles of controller and controlled. It seems these roles are determined energetically: The (traditional) controller uses little energy to affect the behaviour of the controlled, which expends much energy (to affect, in turn, the behaviour of the controller). Accepting that cybernetics is concerned with the form of systems (rather than their physics), the energy argument disappears. When linearity is considered as circularity where *feedback* is ignorably insignificant, we no longer assume those absolute roles (controller and controlled), along with other familiar concepts, such as coded (as opposed to conversational) communication and linear causality, and so forth.

Generalisation to the circular characterises cybernetic systems and the cybernetic way of understanding the world, where interaction, conversation and other similar actualisations of circularity provide both material for study, and cybernetic models through which to carry out that study. Understanding circularity-as-form must include the observer (as an actor in the system), and admitting that which is examined as examinable: confirming a separation between form and content that allows us to, for instance, discuss experience-in-general as form, while insisting that each particular experience is unique, its meaning belonging to each occasion-and-(actor-)observer.

The cybernetics of such explicitly circular systems was called *second-order cybernetics* (see e.g., Glanville, 2002b): a distinction important when we first realised circularity was crucially central to cybernetics. Second-order cybernetics particularly

---

5. The Josiah Macy Foundation supported ten conferences from 1946 to 1953, chaired by Warren McCulloch, on "Circular Causal and Feedback Mechanisms in Biological and Social Systems." Much of the thinking that established cybernetics was developed here: Wiener was a participant. Wiener's MIT dinners and a prior Macy Conference (1942) developed a basis for an transdisciplinary meta-subject, which Wiener named "cybernetics".

insisted on the involved observer making (and accepting responsibility for) his/her observations: a circular process where each observation changes both observer and observed, leading inexorably to new observations!

The observer observes; what is observed changes; a new observation is made. Observation is circular, and circularity is the necessary form for interaction (a key notion in de Zeeuw's approach, see Glanville, 2002a.)

Third Friend: *The Turing Test*

The Turing Test is a conceptual tool, like Occam's Razor. Both are hard to pin down precisely, yet share an intuitive obviousness. The test was introduced by Alan Turing (1950) in the article "Computing Machinery and Intelligence." Its original formulation is frequently considered over-complicated and it is often presented in a simpler form, as here.

To transcend questions originating in Lady Lovelace's assessment of Babbage's engines, dating from the 1830s, concerning whether Artificial Intelligence might, in theory, be possible, Turing proposed changing from a test based in definitions of intelligence to one based on recognising intelligence in operation.

The paraphernalia of the Turing Test is a communication link that can be used with equal facility by both human and computer. Our task (as the human involved) is to judge whether an interactive behaviour with some respondent is intelligent (within a particular context). We (humans) are in a separate space from the respondent (either human or machine), connected only by the link. By definition, we cannot know which our respondent is, but, by interacting with it we may guess (see the next, Black Box, section). Judging it intelligent depends only on us recognising the quality intelligence in the interaction: whether human or machine is of no significance. If we determine the behaviour is intelligent, finding our partner in interaction is a machine should make no difference to our judgement.[6]

Behind the Turing Test is the remarkable assumption mentioned above. Turing does not assume intelligence is a property, but a quality attributed by an observer (you or I) to the behaviour we observe of some entity (object) we are in interaction with: thence, a quality attributed to an object by an observer, consequent upon their interaction. It is recognised rather than measured, not belonging to the "intelligent" object, but is rather a gift from the observer to that object, resulting from the interaction. Thus, questions about whether the object can be intelligent or not become irrelevant: intelligence is not seen as being in the object, but in behaviours in interaction, an attributive gift from an observer (Glanville, 2001a).

Turing's Test implies one further assertion: We should trust experience. We should question what theory tells us, if it counteracts "pure" experience. This does not

---

6. The Turing Test can be used, in generalised form, to determine the existence of any quality in any interaction: It can remove problems of prejudice including those based on race, colour, religion, gender and sexual orientation, although logic does not, of course, preclude emotional responses. Nor can the excuse of trickery on the part of our partner be sustained: for we observers judge that we recognise a particular quality.

dismiss theory, but demands a relationship between theory and experience in which experience is given proper authority. Experience is all we have.

The outcomes of Turing's Test are owned by and the responsibility of the observer(s) in interaction with their partner other(s).

Fourth Friend: *The Black Box*

The concept of the Black Box was introduced into cybernetics primarily by W. Ross Ashby (1956). Attributing the notion to James Clerk Maxwell,[7] he suggested everything might be considered a Black Box. The Black Box allows us to remain profoundly ignorant, yet to act: While we do not know, we can, nevertheless, build descriptions (acquire knowings) allowing us to act, as if we knew. I have elaborated Ashby's position in this journal recently (Glanville, 2007a), where I summarise how the (Ashby) Black Box works thus:

> An observer notices a change. To account for this (s)he installs a device where (s)he observed the change. The device is a Black Box, which has an outside and is assumed to have an inside, which, however, cannot be examined. The purpose in installing this device is to postulate a mechanism accounting for (generating) the change (in the observer's realm of observations). No matter that we believe we understand what's going on inside, the device cannot be opened: it remains black.[8]

> The observer develops and tests suppositions about the Black Box's mechanism by interacting with it (providing inputs and observing outputs). When, through this interaction, the observer has constructed a mechanism accounting for the observed changes, we often say the observer has whitened the box. This whitening takes place, however, between observer and Black Box, existing in the description built of the proposed mechanism: it is not in the Black Box, which we cannot (by definition) look into. Indeed, the Black Box is a fiction inserted to allow the construction of a description giving us a mechanism. We observe and extend the change and construct the account, through interaction with what is, in effect, a fantasy.[9]

But Ashby also suggested the Black Box might be considered universal. I believe this is a prescient understanding: The Black Box is the best available description of how we confront the world. However, accepting this entails we remain fundamentally ignorant of any posited, external, mind-independent reality—or even whether there could be such a thing. We cannot know. With the Black Box, we do not need to. Thus, the Black Box can be understood as the root device of what is now called *radical constructivism*.[10] These extensions of how we understand the Black Box are mine (Glanville, 1979, 1982). They tell us that the outcomes of installing and observing a Black Box are owned by, and the responsibility of, the observer.

---

7. It has always been difficult to trace this attribution. I tried for years before Dr Albert Mueller (at the University of Vienna) informed me the source is Maxwell's (1881) "Theory of Heat."
8. Remember, we invented and placed the device.
9. This is no longer quite Ashby's account, for he appears to consider the Box may be whitened, without being clear how.
10. Although it is possible to cite a key Glasersfeld paper, the publication of a collection edited by Marie Larochelle gives a much wider source, and is a delight. See Glasersfeld (2007).

The Black Box is the epitome of Bateson's *explanatory principle*. It shows us clearly why no scientific theory can be held to be absolutely true: for, no matter how well the description we develop with a Black Box stands up, we do not see inside and so the Box can never be whitened.[11]

The Black Box isn't really there,[12] and it has no connection with what, if anything, happens in whatever mind independent reality there may or may not be.

Fifth Friend: *The Principle (Law) of Mutual Reciprocity*

The Principle (or Law) of Mutual Reciprocity states that, if through drawing a distinction we are willing to give a certain quality to that we distinguish on one side of the distinction, we must also permit the possibility of the same quality being given to that which we distinguish on the other side of this distinction:[13] If I distinguish myself from you and I consider I am intelligent, I must consider that you (which I distinguish from I) might also be intelligent.

The principle does not require the quality be claimed for both sides of the distinction, only that it might be: The principle concerns possibility and potential, not actualisation. This relates to the act of valuing: If we are to value something, we must accept the value might be zero. A quality may appear on either side, but, its value being zero, it may appear absent. However, the potential remains.

This Principle derives from the condition of drawing a *first* distinction. I have argued (Glanville, 1990b), that, distinguishing ourselves, we must also distinguish an other: There is no distinction in a world of one, so there is no point if I distinguish myself, but distinguish no other from which I am distinct (what does it mean, to be distinct, when I am alone?). This is the source of the principle: On either side of the distinction is an assumed potential sameness: In the first distinction, we may call this a sense of self. As a consequence of (the reason for) distinction drawing, it is present not only in the first distinction, but in all distinctions. It is general.

This principle explains how qualities such as intelligence may be understood to belong to both participants in an interaction; shared, in the between. Unfolding, I can say that, recognising intelligence in you I confirm it in me; and that you, acting in the intelligence I recognise in you, confirm my intelligence. This suggests that generosity of approach is important. We should look to find and affirm qualities both in another and in ourselves. We seek to welcome these qualities, rather than deny them.

In this journal, I have argued that favouring such positive qualities is a major benefit of second order cybernetics (Glanville, 2004). We can develop a richer account of being human than the impoverishing approach so familiar in the materialist,

---

11. It can be seen as providing a mechanism (metaphor) supporting Piaget's views of how children build their pictures of their worlds.

12. I cannot resist a reference to the great Captain Beefheart, aphorism author, painter and rock star, who said: "I'm not really here. I just stick around for my friends." A true Black Box!

13. I am using the notion of distinction introduced by George Spencer Brown in his *Laws of Form* (1969), in the extension I argue in Glanville (1990b), where I insisted a distinction consists of 3 distinguished elements. I first introduced the principle in Glanville (1990a), written a couple of years before my 1990b paper.

utilitarian interpretations, which assert our essential selfishness, suggesting the model for human behaviour is mean and grabbing. In contrast, I revel in our generosity (Glanville, 2001c).

Thinking with My Friends

Why have I referred to these thinking devices as friends? Because, as with my human friends, I like to be with them. I enjoy their company. I like doing things with them, especially when I am surprised in our interaction and can consequently increase the range of my ideas. I will demonstrate this by thinking with them about the already mentioned subject, intelligence.

Locating Intelligence[14]

How do we come to consider intelligence? Traditionally, we have thought of intelligence as a property of the individual in whom we have recognised it. However, our experience of intelligence is, I believe, through interaction. We assume the other may be intelligent,[15] and confirm it by interacting with the other's behaviour, recognising the presence of intelligence in the behaviour of the interaction.

Consider further! Intelligence is a quality we recognise in others as we account for their behaviour. This behaviour is formed in interaction. So intelligence is recognised as arising between us (as shared) in this interaction, not in one participant or the other, no matter that we may express it by a statement such as "You are clearly intelligent." We give it because we recognise (and can recognise) it in our shared behaviour, in our interaction, and it is through this that we can come to consider ourselves intelligent. Thus the attribution to another is a sort of mirroring activity.

The intelligence we recognise is not recognised in individuals but it in behavioural interaction. Although we maintain intelligence is caused by individuals in the interaction, this intelligence is not observed in them, but in the interaction that is their shared behaviour. I believe this is how we meet intelligence, in everyday life. Attributes do not emerge. We recognise them. Their commonality is not as properties of objects, but as attributions to (and from) interactions in the mind of the attributor. (I will, however, accept that we may consider the self-attribution of a quality as treatable as a property.)

---

14. De Zeeuw's text for the conference "Problems of Individual Energence" included intelligence as a key example. Signalling intelligence out as a key example also makes it more than an example, perhaps an exemplification.

15. We have traditionally associated intelligence with human beings: hence we question the possibility of intelligence in machines, the original reason for the invention of the Turing Test, on which this thinking is based. We do not question intelligence in humans!

My Friends and Intelligence

Finally, I will examine the contributions to this understanding of intelligence of my five friends (in reverse order). In this manner, I will show their power as thinking companions.

My description of the way we experience behaviours we come to call intelligent exemplifies the Principle of Mutual Reciprocity in action. The intelligence I recognise in the other is the intelligence I recognise, existing in shared behaviour, arising in interaction (as I observe it). I think of this as occupying a space between (hence the importance of the in-between in the interface, discussed in Glanville, 1997). I recognise intelligence as a quality I construct from observed behaviours in a shared interaction. It is both mutual and reciprocal: What I have you have. I know I have it, because I give it to you and you give it to me: We are co-partners. This is Friend Five.

Yet I have made no assertion about properties I take to belong to my co-participant(s) in the interaction. I know nothing of you – my other – except what I observe in interaction with what I call your behaviours, where I recognise intelligence. Note that I did all this. I have treated my other as a Black Box. In the sense in which I have qualified the term, I know, and can know, nothing of what happens in this other. I can observe behaviour in interaction with me (which is how I come to believe (s)he is present in our world). From this, I can build a description allowing me to attribute the quality intelligence to the interaction and to each participant. Thus, we attribute (if we do) the quality to the other, without having to know what happens inside the insideless and fabulous Black Box (and, hence, not knowing any properties). This is Friend Four.

The means, by which we do this, is the Turing Test, which can be seen as the Black Box, made operational. The Turing Test allows us to attribute the quality of intelligence regardless of the nature of the object to which we attribute it (it allows us to step outside our prejudices)! The Turing Test achieves this because its operational premise is, in effect, the Black Box. We never know what is inside the Black Box. We observe behaviour, interact with that, and build descriptions that seem to account for the behaviours. We express the building of the description, in this case, in giving the quality of intelligence, thus performing the Turing Test. This is Friend Three.

The way, we build descriptions that work, is through interaction: that is, productive circularity in shared behaviour. The processes mentioned above are circular in form: I do something, and you do something else (which I take to be in response). As I begin to build my description (and, I suppose—by the Principle of Mutual Reciprocity—you do too) I extend the value of my description by adjusting (controlling) the input in order to test how the description continues to work. Such testing lies at the base of most accounts of science.

Circularity is further involved because it creates a form for interaction, passing both the interaction itself and the quality under consideration (i.e., intelligence) between the participants. This is Friend Two.

Finally, intelligence is recognised in the behaviours exhibited in interaction. It exists in a description of these behaviours. Firstly, in the description by which we attach the label *intelligent* to this behaviour. Secondly, and as importantly, in the recognition that the behaviour expresses (describes) the object. Intelligence is seen not in the object to which we will attribute it (if this object is a Black Box, we cannot see in it), but in a description of the object's behaviour-in-interaction. The attribution of the quality (i.e., intelligence) is not in the object but is in the description (of the behaviour). Since the quality is not in the object, it cannot be (inherently) a property of the object. This is Friend One.

Conclusions

It is, perhaps, clear that my Friends are inter-connected: They work together as a team, and they imply each other. They are related in other ways, too. For instance, the Black Box, Turing's Test, and the difference between the description and what is described are all related to a notion of ignorance, a much underrated condition. I believe, if we have anything at all, what we have is experience: If we seek reality, that is where our realities can lie. I believe this way of thinking is powerful and general. Many qualities other than intelligence are well treated in this manner. Perhaps all qualities are.

Of course, this sounds like a creed. It is. The premise it is developed from is no less a belief than any other premise. And the argument leads to positions firmly founded in belief.

References

Ashby, W. R. (1956). *An introduction to cybernetics*. London: Chapman and Hall.

Bateson, G. (1972). *Steps to an ecology of mind*. New York: Ballentine

Glanville, R. (1979). The form of cybernetics: Whitening the black box. In J. Miller (Ed.), *Proceedings of 24 Society for General Systems Research/American Association for the Advancement of Science Meeting*, Houston, 1979. Louisville: Society for General Systems Research

Glanville, R. (1980). The same is different. In M. Zeleny (Ed.), *Autopoiesis*. New York: Elsevier

Glanville, R. (1982). Inside every white box there are two black boxes trying to get out. *Behavioural Science, 12* (1).

Glanville, R. (1990a). Sed Quis Custodient Ipsos Custodes. In F. Heylighen, E. Rosseel, & F. Demeyere (Eds.) *Self-steering and cognition in complex systems*. London: Gordon and Breach

Glanville, R. (1990b). The self and the other: The purpose of distinction. In R. Trappl (Ed.), *Cybernetics and Systems '90: The Proceedings of the European Meeting on Cybernetics and Systems Research*. Singapore: World Scientific.

Glanville, R. (1997). Behind the curtain. In R. Ascott (Ed.), *Consciousness Reframed I*. Newport: UWC Newport

Glanville, R. (2001a). An intelligent architecture. *Convergence, 7* (2).

Glanville, R. (2001b). Listen! (The Listen Inn). In G. de Zeeuw, M. Vahl, & E. Mennuti (Eds.) *Problems of participation and connection*. Lincoln: LRC

Glanville, R. (2001c). The man in the train: Complexity, unmanageability, conversation and trust. In H. Wüthrich, W. Winter,& A. Philipp (Eds.) *Grenzen Ökonomischen Denkens*. Wiesbaden: Gabler.

Glanville, R. (2002a). Doing the right thing. *Systems Research and Behavioural Science, 19* (2). (Special issue : Gerard de Zeeuw—a Festschrift. R. Glanville, Ed.)

Glanville, R. (2002b). Second order cybernetics. Retrieved September 17, 2004 from the Encyclopaedia of Life Support Systems at http://www.eolss.net

Glanville, R. (2004). Desirable ethics. *Cybernetics & Human Knowing, 11* (2).

Glanville, R. (2007a) A (cybernetic) musing: Ashby and the black box, *Cybernetics & Human Knowing, 14* (1).

Glanville, R. (2007b). A t' Tribute: Qualities: Properties and attributes. *Systemica, 14 (1–6)*. (Problems of Individual Emergence. G. de Zeeuw, M. Vahl, & E. Mennuti, Eds.)

Glasersfeld, E. von (2007). *Key works in radical constructivism* (M. Larochelle, Ed.). Rotterdam: Sense Publishers.

Pask, G. (1968). Man as a system that needs to learn. In D. J. Stewart (Ed.), Automaton theory and learning systems. London: Academic Press.

Pask, G. (1975). *Conversation theory*. London: Hutchinson.

Saussure, F. de (1966). *Course in general linguistics*. New York: McGraw Hill.

Spencer Brown, G. (1969). *Laws of form*. London: George Allen and Unwin.

Turing, A. (1950). Computing Machinery and Intelligence. *Mind, LIX* (236).

Wiener, N. (1948). *Cybernetics, or communication and control in the animal and the machine*. Cambridge, MA: The MIT Press

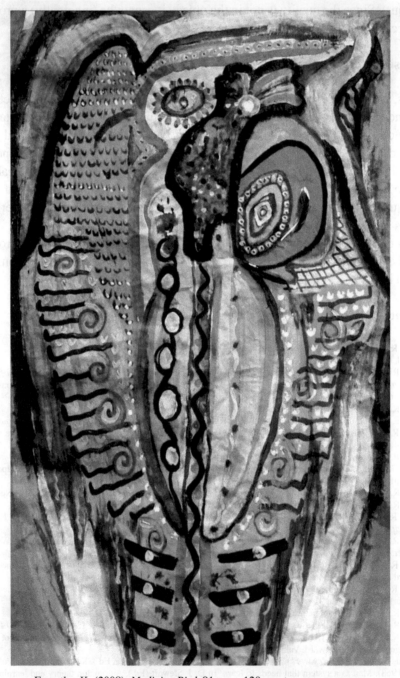

Forsythe, K. (2008). *Medicine Bird*. 91 cm x 120 cm, tempera on paper.

Cybernetics And Human Knowing. Vol. 15, no. 1, pp. 173-184

ASC
American Society for Cybernetics
a society for the art and
science of human understanding

Cybernetics's Reflexive Turns

Klaus Krippendorff[1]

In the history of cybernetics there have been several attempts by cyberneticians to put themselves into the circularities of their theories and designs, invoking a shift from the cybernetics of mechanisms to a *cybernetics of cybernetics*. The latter is the title of a book chapter by Margaret Mead (1968) and of Heinz von Foerster's (1974) compilation of articles on cybernetics. The latter introduced the concept of second-order cybernetics which may have overshadowed or sidelined other reflexivities. I am attempting to recover three additional reflexive turns, describe their origin, implications, and suggest ways in which they continue what Karl Müller (2007) calls an unfinished revolution. These turns are not discussed here in their historical succession but as conceptual expansions of the horizon of cybernetic inquiries and designs.

(1) Cognitive autonomy and the observer

There is widespread consensus that nervous systems are operationally closed, that humans are *cognitively autonomous* beings, responding in their own terms to what should be regarded as perturbations from their environment. This is the starting point of Ernst von Glasersfeld's (1995, 2008) radical constructivism, Humberto Maturana and Francisco Varela's (1980) biology of cognition (also Maturana, 2000; Maturana & Poerksen, 2004), Varela's (1979) principles of biological autonomy, Gordon Pask's (1961) cybernetics of the observer, and underlies von Foerster's (1974, 1979) second-order cybernetics. The earliest mechanical simulation of cognitive autonomy is Ross Ashby's (1952) homeostat. All of these cyberneticians draw conclusions from the acknowledgement that whatever is outside our nervous system is accessible only through that nervous system, and cannot be observed directly and separated from how that nervous system operates.

---

1. Gregory Bateson Professor for Cybernetics, Language, and Culture, The Annenberg School for Communication, University of Pennsylvania. Email: kkrippendorff@asc.upenn.edu

There are significant differences among these theorists. Ashby designed his homeostat in an effort to understand how a brain could adapt to its environment, known only through how it disturbs brain activity. Von Glasersfeld, educational psychologist with a Piagetian orientation, roots his radical constructivism in (subjective) experiences and describes how individuals learn by constructing realities, one on top of or in place of another, whose criterion is not truth but the viability of the observer. Maturana and Varela speak of the nervous system in mechanistic terms as strictly structurally determined, presupposing the autopoiesis (continuous self-production) of the organism. For Maturana (Maturana & Poerksen, 2004, p. 35), observers act in the awareness of distinguishing what they are observing. Von Foerster, the most pronounced critic of the enlightenment project's objectivism, suggests that believing one could observe the world without the realization of being an observer is but an illusion. His reflexivity consists of observers entering their domain of observation and describing their own observing, not what causes them. Like von Glasersfeld, von Foerster considers the reality we see as a construction or invention. Being not determined by external causes, the reality that is seen could be otherwise, thus manifesting human agency. Despite these differences, acknowledging cognitive autonomy leads to the common conception of the rather abstract notion of an observer who attends to his or her own observing, understands his or her understanding, and describes that process in his or her own terms.

I should mention that the idea of second-order cybernetics developed only slowly. In his *Cybernetics of Cybernetics or the Control of Control and the Communication of Communication,* von Foerster (1974) merely distinguishes first and second-order cybernetics by defining the former as the cybernetics of observed systems, and the latter as the cybernetics of observing systems, offering no further articulations. Much of his reflexivity emerged later, in provocative aphorisms and interviews (Foerster, 1979, 1992; Foerster & Poerksen, 2002, pp. 109-111). In his 2003 collection of essays on cybernetics and cognition, he suggested that the essentials of a theory of the observer had been worked out (Foerster, 2003, p. 285).

I agree with Karl Müller's (2007) characterization of second-order cybernetics as an unfinished revolution in the conception of science and of the world more generally. I am suggesting, though, that further development of cybernetics's reflexivity is constrained by three commitments inherent in second-order cybernetics.

1. The commitment to *cognitivism* – taking the autonomy of individual cognition as the exclusive source of explanation, in effect ignoring the social nature of human beings, reducing it to mutual accommodations of individual conceptions (Glasersfeld, 2008), or merely affirming that human beings live in language
2. The commitment to the *primacy of observation* – identifying human beings as observers who seek to *understand* their experiences of observing (the world), rather than, say, as engineers of technology, governors of their society, encouraging meaningful practices of living, including for others

3. The commitment to rely on a *representational language* (Rorty, 1989) –
    consisting of *descriptions*, not necessarily of reality, but acceptable within a
    community of (scientific) observers.

It should be noted that cognition, the process presumed to underlie the attention paid
by observers to their observations, is a highly individualistic construction. This is not
to say that second-order cybernetics has no place for language, which is a collective
artifact. Indeed, von Foerster playfully extended Maturana's proposition that
"everything said is said by an observer" by adding "everything said is said to an
observer" (Foerster, 1979). This echoes Maturana and Varela's (1988) conception of
scientific observers as providing explanations and hypotheses that are testable by the
phenomena the environment continues to bring to the observer's attention and
acceptable by a community of scientific observers. However, the conception of
language underlying these assertions is descriptive, not of an external world but of the
individual understandings shared within a scientific community.

Moreover, descriptions are not meant to act on what they describe. For example,
Maturana and Varela's conception of autopoiesis as an account of the process of living
of living systems has no necessary relation to how living beings operate. Living beings
existed before the concept of autopoiesis was invented in the 1970s and are not
assumed to have changed since the inception of this explanation. Evidently,
descriptions do not change the phenomena they describe only an observing theorist's
understanding of them.

I maintain that these three commitments keep second-order cybernetics with one
foot in the enlightenment project for a positive science, which is committed to
providing truth-verifiable descriptions, in second-order cybernetics, however, from the
perspective of the rather abstract concept of a self-reflecting observer.

(2) Participation – use, design, and conversation – instead of observation

The second reflexivity arises by shifting attention from the limiting concept of an
observer to that of a participant. Consider three situations.

First. Just like von Glasersfeld, Maturana, Varela, Pask, and von Foerster, Ashby
too was preoccupied with cognition, with the mysterious complexity of the human
brain. However, already in his *Design for a Brain*, Ashby (1952) positioned himself
not as an observer but as an experimenter with mechanisms he treated as black boxes
(Ashby, 1956), that is, presuming no knowledge of their design. In this capacity, he
acknowledged that acts of experimentation rendered experimenters as participants in a
larger system composed of them and their objects of interests. Of this larger system,
he concluded, experimenters have access only to the observable consequences of their
own actions. The remainder of the system is left unobserved, hypothetical or hidden
from view. Thus, experimenters do not merely reflect on their own observations, they
must reflect on their participation in systems they actively vary for observable

effects—always acknowledging that an understanding of these systems can never be complete, that one's horizon is always expandable through further actions.

I feel compelled to note that participants rely on what observers regret as undesirable and unintentional observer effects or biases. Heisenberg's uncertainty principle, for example, suggests that whenever observations affect the observed, one can no longer determine with accuracy the properties of the object of one's attention before it was observed. He showed that in quantum physics, one can determine either the location or the momentum of particles, but not both simultaneously. Heisenberg's principle states a limit of the enlightenment ideal of accurate observation. Ashby, however, did not subscribe to this ideal. He acknowledged without regret to be the source of disturbing the object of his attention and constructed models that accounted for both the variations he introduced and the changes he could subsequently observe. By modeling the observable consequences of his actions, Ashby entered the system he constructed as an active participant, not merely as a detached observer, describing or explaining his observations.

Human-computer interfaces provide a good example. What users come to know about their personal computer is limited to the options they were willing and have the time and resources to explore. For competent users, who have learned to navigate a computer along desired paths, that limit may be unproblematic. It may be noticed however, when experiencing their interface to break down, observing different users, or learning something about its architecture.

Second. Designing and building artifacts amounts to a participation that is quite unlike using or experimenting with them. While users' competence results from developing conceptions that are adequate for interacting with what they face, designers' competence is demonstrated by actions that realize intended artifacts in their environment, artifacts whose known structure and functionality conforms to how their designers conceived of experiencing them. Here, human agency shifts from cognitive accommodation to an existing environment to adapting that environment to one's conceptions. Introducing known structures and functionalities into their environment, designers have a far more extensive grasp of what their artifacts can do than users could acquire by examining the options they afford. Despite this extensive grasp, designers too face the limitations of their horizon. Of a working artifact not everything is determined by design. Artifacts may break down unexpectedly, exhibit structurally unanticipated behaviors, may be used in unintended ways, or develop a life of their own, especially when others are involved. Thus, what can be known by design is always only part of the system involving designers, users of designs, and the environment they experience.

With an interest in brains, which are not designed, Ashby built mechanical artifacts to simulate certain brain functions, convinced he could learn something about the structure of the brain from the knowledge of how his models were designed. But the structure of a model is always only one of several hypotheses of the makeup of the modeled.

In his epistemological explorations of black boxes, Ashby encountered informational or computational limits of experimentation or use by building artifacts that exceeded these limits. Subsequently, von Foerster (1984) called the latter "non-trivial machines." The distinction between trivial and non-trivial machines points to fundamental differences between observation, use, and design (Krippendorff, 2008b). Clearly, observers are at the mercy of how the world manifests itself: unfolding sequentially. Only the most trivial machines turn out to be intelligible by observation. Non-trivial machines, contemporary computers, for example, are designed and manufactured for use and the act of designing leaves their designers with insights into possibilities of use far exceeding any users' ability to explore all alternative paths. Ashby and von Foerster are clear in relating the distinction between trivial and non-trivial machines to human abilities – observation, experimentation or use, and design. Their accounts did not, however, extend to the language that made this comparison possible, which is my next point.

Third. The use of language, languaging, is essentially embodied in their speakers and participatory. Most cyberneticians are quick to affirm the importance of language, for example in drawing distinctions and understanding. When von Foerster (1979) playfully extended Maturana's proposition "everything said is said by an observer" by adding "everything said is said to an observer," he embedded the description of observations in a communicational paradigm. Von Glasersfeld, following Piaget, demonstrated how the grammatical structures of linguistic expressions reflect cognitive constructions much like Benjamin Lee Whorf (1956) did. Maturana (2000) defined language as the consensual coordination of consensual coordination of behavior, introducing coordination as the defining function of language. However, detailed conceptions of structures in languaging, what a language does and how it is altered in conversations is rarely found in the discourse of cybernetics.

To me, a cybernetic conception of language needs to be built on conversation, echoing Pask (1975) but avoiding his computer metaphors and embracing instead Maturana's consensual coordinations, Austin's (1962) performatives, C. Wright Mills's (1940) and Marvin Scott's (1968) accountability, Searle's (1968) speech acts, and, most importantly, Ludwig Wittgenstein's (1958) language games (see also Krippendorff, 2008c). I take conversation as

1. Constituting itself in the practices of its participants, what they say and do, especially affirming their participation in the conversation
2. Involving naturally embodied and mundane verbal, gestural, and mediated interactions or turns, not requiring any theory of conversation to engage in one
3. Self-organizing. Participants mutually regulate each others conversational practices without outside intervention, instruction, or management
4. Preserving dialogical equality among participants (e.g., Holquist, 1990, pp. 40-66), which entails contributing in response to the contributions by others and maintaining mutual accountability, the possibility of holding each other accountable and a commitments to offer accounts when requested (Krippendorff,

2008c) or deemed constructive, especially including the willingness of (re)articulating one's understanding of other participants' understanding (second-order understanding, see Krippendorff, 1993). This would exclude the role of (detached scientific) observers.

5. Producing a diversity of jointly constructed artifacts: coordinated understandings, plans of action, designs, and novel use of language

Cybernetically informed family systems theory, for example, has embraced this reflexive turn by considering therapists as dialogically equal participants in conversations with their clients (Anderson, 1997). I have proposed a conception of social organizations as reconstitutable networks of conversation through which members of organizations move more or less freely (Krippendorff, 2008c).

As Gregory Bateson (1972) taught us, we always participate in the circuitry of the world. Acknowledging one's participation in a larger system, whether as explorers, designers, or constituents of social formations, is a reflexive turn that reveals reality, its parts, and the self as interactively or dialogically constructed, and admits that individual knowledge is necessarily incomplete, expandable with efforts. By contrast, observers are more likely to take the position of masters of their observations and building monological models of their world. One could say that participation is based on know-how, observation on know-what (Krippendorff, 2008b).

(3) Realizing human agency in the relativity of discourses

Ashby argued that cybernetics had its own foundation, distinct from established disciplines like physics, psychology, and general systems theory, to name but three, and began to develop that foundation in his *An Introduction to Cybernetics* (Ashby, 1956). While his project could only be accomplished in language—he wrote the text—he did not see his writing as an essential part of this foundation. I consider Ashby's *Introduction* as constituting an inter-disciplinary discourse for cybernetics.

But what is discourse? Dictionaries tend to define discourse an extensive body of writing. I am relying on a more inclusive definition.

To me, *discourse* is systematically constrained conversation (Krippendorff, 2009, pp. 217-234). It exhibits five defining properties:

1. Like conversation, a discourse *produces artifacts*, be they textual matter (designs, theories, and explanations), particular practices (rituals, legal decisions), a system of tangible artifacts (technologies), or constructions of reality (ranging from facts to coherent universes)
2. It *requires a discourse community* whose members are committed to maintain, rearticulate, reconstruct, elaborate, or invent these artifacts
3. Members of its discourse community *institute their recurrent practices,* for example, in the form of requiring the use of particular methods, providing regular publications, manning educational programs, certifying of membership, and setting standards for communication within the community

4. It *maintains a boundary* at which decisions are made regarding who or what belongs and who or what does not. This binary distinction may be made on various grounds, a paradigm, set of axioms, epistemology, or the kind of artifacts it produces
5. It *justifies itself – its artifacts and practices –* to other discourses, so as to sustain it in the continuous through flow of discourse practitioners, available resources, and reality constructions supplied by or to other discourses.

Physics, for example, is a discourse that constructs a universe that is coherent and can be observed and experimented with by the methods of physics, which presumes, among other things, that this universe is causally determined, has no agency, and does not understand how it is being investigated. Within its boundary, the discourse of physics is self-organizing in that it is physicists who educate new physicists and determine whether the theories proposed by physicists are consistent, valid, and further the standing of the discourse. Psychology is another discourse. It creates models of individual human beings' behavior, now largely of human cognition. Biology is a discourse. It creates theories purporting to explain the operation of living systems as distinct from systems of interest to other disciplines. Cybernetics is a discourse as well – cyberneticians decide who is one, settle on their own conceptual repertoire in conversations, and introduce circular systems into their environment – although in the past, it failed to develop strong institutions and its inter-disciplinarity and widespread fascination with its artifacts has left its boundary open for other discourses to forage what suits them.

Owing to the ability of humans to travel across discourses, discourses are not entirely independent from one another. Some discourses mine other discourses for their ideas, as computer science, artificial intelligence, and biology did from first-order cybernetics and Luhmann's (1995) sociology has done from second-order cybernetics, autopoiesis in particular. Some colonize other discourses as cognitive science is attempting to do regarding linguistics and psychology; or the chemical/pharmaceutical discourse does regarding psychiatry – encouraging psychiatrists to administer drugs in place of engaging in talk. There are also discourses that assume foundational status, for example, by insisting that everything real is physical, physics considers itself foundational to all other "less perfect" or "underdeveloped" natural sciences. Similarly, by claiming that all social phenomena are ultimately economic transactions, economics assumes a foundational role in relation to other social sciences. In view of these interactions, discourses that do not claim to be foundational to other discourses often struggle to maintain their autonomy.

One manifestation of human agency is the ability to reflect on one discourse from the perspective of another. Foundational discourses tend to prevent that reflection, equating the artifacts they construct with the universe that exists. Physicists, for example, construct so-called laws of nature that are presumed to underlie nature as observed. This conviction discourages physicists to go outside their discourse and experience the agency they always have in moving from one discourse to another unable to acknowledge their artifacts as human constructions. I am invoking Bateson's (1979) insight that information arises from multiple descriptions, Werner Ulrich's (1996, 2000) boundary critique in critical systems thinking, Wittgenstein's (1958) account of meaning as the awareness of alternative ways of "seeing as," and suggest that the belief in a singular truth amounts to being entrapped in one privileged discourse and hence blind to it.

Biology is a discourse, of course. It encourages conversations that follow its (bio)logic for explaining the operation of living beings. Maturana and Varela (1980) take autopoiesis – a biological artifact invented to explain the process of living of living beings – as a prerequisite for all other features of living beings: reproduction, cognition, adaptation to their environment, and speaking a language. The belief that autopoiesis is primary, prior to, or a prerequisite for the human use of language distinguishes *biological foundationalism* (reiterated in Maturana, 2000, 2008) from non-foundationalist acknowledgements that humans have the option of discursively constructing themselves, each other, their bodies, their worlds, including their vocabularies and conversations. Not that Maturana and Varela are wrong. Their biology is impeccable. However, taking the reflexivity of Heidegger (Dreyfus, 1992) to heart, one can also argue that it is our attention to our being-with-others that makes us, our body and relationships to each other, real for us. Biology is limited to what its discourse highlights. Our body does more, is far richer than our explanations of it. Furthermore, it presupposes linguistic competencies to enter the discourse of biology and rearticulate its artifacts, including autopoiesis, comprehension of which is subordinate to linguistic competence and entirely optional to the living of living beings, as above suggested.

To preserve this reflexive turn, I am suggesting that cybernetic discourse not be grounded in foundationalist conceptions such as of physics, biology, cognitive science or semiotics, that it should rely instead on a conversational conception of human beings, replace observers by participants and the representational conception of language by constructive, interactive, or performative ones, which are capable of acknowledging human agency and the ability of redesigning reality.

(4) Inclusion or social contextualization of cybernetics

Von Foerster cites Margaret Mead's (1968) talk on the cybernetics of cybernetics as the starting point of second-order cybernetics. In personal communication, von Foerster claimed to have clarified Mead's "somewhat confused ideas." However, rereading her talk (at which I was present) reveals that she may have had something quite different in mind.

As an anthropologist, Mead was of course keenly aware of the role of language in directing the attention of its speakers. She characterized "cybernetics as a way of looking at things and as a language for expressing what one sees" (1968, p. 2). This quote could be interpreted in support of the cognitivism in von Foerster's second-order cybernetics. But then she expressed concerns about what the "language of cybernetics" did to society, how society becomes organized as a result of implementing cybernetic systems, calling on cyberneticians to assume responsibilities for how these systems are changing society in unprecedented ways.

Mead's talk was delivered during the cold war. She saw how the Soviet Union embraced cybernetics quite unlike the U.S. did, fearing "the possibility that the Soviet system may become totally cyberneticized, in the technical sense, as a way of controlling everything within its borders and possibly outside, with thousands of giant computers linked together in a system of prodigious and unheard-of efficiency" (1968, p. 3). In contrast and regarding the West, she spoke of the "possibility of using cybernetics as a form of communication in a world of increasing specialization" in the hope of being able to develop sophisticated ways of handling the complexities that cybernetically designed systems are introducing in society (1968, pp. 4-5). She saw that the automation of social institutions made society less governable—a phenomenon that we now know in retrospect eventually undermined the Soviet Union and networked individuals and institutions in unprecedented ways, opening cyberspaces for us to explore but also causing global instabilities for which we have no ready-made answers. Mead's proposal to account for the organizational/ technological consequences of implementing cybernetic ideas was one of expanding the discourse of cybernetics to embrace the context of its social consequences. It amounts to suggesting that cybernetics take up what sociologists push to their margins as the unintended consequences of actions, and economists consider the externalities of their theories.

Warren McCulloch (1945) had discussed a similar reflexivity before Mead did, suggesting that physicists account for themselves in terms of the discourse of physics, which would, he thought, transform physicists into neurophysiologists. Mead, however, was an anthropologist, not a logician, and advocated a move from the early first-order cybernetics to where it becomes embodied. Keenly aware of how the application of cybernetic discourse was complexifying society, she turned McCulloch's logical inclusion problem into an inter-disciplinary challenge.

The reflexive turn that Mead advocated renders cybernetics as a socio-technological discourse that acknowledges the discourses of other disciplines, addresses the social embeddedness of their artifacts, and calls on cyberneticians to not only attend to how they contribute to the ongoing transformations of society but also be accountable for their effects. Mead recognized that all sciences are part of society. One would hope that all sciences therefore address the consequences of their products. However, the convenience of partitioning the world into separately manageable fields, the widespread illusion of objectivity, and the blindness of established sciences to their own discourse, leaves cybernetics as a unique inter-discipline, able to address the very socio-technological complexities it gives birth to. One might add that at the time Mead made her proposal, the cybernetic revolution, commonly but mistakenly called the information revolution, had barely begun and the complexities it created were difficult to foresee.

The emerging cybernetic epistemology

These four reflexive turns jointly encourage a new epistemology:

> an epistemology of participation in social systems under continuous reconstruction (rearticulation and redesign) by their human constituents, able and willing to hold each other accountable for what they contribute, say and do, and how they move through discourses and networks of conversations among them.

This cybernetic epistemology (theory of knowing) does not claim to represent anything outside of it (an ontology or description of reality, absent its knowers). It must merely be livable by knowledgeable actors in and on their environment. It acknowledges various roles of language – networks of conversation and multiple discourses – in how the human constituents of social systems coordinate themselves in the creation of artifacts that constitutively enter and alter the very systems of which they are a part.

Specifically, it recognizes that promoting theories, proposing courses of actions, designing and building artifacts commensurate with one's understanding of a system of interest, and communicating with other constituents of that system changes the system as understood.

By locating abstractions and meta-perspectives in the language used in conversations and discourses, which are self-organizing, it is an epistemology that is embodied in human practices.

As such, it abandons the unattainable and unethical God's eye view of the universe, common to enlightenment scientists and the adherents of universalism, for the admission that one can experience only one's own contributions to a continuously evolving social reality.

Conversely, it suggests that observing social systems from their outside precludes access to what constitutes them: participation. Knowing a social system is demonstrable only by constructively participating in it.

It invokes a communication ethic that grants all human constituents of social systems a measure of dialogical equality (participation), adequate agency (choices) and accountability (see Krippendorff, 2008c), cognitive autonomy (holding individually constructed and potentially unlike conceptions), and an ability to communicate with one another (coordinating each others' understandings).

It affirms that social organizations are repeatedly reconstitutable by their members and, once enacted, under continuous reconstruction by their constituents.

It favors the construction of realities that preserve the circularities of participation in networks of conversation.

While participation is common and unavoidable in everyday social life, the difference between an unreflective being-with-others and cybernetically guided participation lies not in claiming privileged access to reality and truths but in accepting accountability to those who may have to live in the realities one's discourse is projecting, supporting, or bringing into being.

The reflexive turns that various cyberneticians have been taking for some time—not always fully articulated or formalized—suggests a convergence on a definition:

Cybernetics – an inter-disciplinary discourse
that brings forth radically reflexive realities.

The attention to reflexivity, which includes a host of well-known circular causalities, self-references, recursions, and autonomies, moves cybernetics from a science of "control and communication" to an effort by the cybernetic community to come to grips with the challenges that its discourse is creating in the world.

References

Anderson, H. (1997). *Conversation, language, and possibilities*. New York: Basic Books.

Ashby, W. R. (1952). *Design for a brain*. London: Chapman & Hall.

Ashby, W. R. (1956). *An introduction to cybernetics*. London: Chapman & Hall.

Austin, J. (1962). *How to do things with words*. London: Oxford University Press.

Bateson, G. (1972). *Steps to an ecology of mind*. New York: Ballantine Books.

Bateson, G. (1979). *Mind and nature: A necessary unity*. New York: Dutton.

Dreyfus, H. L. (1992). *Being in the world*. Cambridge, MA: The MIT Press.

Foerster, H. von, et al. (Eds.) (1974). *Cybernetics of cybernetics or the control of control and the communication of communication*. Minneapolis: Future Systems.

Foerster, H. von (1979). Cybernetics of cybernetics. In K. Krippendorff (Ed.), *Communication and control in society* (pp. 5-8). New York: Gordon and Breach.

Foerster, H. von. (1984). Principles of self-organization. In H.Ulrich & G.J. B. Probst (Eds.), *Self-organization and management of social systems* (pp. 2-24). New York: Springer.

Foerster, H. von. (1992). Ethics and second-order cybernetics. *Cybernetics & Human Knowing, 1* (1), 9-19.

Foerster, H. von. (2003). *Understanding understanding: Essays on cybernetics and cognition*. New York: Springer.

Foerster, H. von, & Poerksen, B. (2002). *Understanding systems: Conversations on epistemology and ethics*. Heidelberg: Carl-Auer.

Glasersfeld, E. von (1995). *Radical constructivism; A way of knowing and learning*. Washington, DC: Falmer.

Glasersfeld, E. von (2008). Who conceives society? *Constructivist Foundations, 3* (2), 59-64. Retrieved December 19, 2008 from http://www.univie.ac.at/constructivism/journal/articles/CF3.2.pdf

Holquist, M. (1990). *Dialogism; Bakhtin and his world*. London and New York: Routledge.

Krippendorff, K. (1993). Major Metaphors of Communication and some Constructivist Reflections on their Use. *Cybernetics & Human Knowing, 2* (1), 3-25.

Krippendorff, K. (2008a). Towards a radically social constructivism. *Constructivist Foundations, 3* (2), 91-94. Retrieved December 19, 2008 from http://www.univie.ac.at/constructivism/journal/articles/CF3.2.pdf

Krippendorff, K. (2008b). Four (in)determinabilities, not one. In J. V. Ciprut (Ed.), *Indeterminacy: The mapped, the navigable, and the uncharted* (pp. 315-344). Cambridge, MA: The MIT Press.

Krippendorff, K. (2008c). Social organizations as reconstitutable networks of conversations. *Cybernetics & Human Knowing, 15* (3-4), 149-161.

Krippendorff, K. (2009). *On communicating: Otherness, meaning, and information* (Fernando Bermejo, Ed.). New York: Routledge.

Luhmann, N. (1995). *Social systems* (J. Bednartz & D. Baecker, Trans.). Stanford, CA: Stanford University Press.

Maturana, H. R. (1988). Ontology of observing. In *Texts in cybernetics*. Felton, CA: American Society for Cybernetics Conference Workbook. Retrieved August 8, 2008 from http://www.inteco.cl/biology/ontology/

Maturana, H. R. (2000). The nature of the laws of nature. *Systems Research and Behavioral Science 17*,5: 459-468.

Maturana, H. R. (2008). Time: An imaginary spatial dimension or life occurs in the no-time of a continuously changing present. *Cybernetics & Human Knowing, 15* (1), 83-92.

Maturana, H. R. & Poerksen, B. (2004). *From being to doing: The origins of the biology of cognition* (Wolfram K. Koek & Alison R. Koek, Trans.). Heidelberg: Carl Auer.

Maturana, H. R. & Varela, F. J. (1980). *Autopoiesis and cognition; The realization of the living*. Dordrecht: Reidel.

McCulloch, W. S. (1945). A heterarchy of values determined by the topology of nervous nets. *Bulletin of Mathematical Biology, 7* (2), 89-93). (Reprinted in *Embodiments of mind* (pp. 40-45). Cambridge, MA: The MIT Press.)

Mead, M.(1968). Cybernetics of cybernetics. In H. von Foerster et al. (Eds.). *Purposive Systems* (pp. 1-11). New York: Spartan Books.

Müller, K. H. (2007). The BCL: An unfinished revolution of an unfinished revolution. In A. Müller & K. H. Müller (Eds.), *An unfinished revolution: Heinz von Foerster and the Biological Computer Laboratory BCL 1958-1976* (pp. 407-474). Vienna: Echoraum.

Pask, G. S. (1961). *An approach to cybernetics*. New York: Harper & Brothers.

Pask, G. S. (1975). *Conversation, cognition, and learning*. New York: Elsevier.

Rorty, R. (1989). *Contingency, irony, and solidarity*. New York: Cambridge University Press.

Searle, J. R. (1969). *Speech Acts; An essay in the philosophy of language*. New York: Cambridge University Press.

Ulrich, W. (1996). *A primer to critical systems heuristics for action researchers*. Hull: Centre for Systems Studies, University of Hull.

Ulrich, W. (2000). Reflective practice in the civil society: The contribution of critical systems thinking. *Reflective Practice, 1* (2), 247-268.

Varela, F. J. (1979). *Principles of biological autonomy*. New York: North Holland.

Whorf, B. L. (1956). *Language, thought, and reality* (John B. Carroll, Ed.). Cambridge, MA: The MIT Press.

Wittgenstein, L. (1958). *Philosophical investigations* (G. E. M. Anscombe, Trans.). Englewood Cliffs, NJ: Prentice Hall.

Forsythe, K. (2008). *City*. 60 cm x 60 cm, acrylic on canvas with encaustic.

Cybernetics And Human Knowing. Vol. 15, nos. 3-4, pp. 183-191

Biosemiotic Bateson

Phillip Guddemi[1]

A review of *A Legacy for Living Systems: Gregory Bateson as Precursor to Biosemiotics* edited by Jesper Hoffmeyer. Published in 2008 by Springer Science + Business Media B.V. Volume 2 in the series Biosemiotics, edited by Marcello Barbieri and Jesper Hoffmeyer. ISBN 978-1-4020-6705-1.

In 2005 a Bateson Symposium was held in Copenhagen as one of the last events honoring the 100th anniversary of his birth in 1904. The Symposium was supported by Copenhagen University's priority theme of "Religion in the 21st Century" and Bateson was honored as someone who had integrated a cybernetic theory of communication with a unique concept of the sacred. Many of the participants in this symposium are affiliated, some more loosely than others, with a largely European movement known as biosemiotics.

Jesper Hoffmeyer, one of the most important and prolific figures in this movement, and a major organizer of the Copenhagen Symposium, has now edited a book, *A Legacy for Living Systems: Gregory Bateson as Precursor to Biosemiotics*. In this book are collected 14 essays on a range of topics related to, applying, or extending Bateson's work and legacy. As Hoffman notes in his Introduction, "Bateson the Precursor," Bateson was one of the few scientists in his day to recognize that such phenomena as life, language, consciousness, and communication require an approach beyond the materialistic and Cartesian one which was dominant in biology and much of anthropology in the 20th Century (2008, p. 1).

this issue (and the symposium on which it is based) may indicate a renewed worldwide interest in the work and approach of this unique thinker. The essays are primarily thought pieces, rather than research reports (though there are a few exceptions to this). But their base is scientific research and knowledge and they presume (and facilitate) a sophisticated literacy in science. This is in keeping with Bateson's own practice which was always to relate even philosophical speculations to a specific scientific corpus. Open minded biologists and semioticians, as well as students of Peirce, will be interested in the essays in this book.

Not all the essays relate Bateson's work directly to biosemiotics, an approach for which Hoffmeyer is a pioneer and spokesperson. Hoffmeyer defines biosemiotics as the field "concerned with studying the sign-character of the processes that take place inside or between living systems (from the single cell to full organisms and further to populational or ecological systems)" (2008, p. 4). Bateson was the precursor to this field because he was among the first to show us the importance of communication and pattern in a variety of fields ranging from anthropology to psychology to biology.

---

1. pguddemi@well.com

Bateson's biography is relevant to his biosemiotics, in some unexpected ways. I was struck by one of these in the course of reading Chapter 5, which is an account of Bateson's idea of double description. Julie Hui, Tyrone Cashman, and Terrence Deacon describe how this Batesonian concept is relevant to the emerging biological field known as *evo-devo* (p. 77). Evo-devo, the study of the evolutionary biology of development, is commonly thought to be a recent field of study, one which has emerged largely in the last couple of decades to challenge the hegemony of molecular biology in the understanding of genetics and evolution. When I first came across this field, I immediately saw its relevance to Bateson's ideas, and wondered if anyone else had noticed this. Turning to the most prominent popularization of evo-devo, Sean Carroll's (2005) *Endless Forms Most Beautiful*, I thought to look in the index for Bateson. I did not find Bateson, Gregory. But I did find Gregory's father, William Bateson.

Gregory Bateson used to say in lectures, "When my father invented the word genetics, what he had in mind was…" Although the younger Bateson never got an advanced degree in biology, he had from his family background a deep understanding (and a set of controversial positions) relating to the evolutionary doctrines of the late 19th and early 20th Centuries. Gregory Bateson was of course named after Gregor Mendel (Lipset, 1980, p. 37), of whom William Bateson was one of the rediscoverers. It is fair to say however that William Bateson's own theories were less "atomistic" than Mendelian genetics, and related more to what we would now think of as the informational aspects of how genetics transforms development. Evo-devo counts William Bateson as its precursor, much as some biosemioticians wish to count Gregory Bateson as theirs.

Given this background it may be just as appropriate to consider Bateson's approach as a kind of metaphorical extension of evo-devo principles, as well as a transform of early cybernetics into the realm of human and ecological interaction. Luis Bruni, in Chapter 6, shows that ideas from Gregory Bateson, particularly from *Mind and Nature*, are applicable to current issues in molecular biology, as this field moves away from reductionist ideas towards a new appreciation of systems.

A tension that runs in a rather subterranean way through some of the contributions in the book comes out of a tangle in our own *zeitgeist* about issues of the relation of epistemology and ontology in the information and semeiotic sciences. Hoffmeyer (Chapter 2), Cashman (Chapter 3), and Brier (Chapter 13) in particular seem to struggle with this issue in one or another form.

Bateson departed from philosophical realism by using his concept of information, *a difference that makes a difference*, to give a new cybernetic twist to Kant's old concept of the inaccessibility of the *ding an sich*, or *thing in itself*. Bateson was no Kantian in general, but used Kant as a proxy for some of the insights and perspectives of what later would be called second-order cybernetics, or constructivism, with its insistence on relating all knowledge to an observer and denying the possibility of any transcendent or ultimately certain knowledge. Bateson was very insistent on this approach to the students he taught and he felt that the undermining of "reality" by cybernetics was part of its value as a scientific advance. He referred always to his *epistemology* and never to his *ontology*—though it can be argued that his contrast between *pleroma* and *creatura* was ontological in practice as well as epistemological in theory.

Hoffmeyer and Brier, in different ways, contrast this cybernetic epistemology of Bateson's with the realistic yet fallibilist semiotic epistemology of Charles Sanders Peirce. However I cannot help but feel that there is less of a difference in spirit than there is in doctrine between Bateson's epistemological observer-centrism and Peirce's fallibilist realism. The key similarity in my opinion is the denial, in both, of the ability of sense and experiment to get things right authoritatively *without process, feedback,* and *cumulative revision.*

Ty Cashman, in Chapter 3 of this collection, proposes a different way of accommodating Bateson's ideas to a realist epistemology. Cashman critiques Bateson's constructivist interpretation of the Korzybski aphorism that *the map is not the territory.* In so doing Cashman never mentions the pioneering second-order cybernetician Heinz on Foerster. But those familiar with von Foerster's rejoinder that no, *the map is the territory* (i.e. because we can know no territory that is not itself a map; von Foerster & Poerksen, 2002 p. 81), will be intrigued by how Cashman shows that Bateson evolved toward almost exactly von Foerster's position. Cashman seems to see this as a result of Bateson's analysis of the self-closure of the neural system and the resulting self-referentialism of *perception.* Therefore Cashman argues that Bateson would have transcended this problem (and addressed the questions of intentionality and aboutness) if Bateson had only taken into account the possibility of *manipulating* the environment, as opposed to (passively) *sensorily perceiving* it.

This casts Bateson rather oddly in the role of Aristotle to Cashman's Galileo. Bateson always thought of sensory perception as active (and human action as perceptual). He discussed even the saccadic movements of the eye in this light. He did not deny action, manipulation, agency, or purpose. But he counted these on the *map* or *perception* side of the ledger. Far from thinking that they gave any better access to the *territory* than "merely sensory" perception would, he believed that they potentially *distorted the map.*

Perception is not passive to Bateson. He famously included the blind man's stick as part of the perceptual system of the blind man; yet what is the blind man doing but *manipulating* the stick in order to navigate around his environment? And note his discussion in *Mind and Nature* of what linguists might call properties and philosophers, qualities, of a nonliving, pleromatic object—a stone.

> To think straight, it is advisable to expect all qualities and attributes, adjectives, and so on to refer to at least *two* sets of interaction in time.
>
> "The stone is hard' means a) that when poked it resisted penetration and b) that certain continual interactions among the molecular *parts* of the stone in some way bond the parts together.
>
> ... A more precise way of talking would insist that the 'things' are produced, are seen as separate from other 'things,' and are made 'real' by their internal relations and by their behavior in relationship with other things and with the speaker. (Bateson, 1979, p. 67)

This seems to argue for a kind of "double description" of constructivism *and* (fallibilist) realism. But the manipulation of the object (when poked it resists penetration) is part of the construction of the object by the observer. The scientific story of molecules, while granted a certain scientific validity, is epistemologically secondary (and ultimately the *result* of constructivist procedures). However we are not here dealing with a dualism between map and territory; we are instead dealing with the dualism between mapmaking procedures and the map they produce—or, to use a visual analogy, between the neural construction of the visual image transforming the retinal image, and the experienced visual field (including its solid, manipulable objects).

This double description is very important to understanding Bateson's *attitude* to human action, manipulation, agency and purpose. It is precisely because Bateson remains curious about the "realist" side of the ledger—that he assumes that propositions about the environment side of the observer/environment membrane can be made and tested—that he, almost uniquely, asks the question of what happens when one assumes that the *environment* has cybernetic features. This contrasts, for example, with much of second-order cybernetics which implicitly seems to treat the observer's environment as a kind of "cloud of unknowing," an epistemological no-go zone.

It is precisely because Bateson sees perception as active rather than passive, that he is able to critique how purposive action *bends* and *biases* perception in the direction of successful short-term action sequences, creating a kind of systematic blindness to the rich ecological interconnectedness of living things. For Bateson this idea of ecology is necessarily one in which cybernetic circular causations and forms of interconnectedness are rife. But our habitual purposive perceptions and manipulations tend toward a simplification of these ecological relations, both in terms of our understandings of them and, in keeping with the double description I proposed above, also in terms of their own internal relations. The place of *aesthetics* and also of *the sacred* are for Bateson here, as correctives to the conscious human agent as *terrible simplificateur*. Harries-Jones, who ranks in my opinion among the deepest analysts of Bateson's work today, is perhaps the contributor to this issue who most clearly brings these precise issues to bear, though in his Chapter 10 he rather pessimistically notes that even some types of aesthetics, for example the "picture postcard" types as invoked by conservation agencies, can obscure the deeper ecologies that Bateson hoped our wider aesthetic sense could lead us to respect.

However, Bateson's vision of purpose and agency as destructive human capabilities may have led him away from theorizing these adornments of human consciousness explicitly. Brier, in Chapter 13, notes that Bateson does not emphasize the inner world of the conscious human agent (p. 236), though Brier attributes this to a materialistic stance deriving from the concept of information as developed by Wiener and by Shannon. But in assessing what Brier (and others) have seen as a materialist first-order cybernetic approach in Bateson, it is important not to take as statements epitomizing Bateson's mature position what Bateson intended to be a historical exposition of his own and others' thought.[2] Bateson often builds his argument step by step from the first principles of cybernetics, which were initially expressed materialistically, but in order to understand Bateson's position as a whole one must consider the wider web of his ideas, the patterns that connect them over the decades of his corpus.

(To use entropy as one example, Bateson's view of entropy as related to an observer is never fully set out except in one amusing yet profound Metalogue in *Steps to an Ecology of Mind*. But he does not in that essay use the term entropy; instead he asks, "Why do things get in a muddle?" [1972, pp. 3-8] The answer always implies an observer, in a second-order cybernetic fashion.) I would argue that a fuller view of Bateson might allow us to see fewer contradictions than Brier does between Bateson's epistemology and that, for example, of Peirce.

Brier's interest in consciousness makes him sympathetic to Peirce's mystic development of certain grand issues of the ontological status of scientific law, and of the origins and development of the cosmos, which involve the Peircean categories of Firstness, Secondness, and Thirdness (about which more below). Bateson, by contrast, was somewhat diffident about matters outside the living world, and would not have linked nonliving processes to consciousness. As Brier perceptively notes, Bateson would see consciousness as a product of a certain systemic organization rather than as potentially inherent in the smallest particles of matter. As for specifically human consciousness, Bateson seemed reluctant on principle to theorize about it, seeing it as something science had not yet the capacity to address, indeed something about which the right questions were yet to be asked.

In Bateson's seminal 1969 essay, "Style, Grace, and Information in Primitive Art," there is a passage whose deep irony is hidden by its obsolete Freudian formulation, using the term *secondary process* for conscious and verbal thought. Bateson writes, "Nobody, to my knowledge, knows anything about secondary process. But it is ordinarily assumed that everybody knows all about it, so I shall not attempt to describe secondary process in any detail, assuming that you know as much about it as I" (Bateson, 1972, p. 139). This is Bateson's ironic approach to consciousness. Further, in a metalogue in the back of *Mind and Nature*, Bateson refers to consciousness as one of two unanswered questions, at least as to how he would map them onto the picture of mind he outlined in that book (1979, pp. 233-234).

Bateson's emphasis on the mind's primary (non-conscious) processes reflected not only the behaviorist and Freudian theories of his period, but also his sense that

2. For example, Brier (p. 250 fn) cites three sentences from *Angels Fear* as "the rules of [Bateson's] work." Here is the quoted text: "in scientific explanation, there should be no use of mind or deity, and there should be no appeal to final causes. All causality should flow with the flow of time, with no effect of the future on upon the present or the past. No deity, no teleology, and no mind should be postulated in the universe that was to be explained" (Bateson & Bateson, 1987, p. 12). However what Bateson is doing in context here is in fact describing the rules of pre-cybernetic materialism, which cybernetics (in his view) made obsolete. He is ironic when he says, "I am glad I learned that lesson well" (*op. cit.*, p. 12), because as he states regarding his anthropological work *Naven*, which he claims to have been pre-cybernetic, "the rigorous limitation of the premises had the effect of displaying their inadequacy." The later Bateson felt that the cybernetic concept of circular causation had eliminated the need for researchers to fear teleology and final cause, or the use of mind, in explanation.

rational and purposive consciousness, far from being the crown of creation, often yields a short-term and limited perspective. Amplified by technology, contemporary Western conscious purpose yields the nuclear arms race and the ecological crisis. Bateson pinned his hope on art and the sacred as potential correctives for this sort of conscious purpose. Mengel's Chapter 12 on "Re-enchanting Evolution" shows in this spirit that the Biblical story of creation, when not interpreted as a literalistic contradiction to the theory of evolution, can supplement the narrow ethical compass and excessive materialism of some reductionist scientific versions of evolution. A similar analysis, but with a broader scope encompassing the debates between science and religion in general, animates Mary Catherine Bateson's wise reconsideration of her father's work in her Chapter 1, "Angel's Fear Revisited."

For the analysis of human communication, Bateson's conscious-actor-decentered perspective yielded intriguing dividends. Two examples in the volume, which take such a perspective, are the study of implicit learning updated by Schillhab and Gerlach in Chapter 8, and the remarkable reanalysis of the co-created ecology of everyday talk by Favareau in Chapter 11. These are research-based papers which show that Bateson's ideas can inspire new ways of looking at empirical data. I recommend Favareau's analysis in particular to anyone who wants a naturalistic fleshing out of the bones of the cybernetician Humberto Maturana's famous description of language as the "coordination of the coordination of behavior." Favareau does not mention Maturana but Maturanans should study him nonetheless.

To return to an earlier point, Bateson never enfolded himself so firmly inside the observer that he lost his interest in how ecological relationships themselves are cybernetically structured. Two chapters in Hoffmeyer's volume which provide grounded hypotheses as to how primeval organisms and ecologies can bootstrap themselves through cybernetic mechanisms are Chapter 4, "The Pattern Which Connects Pleroma to Creatura: The Autocell Bridge from Physics to Life," by Terrence Deacon along with Jeremy Sherman, and Robert Ulanowicz's Chapter 7, "Process Ecology: *Creatura* at Large in an Open Universe."

These two chapters refer to the famous distinction of Bateson's between *pleroma*, which is the world of forces and impacts as seen through materialistic science or physics, and *creatura*, which is the world seen through cybernetic sciences involving information (i.e., for Bateson, the living world). Jesper Hoffmeyer, in the course of his very informative and provocative article (Chapter 2) delimiting what he calls Bateson's bio-anthropology, makes an intriguing link between this Batesonian distinction and Peirce's categories of Secondness and Thirdness, with *pleroma* corresponding with Secondness and *creatura* with Thirdness. As Hoffmeyer points out this would make Bateson's distinction depend on epistemology explicitly. (Eicher-Catt in Chapter 14 also, but differently, juxtaposes Bateson's and Peirce's categories, while as mentioned, Brier in Chapter 13 discusses Peirce's ontology at length. Brier shows parallelisms and contrasts between the two thinkers as theological in nature, noting their similar immanence and pantheism.)

While I was originally very sympathetic to Hoffmeyer's comparison of the two categorical systems, I believe I can see a subtle difference. I agree with Hoffmeyer that *Peirce's* categories are intrinsically epistemological in nature. Secondness and Thirdness (and for that matter Firstness) are not properties of phenomena, but of the observer's relation to phenomena, and/or her experience of phenomena. In spite of Peirce's avowed realism, these categories can be seen as even more purely epistemological and relative in inspiration than Bateson's. (Yet, as Brier shows in his chapter, this is not the whole story, for Firstness, Secondness, and Thirdness are also for Peirce metaphysical and ontological worlds, see p. 246).

Bateson, as opposed to Peirce, seems always to have made it a principle to be epistemological *rather than* ontological, even (as Hoffmeyer notices) with respect to his distinction between *pleroma* and *creatura*. Nevertheless this distinction often registers more as one between realms of being (though this is a phrase Bateson would never use), which are divided according to which processes serve best as explanatory principles for them.   Since he is interested primarily in *creatura*, this means that *pleroma* becomes for him something of a residual or throwaway category, often implicitly Newtonian. (Bateson was almost aggressively uninterested in quantum physics, as part of his strong reaction against all forms of "physics envy" by social scientists, biologists, and the New Age.) A more fully epistemologized use of Bateson's categories might have anticipated the possibility of a *creaturic* physics (for which Stephen Wolfram's work may provide an example, as well as much of recent chaos and complexity theory). Privately when such a possibility was mentioned to Bateson (that processes of *creatura* might be found underpinning aspects of the nonliving world), this intrigued him.

By almost totally limiting *creatura* to the cybernetic processes he feels characteristic of life, Bateson makes a move which is similar to that of Humberto Maturana, who limits autopoiesis to the operations of living organisms. Both of them are in some deep sense biologists who feel that they have cracked the secret of the difference between the living and the nonliving. The extension of the explanatory principles they use to the nonliving world must for them be approached with skepticism and caution. (Bateson is in this respect less fastidious than Maturana, however, for Bateson includes social and ecological systems as cybernetic "minds," while Maturana is notably skeptical of Luhmann's application of autopoiesis to some such social systems.)

Hoffmeyer, like Cashman (and perhaps by implication, though not explicitly in this book, Brier), would like to use the parallels between Peircean and Batesonian categories to subvert Bateson's claim that direct knowledge of *pleroma* is impossible. Again, this is related to problems they have with the anti-realist, constructivist second-order cybernetic stance (and in Kant's anticipation of this by postulating the impossibility of direct apprehension of the *ding an sich*). I do not see any grounds in Bateson to see either *creatura* or *pleroma* as in any way more amenable to direct apprehension than the other. The same constructivist arguments against "direct" knowledge apply to both. In Peircean terms the indirect knowledge characteristic of *creatura* corresponds to Thirdness which always requires an interpretant. Secondness is not directly perceived, but it should not thereby be denied, which indeed Bateson does not do.

Thus it is that Bateson does not *use* his constructivism in the same way as many of his contemporaries in the second-order cybernetics movement. His constructivism does not lead him to practice the same ascetic agnosticism about "thingish" things as might be attributed to a von Foerster. He does not refuse to investigate or discuss the characteristics of the environment, of the world external to the observer. Maturana and von Foerster may seem at times to invoke cybernetics primarily to insist that one must never claim truth, and epistemologically, Bateson would not disagree.[3] But Bateson—looking ecological disaster in the face decades before most of us—was equally concerned to invoke our epistemological limits to tell us that we can be WRONG (and he sometimes capitalized this).

For Bateson this *wrongness* is itself a manifestation of what the best arguments in this book might call our biosemiotic fallibilism. In the end Bateson wanted an integrated theory of evolution and, though he criticized the term, of adaptation. His cybernetics enabled him to pursue criticisms of the materialism of twentieth century Darwinism, of the inhumanity of human beings to each other, and of the dangerous misapplication of applied science. It pointed him to a respect for art and for the sacred, and for dreams and the unconscious, in a world in which the organization of rational knowledge seemed only to lead to the planning and systematic execution of the unthinkable. The conscious subject may have seemed to possess an unbearable lightness in such a context, and he did not much address it. In our own times his cautions and his rigor still deserve to be studied and emulated, and this book is a major example of the fruitfulness of doing so. I recommend it highly.

References

Bateson, G. (1972). *Steps to an ecology of mind*. New York: Ballantine.
Bateson, G. (1975). "Reality" and redundancy." *The Co-Evolution Quarterly, 6* (Summer), 132-135.
Bateson, G. (1977). Afterword. In J. Brockman (Ed.), *About Bateson* (pp. 235-247). New York: E. P. Dutton.

---

3. Nonetheless, an obscure excerpt published in the Summer 1975 *Co-Evolution Quarterly* entitled "'Reality' and Redundancy" shows Bateson's reluctance to position himself as a conventional anti-realist or realist. Even though his cybernetic epistemology leads him to a critique of what can be known, he does not as a result accept that "every human being must have his or her own idiosyncratic reality" (a word which he in any case sees as "so loaded with ambiguity and *double entendre* as to be useless except as an interesting example of linguistic and epistemological decay)." Instead he posits that human observers share in some sense "the same outside world" (he uses this phrase) though observers perceive it differently according to differences in epistemology and culture. "But to suggest that this outside world will *be* different [to different observers] is to accept the premise that "reality" is completely un-thingish, that it indeed has none of that value in contrast to which the 'unreal' was devalued." This fragment which was intended as part of the glossary for the book which eventually became *Mind and Nature* shows a Bateson struggling with his thought, and he did not in fact include any version of it in the eventual book, a fact which may indicate that he felt it did not live up to his standards of rigor. But it shows an interesting intention on his part to decenter or destabilize both realism and anti-realism, by claiming that both participate in a "Cartesian dualism" which should be obsolete. (Bateson, 1975, p. 132). In a similar vein, in the "Afterword" to the *festschrift* organized by the science editor John Brockman, Bateson also noted that his epistemology made the concepts "objectivity" and "subjectivity" both obsolete (Bateson, 1977, p. 245).

Bateson, G. (1979). *Mind and nature: A necessary unity.* Toronto: Bantam Books.

Bateson, G., & Bateson, M. C. (1987). *Angels fear: Toward an epistemology of the sacred.* New York: Macmillan.

Carroll, S. (2005). *Endless forms most beautiful.* New York: W.W. Norton & Co.

Hoffmeyer, J. (Ed.) (2008). *A Legacy for living systems: Gregory Bateson as precursor to biosemiotics.* Berlin: Springer Science / Business Media B.V.

Lipset, D. (1980). *Gregory Bateson: The legacy of a scientist.* Englewood Cliffs, NJ: Prentice-Hall.

Von Foerster, H., & Poerksen, B. (2002). *Understanding systems: Conversations on epistemology and ethics.* IFSR International Series on Systems Science and Engineering, Volume 17. New York: Kluwer Academic/ Plenum.

Forsythe, K. (2005). *Signature.* 22 cm x 35 cm, collage on paper.

Forsythe, K. (2005). *In the Garden 1*. 30 cm x 35 cm, mixed media collage on paper.

www.ingramcontent.com/pod-product-compliance
Lightning Source LLC
Chambersburg PA
CBHW060129060326
40690CB00018B/3813